D1563765

NORTHERN EXPOSURE

The Cultural History of Television

Mad Men: *A Cultural History*, by M. Keith Booker and Bob Batchelor
Frasier: *A Cultural History*, by Joseph J. Darowski and Kate Darowski
Breaking Bad: *A Cultural History*, by Lara Stache
Star Trek: *A Cultural History*, by M. Keith Booker
The Simpsons: *A Cultural History*, by Moritz Fink
Cheers: *A Cultural History*, by Joseph J. Darowski and Kate Darowski
Gilmore Girls: *A Cultural History*, by Lara Stache and Rachel Davidson
Friends: *A Cultural History*, by Jennifer C. Dunn
Seinfeld: *A Cultural History*, by Paul Arras
Northern Exposure: *A Cultural History*, by Michael Samuel

NORTHERN EXPOSURE

A Cultural History

Michael Samuel

ROWMAN & LITTLEFIELD
Lanham • Boulder • New York • London

Published by Rowman & Littlefield
An imprint of The Rowman & Littlefield Publishing Group, Inc.
4501 Forbes Boulevard, Suite 200, Lanham, Maryland 20706
www.rowman.com

6 Tinworth Street, London SE11 5AL, United Kingdom

British Library Cataloguing in Publication Information Available

Library of Congress Cataloging-in-Publication Data

Names: Samuel, Michael, author.
Title: Northern exposure : a cultural history / Michael Samuel.
Description: Lanham : Rowman & Littlefield, [2021] | Series: The cultural history of television |
    Includes bibliographical references, filmography, and index. | Summary: "This book revisits and
    celebrates the cultural legacy of the cult television series Northern Exposure. With a focus on its
    production history, fan culture, and individual episodes, it reveals the show's profound influence
    and argues its status as the prototype contemporary television series"—Provided by publisher.
Identifiers: LCCN 2021013139 (print) | LCCN 2021013140 (ebook) | ISBN 9781538117446 (cloth) |
    ISBN 9781538117453 (epub)
Subjects: LCSH: Northern exposure (Television program) | Television comedies—United States—
    History and criticism. | Medical television programs—United States—History and criticism. |
    Television—Production and direction—United States. | Alaska—On television.
Classification: LCC PN1992.77.N67 S26 2021 (print) | LCC PN1992.77.N67 (ebook) | DDC 791.45/
    72—dc23
LC record available at https://lccn.loc.gov/2021013139
LC ebook record available at https://lccn.loc.gov/2021013140

CONTENTS

Notes to the Reader   vii

Acknowledgments   ix

Prologue: On a Personal Note   xi

1 Roslyn   1

2 Paging "Dr. Snow": Joshua Brand, John Falsey, and the
       Making of *Northern Exposure*   15

3 "The Paris of the North": The Characters, Setting, and Stories 43

4 From Critically Acclaimed to Canceled   67

5 *Northern Exposure*: A Cultural Legacy   81

Epilogue   101

Appendix A: Episode Summaries   103

Appendix B: Fan Survey   157

Appendix C: Books about *Northern Exposure*   165

Notes   167

Bibliography and Filmography   179

Index   189

About the Author   193

NOTES TO THE READER

This book assumes that you have watched the series *Northern Exposure*, which ran on CBS in the United States between 1990 and 1995. It will therefore not only contain spoilers but will take certain liberties in its overall structure and flow. While this book mostly follows a logical order, from *Northern Exposure*'s conception to its legacy, at times it will jump forward and backward as it explores the many facets of this 1990s cult television series. Like a torrent, let it wash over you. *Northern Exposure* is a state of mind.

* * *

When referencing quotes from characters, or overall episodes of *Northern Exposure,* this book will include information in an endnote. These notes will include the character's name (if relevant), along with the episode title, the number of the season, the number of the episode, and the date it was originally broadcast in the United States. All details related to all episodes of the series can be found in appendix A, Episode Summaries, in the latter half of the book.

ACKNOWLEDGMENTS

Sometimes it is hard to know for whom a book about a thirty-year-old television series is written. At the start of this journey, the question came up a number of times. However, during the process of writing this book, it became overwhelmingly clear. A television series like *Northern Exposure* is kept alive by its fans, who, with each passing year, sustain its memory and embrace its message and philosophy. In our conversations, online and in person, you, the fans, have been more than generous to me. Therefore, I would like to dedicate my first acknowledgment to you, my fellow Ciceleans.

Though we never met, I would like to personally acknowledge an incredible debt to the late John Falsey, who sadly passed in January 2019. Along with his longtime collaborator Joshua Brand, Falsey pioneered this wonderful television series and many others that continue to be widely celebrated and valued. Falsey's contribution to television is profound. Through his work, and through the extensive community that *Northern Exposure* has fostered, Falsey will be fondly remembered. Thank you.

I could never have completed this project without the continued friendship, interest, and encouragement offered by a select group of people. They include Daniel Harris, Agata Frymus, Daniel Clarke, Rob Stone, Esther Santamaría, Travis Wicklund, Josette Wolthuis, Stephanie Prugh, Luis Friejo, Will Carroll, Darran Patton, Todd Sodano, Christopher Whitehouse, David Forrest, Paul Cooke, Rachel Moseley, Helen Wheatley, Karl Schoonover, José Arroyo, Tracey McVey, Richard Wallace, Leanne Weston, and all the students I had the pleasure of teaching and exploring television with at the University of Bristol, the University of Warwick, the University of Birmingham (B-Film), Royal Holloway University of London, and the City University of New York (CUNY).

I would like to acknowledge the collective efforts of the team at Rowman & Littlefield for their efforts in bringing this book to print.

I would like to give special credit to my friend and mentor, Scott F. Stoddart, whose years of kindness and support have not only inspired my work but profoundly shaped me as a scholar and as a person.

Likewise, I would also like to extend special thanks to Louisa Mitchell for her friendship and for her editorial work on this project.

I would like to recognize the encouragement and generosity of my ever growing family, Steven, Simeon, Sarah, Rachael, Ryan, Ellie, John, Pauline, David, and Chioma (and all pets), to whom I owe a great debt of gratitude. And lastly, I must acknowledge the inspiration, support, and love of Julia Tanner. In return, you have my love and respect.

PROLOGUE

On a Personal Note

Throughout the 1990s, each night our family home in the quiet ex–coal mining town of Treharris in South Wales became an extension of America. With the late arrival and repeat broadcasts of imported American television series onto our small screens, our living room became a Boston tavern with *Cheers*, a Chicago emergency room with *ER*, a Seattle radio station with *Frasier*, a West Village apartment with *Friends*, the fictional any town of Springfield with *The Simpsons*, a California high school above a demonic gateway with *Buffy the Vampire Slayer*, and the Oval Office with *The West Wing*. At 10 p.m. on 16 March 1992, the television transported our family to the fictional outpost of Cicely, Alaska, as *Northern Exposure* was broadcast for the first time in the United Kingdom on terrestrial television.

Northern Exposure appeared on British television on Channel 4 two years after it was first shown on CBS in the United States, where it had already achieved "cult" status according to the original Channel 4 press pack. I was four years old in 1992 and therefore do not remember *Northern Exposure*'s original broadcast on British television. However, I do remember catching my first glimpse of Cicely (which I now know was the town of Roslyn, Washington, in real life) on-screen. It was in the winter of 1995. According to records, it was the coldest winter in the United Kingdom since 1981, and we were snowed in. It was late, and I had gone downstairs for some reason or another. Through the banister rails, I looked down over my father, Steven, who was sitting on the sofa, wrapped in a wool blanket, watching television. The volume was turned down low so as not to wake my youngest sister who was one at the time. Like Alice being led down the rabbit hole, I descended the stairs slowly, and for several minutes I was transfixed on the television screen, following a curious moose as it ambled through the main street of the small town in the series's opening credit sequence.

I was too young then to appreciate *Northern Exposure* and the impact it would one day have on me. It was not until the mid-2000s, after buying the DVDs during my first year at university, that I would realize the value of the television series. From the moment I loaded the first disc into the DVD player, navigated the terribly low-resolution DVD menu complete with David Schwartz's iconic theme tune, and pressed play on the "Pilot" episode (1.1), I felt an immediate connection to the series. Having left my hometown to attend university, I had been thrust from my everyday life into a new situation. Away from home, I was adapting to change: a new place, a new community of people, a different pace of life.

Like a comfort blanket, *Northern Exposure* provided me with warmth. Unlike the series protagonist, Dr. Joel Fleischman (played by Rob Morrow)—a big fish in a small pond, frustrated, angry—my relationship with Cicely and its denizens was somewhat different. I found its small –townness—a place where everyone knows everyone else's business—both familiar and comforting. At a time when my hometown and neighbors seemed so far away, every episode extended an invitation to me to be a part of what was happening on-screen. At the end of a busy or stressful day, or when I was nursing a hangover, *Northern Exposure* was like a "welcome back" from the townspeople of Cicely. In short, through *Northern Exposure*, and through Cicely, I found home.

In the Welsh language, this feeling can be described by the unique word *cwtch* (which rhymes with "butch"). The word *cwtch* has no English cognate. It is often mistaken by those from outside of Wales as just meaning to give someone a hug. However, a *cwtch*, or the action *to cwtch*, is significant of much more. If you ask a person from Wales what a *cwtch* is, or what it means to them, they will likely express a "fond smile."[1] This is because the word *cwtch* triggers multiple emotional registers; it "has the magical quality of transporting someone back to the safety of their childhood."[2] As the University of South Wales website explains, this emotional response is rooted in the word's secondary meaning, which is "a place to safely store things."[3] Therefore, to offer or to give someone a *cwtch* is to offer or give someone a "safe place."[4] It is not too far-fetched to suggest that *Northern Exposure* provided me, back then, as it continues to provide me today, with sanctuary or a "safe place."

With time, and with many rewatches, *Northern Exposure* has secured a special place in my heart. Beyond its unique personality, I am constantly surprised by the complexity of its script. I revel in its vision of a small-town utopia, defined by understanding and diversity, and its mythic and magical quality. Likewise, I am warmed by its diverse representations of other cultures—cultures and characters I otherwise seldom saw on American television growing up in the 1990s, and arguably since.

I wrote this book in pursuit of a deeper understanding of *Northern Exposure* and to provide a portrait of the cultural moment that gave way for and shaped the series. Furthermore, I was driven by a desire to explore the series's cultural impact since it was first broadcast in 1990. When I embarked on this project, I wanted to explore these aspects, while also attempting to pinpoint the reasons why I continue to return to the series time and time again. What I find is that my reasons keep changing. However, as I sat down to watch the series for the *n*th time to research this book, I realized that one thing still has not changed: my emotional response to the opening credit sequence. Every viewing rekindles the feeling of wonder encapsulated in that moment in South Wales in 1995, age seven, when I found myself transfixed as I watched the series for the first time with my father. This book, like my love of *Northern Exposure*, is therefore dedicated to him.

I

ROSLYN

Roslyn is a small town located eighty miles east of Seattle in the middle of upper Kittitas County, Washington. Founded in 1886 by Logan M. Bullet, vice president of the Northern Pacific Coal Company, Roslyn was established as a settlement for the company's employees, mainly coal miners and their families, who "fed the engines of the Northern Pacific Railway."[1] In its heyday at the turn of the twentieth century, the population of Roslyn peaked at just over three thousand people. The promise of mining work just two decades earlier had attracted people from the world

over to this particular region in the Pacific Northwest. Both committed to and equally dependent on the coal industry as their primary source of income, people from the United Kingdom, mainland and Eastern Europe, and even the Asia-Pacific upped sticks and made way for the northwest shoulder of the United States. It is for this reason that Roslyn is described as "one of the most ethnically diverse towns in the state."[2] For a while, the town and its population prospered as the surrounding areas produced "a million tons of coal annually."[3] But, while a beacon of promise, the coal industry also provided a false sense of security. After several prosperous decades, the town's production and population plateaued in the first decade of the 1900s. It was a reminder that Roslyn's days of growth were numbered.

The nationwide move from coal to diesel power in the mid-1910s to early 1920s resulted in the gradual closure of many coal mines across North America. Roslyn was no exception. The last of its coal mines closed in 1963. While the closure of the mines signaled the looming end of industry in Roslyn, its death was far from unexpected. Indeed, the town's population had dwindled long before the 1960s, with many of its residents having left Roslyn to work elsewhere. For a portion of ex-miners, they either stayed in, or only remained a stone's throw away from, Roslyn, taking advantage of alternative and relatively local ventures, such as "logging, railroading, trucking, or building dams and highways for the federal government."[4] Meanwhile, for others, the end of the mining industry resulted in large swathes leaving the town, migrating south to California or east to Detroit or New York with the industrial shift toward mass production during the economic boom of the early 1920s.

In the wake of the collapsed industry and the closure of its mines in the early 1960s, Roslyn experienced a long period of economic decline. This caused the town's population to decrease substantially over the years, reaching as low as nine hundred by the 1990s.[5] Without industry, Roslyn, like so many small industrial American outposts, became a ghost town. Will Carroll at the University of Birmingham sheds some light on this matter. In an interview with Carroll conducted in 2020, he explained that "America's frontier history is packed with the ghost towns of former industry. Mills sit vacant. Logging yards, overgrown. Each betrays the stories of those who lived and died in such places, their histories hidden and awaiting exhumation." In summary, Carroll characterized America as "nothing if not an archipelago of small towns, each bearing the telltale scars of industrial boom and bust."[6]

Roslyn wore its industrial heritage on its sleeve. But after the closure of its mines in the 1960s, the town found itself in something of an identity crisis. For decades, Roslyn became a real estate haven for the city dwellers of neighboring Seattle. As Bryan Di Salvatore writes, the citizens of Roslyn "watched the Seattle rich—attracted to nearby lakes and forests—pick up properties in town and out, for recreation, for retirement, for investment."[7] While on one hand the second-home economy was something of a short-term lifeline for the town, without permanent residents, a community, or an industry, Roslyn was endangered. In order to survive, the town had to adapt.

Since the 1960s, Roslyn has thus turned to other industries (besides coal mining) as a source of revenue. In terms of its geography, Roslyn is located in the Cascade Mountains National Park. Dubbed by *National Geographic* as "the American Alps," Washington's North Cascade National Park boasts 684,000 acres of "snow-topped mountains, rivers, and valleys," as well as being "home to a diverse ecosystem that includes wolves, lynx, and moose."[8] Considering this, it is only logical that when it came to finding an alternative and reliable source of revenue, the town focused on forestry before capitalizing on the tourism potential of its surrounding areas. Tourism has since played a significant role in Roslyn's economic recovery and prosperity, offering visitors the opportunity to enjoy a broad range of winter and summer recreational activities, such as skiing, fishing, camping, and golfing. From the early 1990s, however, Roslyn's luck and economic outlook improved dramatically, and not just because of its outdoor culture and industry. From 1992, the town's annual footfall increased rapidly as an unexpected rush of tourists traveled from all over the world to visit the small ex-mining town. Lured not by history, nor persuaded by the majesty of the great outdoors, these tourists instead traveled to see what had quickly become one of primetime television's "most recognized and appealing stars,"[9] the town of Roslyn itself, which had, just two years prior, made its small-screen debut as the fictional Alaskan outpost of Cicely in the hit television series *Northern Exposure*.[10]

Northern Exposure was created by veteran television writer-producer duo Joshua Brand (b. 1950) and John Falsey (1951–2019). The television series is a fish-out-of-water story that documents the trials and tribulations of Dr. Joel Fleischman (played by Rob Morrow). Joel, a quintessential New Yorker and recent graduate of Columbia University Medical School, has been sent to practice medicine in Alaska for four years to fulfill the terms of his scholarship from that state. As Brian Doan aptly puts it in his breakdown and examination of the characters that make up *Northern Exposure*, "the secret to Dr. Fleischman was in his eyes."[11] Indeed, it is in his eyes, and through his eyes, that Joel's journey and personal growth is documented. Told through worried glances, confused observations, and eyebrow-raising expressions of utter bewilderment, Joel's journey begins on the red-eye from JFK to Anchorage in the opening scene of "Pilot,"[12] as Joel observes the facial expressions of his fellow passenger (John Aylward) when he tells him that he is traveling to Alaska to be the state's "indentured slave for four years."[13]

"You ever been to Alaska?" the unnamed passenger sitting beside him asks.

"Of course," replies Joel. "What kind of schmuck do you think I am?" Joel explains that he and his girlfriend Elaine (played by Jessica Lundy), a third-year law student at Yale University, had indeed visited Alaska the previous summer and "loved the place." Joel backtracks: "All right, not loved, but we both agreed it's definitely doable."

The passenger offers Joel an unconvinced look.

"What? What are you trying to say? Are you trying to tell me something?" Joel asks, puzzled by the passenger's line of questioning and his suggestive facial expressions. Laughing to himself, the passenger responds with a "Good luck" before turning off the cabin light.

The turning off of the cabin light at the end of the brief exchange between Joel and the unnamed passenger invites the opening drumbeats and distinct rhythmic bass line of the series's iconic and award-winning opening credit score from the then unknown television composer David Schwartz. Schwartz would go on to score the likes of *Beverly Hills, 90210*, *Arrested Development*, *Deadwood*, *Rules of Engagement*, and *The Good Place*, among many others. Scoring *Northern Exposure* was Schwartz's first job. Fortunately, his theme tune would not only go on to feature in the remaining 109 episodes of the series but would later earn Schwartz three consecutive BMI Film & TV Awards for Best Original Soundtrack in 1992, 1993, and 1994.[14] While the theme tune made the series instantly recognizable, the opening drumbeats also ushered onto the screen one of the 1990s most memorable yet uncredited television characters, Morty the moose,[15] through whom we, the audience, are provided with our first glimpse of Cicely, Alaska—in real life Roslyn, Washington—on-screen.

Emerging from behind a storefront advertising Village Pizza, Morty ambles through the small town during what appears to be early morning. He glances at a mannequin in a closed storefront. He looks up at mounted antlers on a wood-clad property. He stares in the direction of the façade of a pale blue building, the words "Northwestern Mining Co." printed on the sign above the door and the name "Dr. Joel Fleischman" poorly written in white ink on the ground-floor window. At the end of his route, Morty walks in front of a painted mural depicting a tropical scene, at the center of which is a camel positioned before the backdrop of mountains and an expansive sky. Large lettering reads, "Roslyn Cafe: An Oasis." The fixed shot of the mural fades out as the series's title card fades in over a final establishing shot of the fictional town of Cicely, Morty's journey setting the stage for the fiction to play out.

Roslyn was the perfect fit for Cicely. Just as John Gast's 1872 painting *American Progress* established in the popular imagination a specific iconography of America, visually symbolic of its history of westward expansion, myth, and ideology,[16] inspiring countless cultural reproductions along the way,[17] the opening credit sequence of *Northern Exposure* functions similarly. The main road, Pennsylvania Avenue, depicted in the opening credit sequence, visually symbolizes the American frontier town, the town, and arguably the nation's history and ambition, physically embodied in the architecture of main street. Roslyn is the quintessential small American town preserved in time from the last decades of the nineteenth century. Isolated, its "turn-of-the-century architecture and character remained relatively intact,"[18] and its tangible heritage earned the town a place on the National Register of Historic Places.

From the time of its conception, cocreator Joshua Brand knew that he "didn't want a yuppified town with a Ben & Jerry's store."[19] As well as an affordable alternative to Alaska for the production team, who were restricted to an $839,000 budget per episode, the ex-mining town of Roslyn represented a combination of "historical presence, climate and geography."[20] With its "weather-worn architecture from the early 1900s and heavy snowfalls," the town "looked the part of a remote Alaskan village."[21] Therefore, when location scouts from Cine-Nevada (*Northern Exposure*'s production team) started their search for alternative locations

to Alaska in which to shoot the series, it did not take much to convince
them that Roslyn was the perfect fit. After surveying several other locations, Matt Nodella of Cine-Nevada took up the offer from Christine
Lewis, then manager of the Washington State Film and Video Office, to
visit Roslyn. As Lewis recalls, after a drive around the areas, the production team's "eyes grew wide" as they turned onto Pennsylvania Avenue.
Upon seeing the view of Roslyn as depicted at the end of the series's
opening credit sequence, Nodella turned to Lewis and said, "Christine,
this is Alaska."[22] Persuaded by its scenic backdrop and its proximity to
Seattle, which had sound studios that the production team could use for
several of *Northern Exposure*'s internal scenes, Roslyn presented the
ideal location to base the series and its production. *Northern Exposure*
had found its Cicely.

Shooting a television series or film in such a location as Roslyn has a
number of benefits. In the case of Roslyn, *Northern Exposure* was, and
has since been, a lucrative asset, both culturally and economically. From
the start, Roslyn's leadership shared the foresight of figures like Lewis in
immediately seeing the potential benefits of offering the town as a location for film and television productions. As Rhonda Phillips reflects,
"The town's leadership was always supportive [of the television industry
filming in Roslyn], recognizing the filming as a much needed boost to the
economy of Roslyn."[23] As Phillips goes on to explain, the mayor recognized the hardships the town had gone through and endured, largely at the
expense of much of its population during its extended period of economic
uncertainty after the collapse of its mining industry. He therefore welcomed the financial boost filming promised to bring to the small town,
and thus also welcomed the television production crews, casts, and eventually tourists.[24]

Production began in Roslyn in 1989. From the moment *Northern Exposure*'s crew first descended on Pennsylvania Avenue, the small town
changed overnight as "the rustic heart of downtown Roslyn was transformed into the fictional outpost of Cicely."[25] Suddenly the sleepy town
of Roslyn was flooded with activity. In the "town where nothing out of
the ordinary happened, the extraordinary soon became the daily buzz,"
writes Renee Skelton of the *Washington Post*, as the small, quiet, postindustrial American town became the location for the eight-episode season
1 shoot.[26] Weekly caravans transported production equipment to Roslyn
from an external base in Seattle, and along with them enough people to

boost Roslyn's population to nearly a thousand.[27] Furthermore, in addition to the cast and crew physically involved in the filming of season 1, the gradual warm embrace of *Northern Exposure* by television audiences around the world attracted fans from across the globe, keen to visit the set and immerse themselves in the fictional world they had seen week in and week out on their television screens. In its first year of production, for instance, it is reported that between three and four hundred fans observed the filming of *Northern Exposure* every day—an extraordinary number for any location, let alone a small town like Roslyn.

Not only was this footfall beneficial for the existing businesses in Roslyn, but it also created new opportunities for the local population. *Northern Exposure* created a hundred new jobs to support the new businesses established in Roslyn. In addition to accommodating the production of the series by opening extra businesses to ensure its smooth run during its prolonged stay in Roslyn, residents also had the opportunity to be directly involved in the series as paid extras. It was an opportunity that dozens embraced.

Roslyn's newfound celebrity status, however beneficial for the town's economy, came with its issues. While *Northern Exposure* revived the town's economy in the 1990s—increasing visitor footfall, creating new businesses, and replenishing its dwindled population—the production also hindered a way of life for Roslyn's inhabitants. The production disrupted the flow of everyday life in the town. A great number of the series's famous locales can be found on, or just off, Pennsylvania Avenue. Thus, the downtown area of Roslyn was both the main site of production as well as a prime tourist hot spot for *Northern Exposure* fans who had come to observe the filming or to pay homage to the series. While the location was convenient for the production crew and tourists, filming proved inconvenient for the town's residents. Roslyn's relationship with the production was thus "tumultuous" in the beginning.[28] "During filming," says Margaret Heide, the city clerk at Roslyn, "the city's main street, Pennsylvania Avenue, [was] blocked to traffic as television crews bark[ed] for silence through bullhorns."[29] The streets were littered with filming equipment accompanied by on-site crews, establishing what Di Salvatore calls "an alfresco factory."[30]

Increased traffic, concentrated production, and hordes of ambling and observing tourists on Pennsylvania Avenue prevented the flow of movement through the town, particularly for those residents going about their daily business. Roslynites began to reconsider the benefits of *Northern Exposure*'s production in and association with their quiet town and its quiet way of life. Following months of disruption, "Roslynites felt that their guest was outstaying its welcome."[31] However, by then it was too late. As the series had proved popular with television audiences, the producers were keen to extend it. At first they green-lit season 2, which would be another small order of episodes, just seven. *Northern Exposure* tourism, like the series viewing figures, continued to grow as fans came in waves to Roslyn to regularly watch the production of their new favorite television series. Meanwhile, others congested Roslyn's streets "snapping pictures and peering into store windows."[32] Very much like Morty the moose from the opening credit sequence, they ambled through Roslyn. With maps in hand and cameras around their necks, they visited, one-by-one, the landmarks that had become so familiar to them week in and week out through their television screens. Moving westward on Pennsylvania Avenue, on one side the fan-tourist would find Joel's practice in the repurposed pale blue Northwestern Mining Co. building, and further on, the historic tavern, the Brick, which dates back to 1889 (it is the oldest continuously operating tavern in Washington State). On the other side of the road, they can visit Ruth-Anne's (played by Peggy Phillips) general store; they can peer through the windows of Maurice's (played by Barry Corbin) office at the Northwest Improvement Company; and next door they can find the KBHR radio studio, where Chris Stevens (played by John Corbett) broadcasts his morning series, *Chris in the Morning*. Finally, their tour ends with their arrival at Roslyn's Cafe, with the infamous mural painted on its side—an essential point of interest on many a fan itinerary.[33] Other sites include various character houses, as well as Roslyn's theater, city hall, church, and museum, all of which feature in the series.[34]

After its second season was broadcast, *Northern Exposure* was renewed for four more seasons. Unlike the first two seasons, however, which totaled fifteen episodes, the production company's contract with Roslyn this time was for an additional ninety-five episodes. "It was not an easy transition for the town or the production crew during the early days of filming," remarks Phillips.[35] However, as Phillips acknowledges, "the production company made efforts to smooth over some of the tension by donating a fire truck to the town, sponsoring a 10-K race, distributing holiday baskets, and other activities."[36]

"Stardom certainly changed Roslyn," writes Skelton.[37] Its years in the spotlight during the production of *Northern Exposure* "turn[ed] it from a sleepy hamlet into a bustling tourist attraction."[38] But while the series had a positive economic effect on Roslyn, and by extension the state of Washington, putting the town that its residents were incredibly proud of on the map, for others, they "would just as soon return to the anonymity and quiet of the pre-'Exposure' days."[39] Eventually, the latter group got their way when, in 1995, entertainment news outlets announced *Northern Exposure*'s cancellation. Following Rob Morrow's exit from the sixth season (which this book will explore later), a dwindling audience share, and something of a fade into obscurity, *Northern Exposure*'s cancellation came as a surprise to nobody. Production in Roslyn came to an end after the filming of season 6 wrapped. Just as quickly as the crews had descended on Pennsylvania Avenue in 1989, they packed up and left in the spring of 1995. When the filming of *Northern Exposure* came to an end in Roslyn, the desire of some of the residents to return to the "pre-'Exposure' days" was somewhat fulfilled. While the absence of the cast and crew members returned life to normal in Roslyn, their departure left a hole in the town. With *Northern Exposure*'s absence, Roslyn took a significant hit. As Phillips writes, "The filming of Northern Exposure resuscitated the stagnant economy of an isolated small town. The old adage, all good things must come to an end, holds particular relevance in this case, for when filming ceased, the economic boost declined."[40] In the wake of *Northern Exposure*'s production, Roslyn immediately felt its absence. But Roslyn's relationship with *Northern Exposure* was far from over; the series continues to have a lasting impact on the town.

The spotlight on Roslyn in the early 1990s, though temporary, provided the town with "the impetus for the community to consider its options to encourage economic development."[41] Thus, immediately, the Roslyn Business Association was formed. Their mission was to develop special events and festivals to renew interest in Roslyn. Once more, the town looked to tourism, though it was film- and television-induced tourism this time around rather than outdoor activities. Due to the positive success of *Northern Exposure* and its continued profile in popular culture, the series has played a key role in sustaining Roslyn's tourism economy. However, as Roslyn's Chamber of Commerce openly admits, their campaigns did not need to do much in order to sell Roslyn as a destination to *Northern Exposure* enthusiasts. *Northern Exposure*–influenced tourism sustains itself through the continued interest the series generates to this day through occasional reruns on television, rewatches on DVD or Blu-ray, and user posts on social media, for example. In regard to the latter, posts featuring scenes from the series and fan photos of key locations in and around Roslyn, in the view of destination marketers, serve as free advertising for Roslyn as a tourist destination. While Morty the moose enjoyed one last stroll up Pennsylvania Avenue in the series finale— walking by the empty storefronts, Joel's office, The Brick, the KBHR studio, the general store, and Roslyn's Cafe—even today, decades later, "fans still show up in real Roslyn for a glimpse into the fake Cicely of yesteryear."[42] So popular was the *Northern Exposure*–inspired tourism that in 1997 and 1998, commercially organized reunions were staged in the town, uniting fans with various cast members to celebrate the series. The first reunion event, for example, was attended by cast members Barry Corbin, Cynthia Geary, Elaine Miles, and Moultrie Patten, while Iris DeMent, whose haunting song "Our Town" brought the series to a close in 1995 in the series finale, performed live. In 1999, a nonprofit event was organized that would become an annual occurrence. Named Moose-fest, this event was a formal convention that would bring together fans to attend tours and guest talks from cast members. However, the annual event was essentially an excuse to connect fans to one another via a shared love of all things *Northern Exposure*. Founded by Kurt Lutterman, Moosefest was a response to the popularity of the official reunions that had taken place the previous two years (1997 and 1998). In the *Seattle Times*, Lutterman explains that "the fans he knows enjoyed getting together so much that they picked up the antlers—so to speak—in 1999, turning Moosefest into a nonprofit event."[43] As the Friends of Roslyn webpage states, Moosefest is a "publicly-supported charity established in 1999 by fans of the television show, Northern Exposure, [who wished] to support the community of Roslyn." Such public events were substantially beneficial for the town of Roslyn. Between 1997 and 2005, for example, the annual gatherings and Moosefest events had generated and donated, in all, profits of $15,000 to the town of Roslyn.[44] Furthermore, "from its first festival in 1999, $10,000 was earned and distributed to the Roslyn Library, the Chamber of Commerce, and other community groups. The funding also helped establish the Northern Lights Theater group."[45]

Sadly, on 24 July 2005, the annual Moosefest events came to an end after just six years. The reason being a steady decline in attendance.

Despite attracting fans from the world over each year, the problem was that the reunion was no longer "attracting enough of them."[46] In short, Moosefest had become unfeasible. But while the formal festivities have come to an end in the small town, the "friendships and kinships [between] fans" have ensured the continued commitment of small groups who get together informally in Roslyn each July.[47] As the Moosefest website states,

> There are no scheduled events, celebrities, nor registration fee. It is basically a "hang out together" weekend. Usually 15 to 30 people show up. Everyone is welcome! The activities usually include: hanging out, talking, going out to dinner, watching some episodes, visiting some filming sites, and other stuff that organically arises from the collective unconscious.[48]

With time, the grievances with the production of *Northern Exposure* as felt by a portion of Roslyn's population appear to have lifted. As Jordan Nailon reflects, "While some hamlets have been known to resent the perpetual glare of Hollywood's spotlight . . . the people of Roslyn are, on the whole, quite chipper about it."[49] With time, the legacy of *Northern Exposure* and the memory of its production in Roslyn is generally positively regarded, given that it created many opportunities for its denizens and treated the town and its people well. Furthermore, as Nailon's interview with Carlena Bern, an employee at the Brick, reveals, the series has brought younger generations of fans to Roslyn over the last few years, some arriving "with foggy childhood memories formed from their parents' TV sets. Other visitors weren't even born when the show originally aired but have come to know and love it through the Internet" or from DVD or Blu-ray box sets.[50]

Lasting narratives, capturing both the excitement and opportunity that *Northern Exposure* presented Roslyn, as well as documenting the problematic aspects of the series's production, reveal a story of challenge and endurance, acceptance and legacy, all wrapped up in the survival narrative of the ex-mining town. And while Roslyn continues to stand, its resuscitation, arguable transformation (from postindustrial small town to television tourist attraction), and continued legacy owe a great deal to *Northern Exposure*. As Carroll states, "The American small town is the nation in miniature, agricultural heritage and former industry are etched upon its rutted streets and weathered frontages. *Northern Exposure* took that same diorama and made of it something sacred."[51] In the series, this is true. But the same can also be said about the relationship between the series and the town beyond the screen—merging historical hamlet with the television set, the industrial histories entwined.

The ghosts of *Northern Exposure*'s production are still visible in Roslyn. They are still standing. As memories of key scenes from the television series live on in the imaginations of fan-tourists visiting Roslyn, tangible reminders of the series's presence also remain in place: memories of Joel first stepping into his office with Maurice, or insulting the entire town by referring to them as "rednecks" over the phone at the Brick in "Pilot";[52] the town gathering around a small parcel at Ruth-Anne's general store in "The Final Frontier";[53] Chris first seeing Bernard outside of the KBHR studio in "Aurora Borealis: A Fairy Tale for Big People";[54] and of course the almost silhouetted Morty the moose standing before the Roslyn's Café mural in the opening credit sequence.

Northern Exposure reshaped, refined, and rebranded the town of Roslyn, for better or for worse, depending on your stance. The likes of the KBHR studio set and the name "Dr. Joel Fleischman" on the ground-floor window of the pale blue Northwestern Mining Co. building symbolize the competing identities of Roslyn, the fusion between its history and heritage as an industrial coal-mining town, and a site of memory for television fans to make their annual pilgrimages to. For fans of the series, Roslyn is not only a symbolic popular cultural site of memory—a location used as the backdrop to a popular drama from the early 1990s—but both the town and the series signify a site of connection, bringing together fans the world over to celebrate a television series that turned thirty on 12 July 2020. While considered a cult classic and a favorite at the time, it was a television series that the producers and networks did not understand and did not think would work, but it did, running for six seasons and earning wide critical acclaim. Likewise, it is a series that has sustained a dedicated and growing fan base that actively keeps its memory alive and advocates its return to small screens. And lastly, it is a television series this book is committed to exploring.

The story of Roslyn, and the impact of *Northern Exposure* on it, is allegorical of the story of the television series of *Northern Exposure* itself and its impact on the landscape of American television in the 1990s (and arguably since). Just as Morty the moose had wandered onto the fictional main street of Cicely, Alaska, in the series's opening credit sequence,

Northern Exposure itself had snuck under the radar and made its way onto the screen and into the homes of television viewers unexpectedly before becoming a sleeper hit for the CBS network. *Northern Exposure* not only managed to wander onto the schedule, but against the expectations of the network producers, it would go on to attract large audience figures (especially in its earlier seasons); earn almost universal acclaim from audiences and critics alike; enjoy an extended five-year, six-season run on television; and collect a number of notable accolades along the way.

This book, Northern Exposure: *A Cultural History*, is not a biography of a television series in the traditional sense. Certainly it has biographical elements that provide insight into the production and reception of *Northern Exposure*, introducing you to the setting, the main cast of characters, and their story lines. However, more than a biography, it is a journey to find out how the series overcame the odds that were stacked against it. Moreover, it is an inquiry into why the series is still being watched and rewatched today, passed on from generation to generation, original viewers and new, and still very much enjoyed thirty years later.[55] This book maps out the story of this groundbreaking American television series, from its conception to cancellation, before analyzing its lasting cultural impact. It asks, What is the enduring appeal of *Northern Exposure*? And how is it that a rule-breaking television series produced thirty years ago found an audience, became a critical success, and enjoyed such an enduring legacy and growing fan base? It is the main ambition of the first two parts of this book to explore these questions.

To begin, though, is to state that the story of *Northern Exposure* is that of an underdog. It begins with two renegade writers-turned-creators named Joshua Brand and John Falsey who, out of equal parts bravery and ignorance, duped a television network and, in the process, arguably created "the prototype modern TV series,"[56] during what is regarded as the height of "television's second golden age."[57]

2

PAGING "DR. SNOW"

Joshua Brand, John Falsey, and the
Making of *Northern Exposure*

When *Northern Exposure* was first sold to the producers at Universal Television and CBS, it was done so under the alias "Dr. Snow." At the end of the 1980s, the CBS programming catalog was overcrowded. The network had commissioned too many series, and they needed to clear the deck of excess projects. With its fall season prime-time slot dominated by the sitcom *Murphy Brown*, about the eponymous title character played by Candice Bergen, news anchor of fictional newsmagazine *FYI*, the only available slots were in the summer of 1990. The network needed what Elena Lazic called a "midseason slot-filler" to bridge the gap in their programming schedule between fall seasons, when new or returning popular series typically air.[1] The network had a gap to fill, and it needed something quick to fill it with.

Already under contract with the network, two television creatives were fortunately on hand to answer the call. Their names were Joshua Brand and John Falsey. Capitalizing on the long popularity of hospital dramas and series about medical professionals on American television, Brand and Falsey pitched the idea for "Dr. Snow." According to Brand, who spoke at a panel discussion at Austin's ATX Television Festival in 2017, "Dr. Snow" was to be a medical drama that would tell a fish-out-of-water story about a "quintessential New Yorker in the final frontier [Alas-

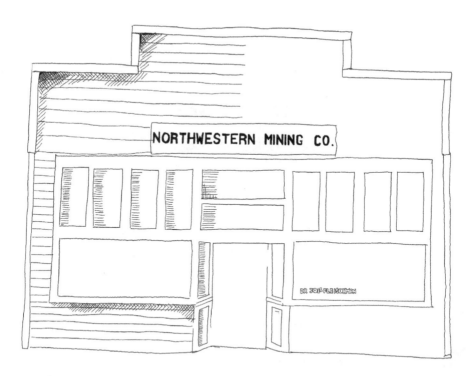

ka]."[2] Before continuing, it is important to establish a sense of the history of the medical drama on American television.

The medical drama emerged in the early 1950s with the likes of *City Hospital* and *Medic*, which starred Richard Boone as Dr. Konrad Styner, a head surgeon who helped his team navigate their personal and professional lives. Quickly, the genre captured the interest of television audiences, providing them with weekly isolated narrative arcs in which, over the course of a single episode, patients would be diagnosed, treated, and discharged. Such primary narrative structures were often paired with secondary narratives, typically borrowed from the soap opera or melodrama genres. These included relationships and affairs, scandalous activities, and crime and legal subplots, and some of these secondary narratives would span several episodes or entire seasons. Since the 1950s, the medical drama had only continued to grow, catering to growing appetites for a diversity of medical narratives on-screen. This evolution is perhaps best reflected in the medical television series of the 1960s and 1970s. Such series include *Dr. Kildare*, about the relationship between a young intern, played by Richard Chamberlain, and his mentor, played by Raymond Massey; the realist hospital drama *Ben Casey*, which pits the titular character, played by Vince Edwards, against the medical establishment; the long-running *General Hospital*, which merges the collective experiences of generations of employees and patients who work in or visit the hectic hospital located in Port Charles, New York; *Marcus Welby, M.D.*, which starred Robert Young and James Brolin as doctors Marcus Welby and Steven Kiley, respectively, who regularly butted heads over traditional and modern medical treatments while also trying to personalize the medical profession; and *Medical Center* (also called *Calling Dr. Gannon*), about the inner workings of a Los Angeles–based university hospital.

The 1970s and 1980s were both decades in which the medical drama arguably evolved. Influenced by the countercultural psyche left over from the previous decade, many of these dramas mobilized their context, becoming vehicles for sociopolitical commentary, while often also experimenting with the parameters of the genre. Typical of this period, medical dramas began to combine workplace and procedural drama with comedy. The satirical "dramedy" *M*A*S*H*, which was adapted from the same source material as Robert Altman's 1970 film (Robert Hooker's 1969 novel, M*A*S*H: *A Novel about Three Army Doctors*), was pioneering in this regard. CBS's hit series *M*A*S*H* influenced the network's relationship with the popular television genre. This dramedy, set during the Korean War, led to a flurry of medical dramas between the late 1970s and early 1990s. These included *Trapper John, M.D.*, which ported a veteran chief surgeon (played by Pernell Roberts) of a MASH unit from the Korean War to a present-day city hospital setting; the short-lived *Kay O'Brien*, which explored a resident surgeon (played by Patricia Kalember) who struggles to prevent her personal and professional lives from colliding; and, again, the short-lived *Island Son*, which saw an internist (played by Richard Chamberlain) return to his native Hawaii to give back to his former community.

Not only did *M*A*S*H* influence these dramas on network CBS, but it also inspired the output of other television stations. NBC, for example, produced and broadcast a number of medical dramas, each with its own unique twist on the genre. *Quincy, M.E.*, for instance, centered on the eponymous character Quincy (played by Jack Klugman), a coroner who investigates suspicious deaths, and in *Nightingales*, the focus is on the stories of five nursing students under the supervision of Christine Broderick (played by Suzanne Pleshette). Meanwhile, on network ABC, *Doogie Howser, M.D.* challenged the doctor paradigm by featuring a teenage physician (played by Neil Patrick Harris), and the ensemble drama *China Beach*—produced by John Wells, who would go on to produce the likes of *ER* and *The West Wing* in the 1990s—was a preview of television to come, with its high-budget production, expanse of characters, and complex technical elements (visuals aesthetics, direction, editing, and sound).

Now, back in the boardroom, given that Brand and Falsey pitched "Dr. Snow" as a medical drama, the network automatically assumed that each episode would strictly abide by the tried and tested formula and follow a tight set of familiar generic conventions: the series would be episodic; at the beginning of each episode, the doctor would travel to remote locations; the doctor would diagnose the patient(s); they would then go about tracking down medication and medical supplies (and have much difficulty doing so); and each episode would conclude with the patient being cured and discharged. It was an easy sell for the network. Given that on paper "Dr. Snow" promised to conform to the formulaic nature of the medical drama genre and shared similarities with some of the popular series released between the 1960s and 1980s, CBS green-lit Brand and Falsey's series.

Initially CBS placed a short order for just eight episodes of "Dr. Snow" and contracted Brand and Falsey to produce the series with the midseason broadcast window in mind. This was not a typical broadcast window for a new drama series, especially a series associated with a popular prime-time genre (namely the medical drama). This midseason window had the potential to be both a blessing and a curse for Brand and Falsey and "Dr. Snow." As Brand remarked in conversation with television critic Maureen Ryan at the ATX Television Festival in Austin in 2017, the network chose a slot in which "they thought no-one would watch."[3] However, Brand also recognized that being relegated to the midseason slot was not all bad. Rather than limiting the production, being perceived by executives as a "midseason slot-filler" actually granted him and Falsey a high degree of creative freedom and control over their project. Simply put, "Dr. Snow" was not a network priority. With the network's attention diverted elsewhere—to the likes of *Murphy Brown*—Brand and Falsey and the rest of the production team responsible for creating the pilot episode of "Dr. Snow" were able to fly under the radar, so to speak. The creatives, and by extension the series, were able to "operate entirely on [their] own terms."[4]

The story of the making of *Northern Exposure* is an underdog tale about a television series brought to life by a pair of renegade creators who duped the studios in order to make the series they wanted to create. Their vision, this book argues, was of a television series that would help pave the way for television as we know it today. They were ahead of their time. Their vision for *Northern Exposure* came about at a time when few were challenging popular formats and were generally failing to recognize the potential of the medium—a realization that would come at the end of the 1990s (especially with the offerings of HBO). This chapter is committed to exploring the development of *Northern Exposure*, from its early conception as "Dr. Snow" to the broadcast of its pilot and freshman season. Before considering answers to these questions and diving into the series story, however, it is vital to explore the biographies—both personal and professional—of its creators, Brand and Falsey. After all, part of the reason for the lack of interference from the studios in the production of "Dr. Snow" was the confidence the network placed in Brand and Falsey themselves as creatives, and in their ability to deliver a medical drama that fit the popular television format. This confidence was placed in the creative duo because of their prior successes in television. To begin to understand *Northern Exposure*, one has to understand Brand and Falsey and their contribution to the landscape of American television between the late 1970s and the 1990s.

BRAND AND FALSEY: AN INTRODUCTION

Born in Queens, New York, in 1950, the youngest child of Polish immigrant parents, Joshua Brand has always viewed the world from the perspective of an outsider. It is a perspective that has creatively informed the outlook of various characters central to the television dramas he has created, produced, or written for. Not least, it is a unique perspective reflected in the central character of Dr. Joel Fleischman in *Northern Exposure*, authenticating his outlook on the situation that he suddenly finds himself in when his plans to serve the city of Anchorage as a medical practitioner are diverted to Cicely, Alaska.

As a creative figure in the television industry, it is Brand's outsider perspective that drives his curiosity and daring to undertake all kinds of experiences and creative endeavors. Moreover, these endeavors are not just limited to his credits in television but extend to other fields. In college, for example, he wrote a children's book and a novel (both unpublished), and in his late twenties and early thirties he wrote plays for the stage, several of which were performed by Los Angeles–based amateur dramatic societies. While he was writing plays, he worked tirelessly to develop countless screenplays for the big and small screen alike. In regard to his work in film and television, Brand attributes his fortune—and before success, his willingness to at least try—to a blatant unawareness. His approach to trying new things, he confesses, comes from a position of "not knowing enough or not knowing too much."[5]

It is Brand's adventurousness, born from his own naïveté, that has afforded him many creative opportunities, some of which resulted in several small-screen successes: in the 1980s and 1990s with the critically acclaimed and highly awarded *St. Elsewhere* and *Northern Exposure*, respectively, and more recently with the FX series *The Americans*, about two Russian agents (played by Matthew Rhys and Keri Russell) operating in America at the height of the Cold War. On *The Americans*, Brand served as a writer and consulting producer. While Brand's career in television is consistent and successful, the start of his career path was purely coincidental. It is a career that has, to a large extent, fallen into place.

As a child, Brand was brought up without knowledge of the television or film industries. The son of a tiler and a houseperson, the television industry was never a professional consideration for a young Brand. He viewed television much the same way that the average American of the 1950s and 1960s viewed it, as an object of pleasure, a source of entertainment, and a signifier of social status for the postwar (World War II) American household. As such, Brand includes *The Ed Sullivan Show*, the incredibly popular American variety show that ran between 1948 and 1971 and premiered the likes of Elvis Presley and the Beatles, as being one of the television series he remembers watching with his family as a child.

In the same way that a career in the entertainment industry was never a consideration for Brand, neither was writing. Not having been brought up in a literary family, Brand's early literary ambitions were as much a surprise to Brand's family as they were to himself. After leaving high school, Brand pursued his literary interests at university, enrolling in an undergraduate degree program in English literature before going on to graduate school at Columbia University on a full fellowship. Leaving college with a master's degree and two unpublished manuscripts under his arm (the aforementioned children's book and a novel) in 1974, Brand admits he was, as generally many twenty-something humanities students leaving college are, completely unaware of what he wanted to do next. It was at his sister's wedding that Brand was first introduced to the prospect of a future in the entertainment industry. It was there that he met a screenwriter from Westport, Connecticut, who spoke to him about writing for the screen. On reflection, Brand credits his education about writing for the screen to this conversation.[6] Not only was a young Brand convinced that a future in screenwriting lay ahead for him, but he was persuaded enough to make the move out west, from New York City to Los Angeles, the exodus of many creative people in American cultural history.

On the advice of some friends in Los Angeles, Brand quickly secured an agent who advised him to write a spec script for a television series. "What's a spec script?" asked an unaware Brand. The agent explained to the budding screenwriter that he needed to write an episode for television that they could forward to the people working in television. "What happens then?" "Well, if they like it, maybe they'll buy it. If not, they give you a job writing something for the television show," the agent replied.[7]

On the advice of the agent, Brand set about writing his first spec script for the short-lived CBS series *Delvecchio*, written by Steven Bochco, who had previous created *Hill Street Blues*, along with Michael Kozoll, writer of *First Blood*, who had, before *Delvecchio*, worked on episodes of *Kolchak: The Night Stalker*, *Switch*, and *Quincy, M.E.* *Delvecchio* ran for one season, with a total of twenty-two episodes. It starred Judd Hirsch as the title character, Detective Dominick Delvecchio, an Italian American detective and law student working for the Los Angeles Police Department (LAPD).

While he submitted his screenplay with enthusiasm, on this occasion Brand was unsuccessful. Based on the rejection of his spec script for *Delvecchio*, Brand concluded that the process of writing a spec script was a waste of time. From that moment onward, he decided that rather than invest his time and efforts into writing a full script, which if rejected would just be thrown away, he would instead commit to just writing a single act of a television episode (approximately fifteen pages), which when completed resembled a play. As far as Brand was concerned, what he chose to write were effectively theatrical scenes. "Three people in a room talking."[8] His rationale was that if the studio rejected it, at least the script had a chance with the amateur dramatic societies of Los Angeles. Brand's instincts were right; often his scripts made it to the stage more than they made it onto the small screen.

Brand's plays did not immediately lead to a job in the television industry. However, after a few years of touring these screenplays–turned–theatrical scripts on stage, one of his plays caught the attention of a valuable audience member and someone Brand knew from New York City. Brand was around twenty-seven at the time. The event would change the young writer's luck. The person was Jeff Sagansky, a young NBC executive who would later run the network CBS TriStar Pictures between 1989 and 1994. Though he did not immediately reach out to Brand, Sagansky remembered Brand and called him up with a job offer a year later. Sagansky invited Brand to write an episode for a television series that, like many others, would sadly never air. Rather than view the incident as a setback, Brand chose to take away a different message: that yes was a better word than no. As Brand explains in his interview, "Yes creates possibilities and no ends possibilities. No is a steel curtain." Of course, Brand is careful in the interview not to advise anyone to say yes to everything. But he goes on to remind us that we "always have the no card in [our] pocket. You can always pull it out any time you want," Brand assures. "I learned that . . . unless you really don't want to do something, then what the hell?"[9]

After a few years of selling scripts and plays and living within a strict financial budget, surviving hand to mouth, Brand made the difficult decision to move back to New York City with the hope of getting a job teaching at one of the city colleges. In the mid-1970s, New York City was suffering. It was on the verge of bankruptcy—a result of the nationwide economic stagnation of the 1970s, which saw large swathes of the urban middle class swapping the cities for the suburbs. The city's fiscal crisis not only created a climate of self-destruction, with the city riddled with crime, but led to a hiring freeze, which immediately dashed the prospects of a returning writer and hopeful teacher such as Brand. The blatant lack of opportunities on the East Coast forced Brand to reconsider his move and resulted in his prompt return to Los Angeles. This time, however, his venture would be more successful. On this professional attempt, he would not only secure a job writing for television but would meet his longtime creative collaborator, John Falsey.

Like Brand, John Falsey was born (1951) into a family that was not interested or involved in the entertainment industry. Falsey was the son of a tax lawyer and a teacher from New Haven, Connecticut. Also similar to Brand, Falsey realized his creativity at college when he left Connecticut for Massachusetts in the early 1970s to gain a bachelor of arts degree in English at Hampshire College. Falsey graduated in 1975 and went on to earn a master of fine arts in creative writing from the prestigious Iowa Writers' Workshop in 1978, where he had attended workshops by Jane Smiley, the 1991 Pulitzer Prize winner for her novel *A Thousand Acres*, and science-fiction master Joe Haldeman, best known for *The Forever War*. It was during his time at the Iowa Writers' Workshop that Falsey's career as a writer, and specifically as a writer for television, began at the age of twenty-seven.

At this time, Falsey wrote and submitted a short story to the *New Yorker* titled "Bachelors"; it later appeared on page twenty-four in the 9 January 1978 issue. "Bachelors" is about three men—the narrator, his father, and his best friend Charles—whose lives are affected by the death of the narrator's mother. The publication in the *New Yorker* was not only a great achievement for the budding writer but caught the attention of director and producer Bruce Paltrow (father of Gwyneth and Jake). The story led to Paltrow hiring Falsey in 1979 to write for a television series on which he was the producer, senior writer, and director (of eight episodes). That series was *The White Shadow*.

THE WHITE SHADOW

Long before the drama *Friday Night Lights* or the Netflix docuseries *Cheer* explored the complicated lives of young sportspeople in the American high school system, there was the television series *The White Shadow*. The series shone a light on the lives of the players and coaches of a mixed-race, inner-city high school basketball team from Los Angeles, coached by ex-NBA player Ken Reeves (played by Ken Howard). Any good sports drama, like any good drama, full stop, whether it be a series about gangsters, lawyers, politicians, or medical professionals, is about the personal lives of its characters as much as it is about their academic or professional commitments. Alongside his duties as the head of a crime family, Tony Soprano (James Gandolfini), for example, juggles his marital and paternal pressures in *The Sopranos*; outside the courtroom, Alicia Florrick (Julianna Margulies) reassembles her personal life after the devastating revelation of her husband's affair shatters her family in *The Good Wife*; and likewise, Don Draper's past and secret identity often collide with his personal and professional lives in *Mad Men*, affecting his relationships and commitments. *The White Shadow* was about the personal lives of the pupils of Carver High School, the fictional high school that provided the setting for the drama, as much as it was about their athletic and academic lives. Like the wave of series with a focus on the lives of teenagers in the high school system that followed it—including *My So-Called Life*, *Dawson's Creek*, *The O.C.*, *Glee*, and *Riverdale*—each episode of *The White Shadow* addressed the myriad of problems that affect the everyday lives of younger people. The characters, known in the series by their nicknames, including the likes of Coolidge (played by Byron Stewart), CJ (played by Erik Kilpatrick), Hollywood (played by Thomas Carter), Go-Go (played by Ira Angustain), Goldstein (played by Ken Michelman), New York (played by John Mengatti), Salami (played by Timothy Van Patten), and Thorpe (played by Kevin Hooks), regularly brought their issues to the attention of Coach Reeves or the various academic staff at Carver High School. These included everything from their personal struggles with addiction, sexuality, bullying, teen pregnancy, and physical and mental disabilities to issues from their home lives, such as domestic violence and absent or unfit parents.

While these story lines are now considered commonplace for young adult drama series, when it was released in the late 1970s, *The White Shadow* was considered trailblazing. For its daring to explore such issues as sexuality and teen prostitution, for example, *The White Shadow* was critically lauded. During its limited run of three seasons on CBS, the series was nominated for consecutive Emmy Awards for Best Drama in 1980 and 1981. The legacy of *The White Shadow* extends beyond its accolades, however. As actor-turned-director Thomas Carter (who played "Hollywood" in the series) reinforces in an interview in the *New York Post*,

It [*The White Shadow*] was very ahead of its time, man. We did so many things that were shocking, unheard of things on TV in the '70s. . . . I really liked that the show from the start didn't want to be simply a show about basketball, but was going to be daring and ambitious enough to try and say important things and make a difference.[10]

John Falsey started work as a writer on *The White Shadow* on episode 8 of its first season, titled "One of the Boys," and he would go on to write seven more episodes. *The White Shadow* is an important addition to Falsey's résumé, signifying his induction into the television industry and representing a series on which he earned his first industry credits as a writer and story editor. More importantly, however, it was behind the scenes of *The White Shadow* that Falsey's life would change significantly: it was during his interview for the job as writer on the series that he first met his long-term collaborator, Joshua Brand, who was also trying out for the CBS drama.

Just before *The White Shadow*, Joshua Brand had earned a regular writing staff credit for his contribution to the television series *Operation Petticoat* (also known as *Petticoat Affair*), after successfully pitching the idea of "*M*A*S*H* in a submarine" to the network. However, after finding out that the network had been adapting his ideas without formal credit, Brand soon quit the series. As Brand put it in his interview with Matz, "Basically I got tired of being fucked up the ass."[11] When he walked away from *Operation Petticoat*, Brand did not leave completely empty-handed. After some resistance, the studio granted him a teleplay credit for his work on the series, earning him a place in the Writer's Guild.

In search of a new job, Brand was invited to pitch some ideas to Marc Rubin, a writer on *The White Shadow*. Rubin had overseen a four-episode story arc and had written over ten episodes of the series. Brand was brought into a room where he was introduced to Falsey, who was in turn introduced as a writer fresh out of the Iowa Writers' Workshop. The two viewed an episode of *The White Shadow* and were tasked with generating new ideas for the series. The process was pleasant and fruitful. The young writers immediately gelled. In fact, they got along so well that Brand, upon hearing that Falsey would be alone during the Thanksgiving holiday, invited him to celebrate with him and his girlfriend at the time. Falsey gratefully declined. The following day, Brand received a phone call from an excited Falsey. The studio had bought his ideas. While Brand

was disappointed that the studio had rejected his own ideas, he nevertheless congratulated Falsey on their acceptance of his. This would be the
last exchange the pair would have for a while.

That Christmas, Brand had returned to New York City to try to get a
job teaching at City College. However, as formerly mentioned, due to the
city's financial crisis, he failed to find one. The odds stacked against him,
he soon found himself traveling back to Los Angeles to try his hand at
writing for the screen once again. Coincidentally, on the flight back to
Los Angeles, Brand overheard a familiar voice coming from down the
aisle. It was Falsey. Switching seats with a fellow passenger, the two sat
next to each other and talked for the remainder of the flight.

Back in Los Angeles, it was not long before Brand heard from Falsey.
Falsey invited him to pitch ideas to Rubin again. This time, based on
Falsey's recommendation, the network commissioned Brand's ideas, but
nothing came of them. However, just a few months later, Falsey called
Brand again. At this point, however, Falsey was not just a writer on *The
White Shadow* but the story editor, and he presented Brand with an offer
to write an episode with him. The only caveat was that they had just three
days to do it. The time pressure did not dampen their creativity, however.
In fact, it had quite the opposite effect. Not only did the deadline motivate
them to produce a script quickly, but the challenge solidified their friendship in the process. The script led to Brand and Falsey working together
on six more episodes of *The White Shadow* before Falsey brought Brand
on board permanently as a story editor. "John was a story editor, and he
was instrumental in me getting my first script assignment on the show,"
Brand said in the *New York Times*.[12] It was a favor that Brand would later
return, inviting Falsey to collaborate with him on his next series. But
more on that soon. The title "story editor" conjures up the image of a
figure overseeing a writer's room. In reality however, this was far from
the truth. Brand and Falsey did not oversee a writer's room. They *were*
the writer's room.

Beyond their friendship, Brand and Falsey's partnership proved fruitful. For Brand, the experience was especially enriching, earning him an
education in how the television industry works. When he got the opportunity to write for *The White Shadow*, Brand committed wholeheartedly.
Not only did the experience teach him about collaborating with others
and the technicalities of writing for the small screen, but he gained a
higher knowledge about the inner workings and the interconnectedness

between media. Fundamentally, this awareness allowed him to cross between the mediums of film and television and to even blur the lines
between genres, such as comedy and drama. More importantly, however,
it allowed him to overcome previously perceived barriers. Brand discov-
ered that the more he worked on the production, the more it was revealed
to him that the line between television and film, which he had always
perceived as a "steel curtain," was "bullshit."[13] The experience of working with Falsey on *The White Shadow* solidified Brand's disposition as a
writer. Furthermore, it validated his outlook on life, which was to always
try new things—a position that came from "not knowing enough or not
knowing too much."[14] However, just as Brand and Falsey were finding
their groove and navigating the television industry through *The White
Shadow*, the industry pulled the proverbial rug out from under their feet.

Despite positive reviews and several accolades, in 1981 *The White
Shadow* was canceled, but this was not the end of the road for Brand and
Falsey's creative partnership. As the networks and those involved in producing the series anticipated *The White Shadow*'s cancellation, they had
already started to consider Brand and Falsey's next project. One of these
people was Grant Tinker, the cofounder of MTM Enterprises, along with
his then wife, the Renaissance woman Mary Tyler Moore. Moore established herself as a jill-of-all-trades over the course of her life and career,
moving from the position of actress, with roles in *The Dick Van Dyke
Show* and the self-titled *Mary Tyler Moore Show*, to producer. In 1969,
along with her husband Grant Tinker, Moore established MTM Enterprises, the production company behind a long line of hits for television,
including *The Bob Newhart Show*, *Rhoda*, *Lou Grant*, and *Hill Street
Blues*, among many others. Moore was also a successful writer and acti-
vist. MTM Enterprises had produced *The White Shadow*. After its cancellation, Tinker approached Brand and Falsey and asked them what projects
they had lined up. For Falsey, his plans were to work on a miniseries
about Northern Ireland. For Brand, he had an idea for a new series.
Inspired by a friend who went to medical school named Lance Luria,
Brand wanted to develop a drama set in a hospital.[15] As Brand admits, it
was really his friend's idea, who one day said to him, "You know, someone really ought to write a show about what goes on in a teaching hospital. You would not fucking believe what goes on; it's unbelievable." His
pitch, while perhaps undercooked, was immediately met with enthusiasm
by Tinker, who responded, "*Hill Street* in a hospital."[16] Tinker was refer-

ring here, of course, to the police drama *Hill Street Blues* that he and Moore had produced, which had just aired on NBC. *Hill Street Blues* was earning sweeping critical acclaim, with many television critics and scholars already hailing the series for redefining television. *Hill Street Blues* earned its reputation for its creative choices as much as for the adult nature of its script. Resisting the gimmicks of the cop drama, *Hill Street Blues* instead adopted a realist aesthetic, like that of a New Hollywood film such as *Serpico*. Rather than appealing to a wide family audience, the script was notably adult in tone, with hard-hitting issues and dialogue riddled with what was regarded as profanity (at least in the context of genre television). In terms of its storytelling, the series opted out of focusing on a single detective or police duo and instead utilized multiple narrative threads to chronicle the interwoven professional and personal lives of an inner-city police precinct, reflected in its large cast of characters. Tinker's vision for Brand's pitch would switch the police setting for a hospital setting, the criminal investigation for the diagnosis and treatment of patients, and the hierarchy of the precinct for the politics of the city hospital—all with the ambition of driving television even further as a storytelling medium.

Fortunately for Tinker, Brand shared his vision, adding that the series should include complex stories inspired by real-world events, and in terms of its genre, it had to fuse comedy with drama, much as earlier series (such as *M*A*S*H*) had in the 1970s. Tinker slept on it but did not keep Brand waiting for long. He called Brand within days of their discussion with the offer of a thirteen-episode order based on his idea. But Brand did not immediately bite.

"Why?" asked a surprised Tinker.

"I want to create the show," said Brand. "I want to be the producer." Tinker agreed, but Brand's conditions did not end there. In addition to producing the series, Brand also wanted his partner Falsey on board as a writer. But to Brand's surprise, when he took the offer to Falsey, he declined. On Brand's second appeal to Falsey, he reworked his offer: "Do you want to produce the series with me?"

The two shook hands.[17]

ST. ELSEWHERE

True to Grant Tinker's initial reaction to Joshua Brand's original pitch, on the surface *St. Elsewhere* appeared to be essentially *"Hill Street [Blues]* in a hospital." In the opinion of Alan Sepinwall, with *St. Elsewhere*, Brand and the producers had succeeded in "transplant[ing] the *Hill Street* formula to a hospital setting" in their exploration of the intersection between the working and private lives of the staff of St. Eligius, a run-down teaching hospital in Boston.[18] But while Tinker's summary of *St. Elsewhere* in one sentence is effective from a marketing standpoint, to characterize *St. Elsewhere* in such a way is, in the opinion of this writer, reductive. *St. Elsewhere* is as ambitious as it is eccentric. In terms of its qualities, it is defined by its experimental plotlines, its unique blend of dark comedy, and its naturalistic visual aesthetics. Beyond its audiovisual stylistic choices and its darkly comic tone, the series is also regarded for its narrative daring and prestige cast of characters, including Mark Harmon as Dr. Robert Caldwell, Ed Begley Jr. as Dr. Victor Ehrlich, Denzel Washington as Dr. Philip Chandler, David Morse as Dr. Jack "Boomer" Morrison, Helen Hunt as Clancy Williams, and many other would-be high-profile actors in film and television alike. While the series invested in such talent to portray its complex characters, *St. Elsewhere* equally earned a reputation long before the likes of *Game of Thrones* for killing off primary characters in unexpected ways. In 1983, for example, *St. Elsewhere* broke ground as the first prime-time television series to depict an HIV/AIDS patient, responding to the tragic epidemic unfolding beyond the screen. Rather than fall in line with the popular narrative that HIV/AIDS was a disease that only affected homosexual men, the writers decided to focus on its contraction by a heterosexual character. Its victim was the notorious womanizer Dr. Robert Caldwell. During their time writing for *St. Elsewhere*, such narratives had earned Brand and Falsey the nicknames "Dr. Death and Mr. Depression" because of their dark humor and the often fatal consequences their words on the page had on the characters on the screen.[19]

While often operating within the parameters of realism, drawing from news headlines and current affairs such as national and global health epidemics, race tensions, urban crime, and class in America, *St. Elsewhere* was no stranger to the surreal. One example of this is the dreamlike flashback narrative in "Time Heals Parts 1 and 2" (4.17 and 4.18). Another, the notoriously controversial finale, "The Last One" (6.12), in which the entire drama is revealed to be the product of the imagination of Tommy (Chad Allen), Dr. Donald Westfall's (Ed Flanders) autistic son. The finale set a new standard for television and its capacity to inspire or provoke (depending on your opinion). Furthermore, when it was broadcast on 25 May 1988, the finale of *St. Elsewhere* was watched by 22.5 million viewers, placing it in the twenty most-watched television finales of all time.

St. Elsewhere's experimental nature, while divisive at times, did not deter audiences and critics. Quite the contrary, in fact. *St. Elsewhere* attracted a steady audience and earned wide acclaim. "If some of its story arcs could be preposterous," writes Emily Todd VanDerWerff of *The A.V. Club*, *St. Elsewhere*'s "finest moments and strongest episodes remain among the best television has ever produced."[20] John J. O'Connor of the *New York Times* referred to the series as "stylish" and "very special and rewarding."[21] And, reflecting back on *St. Elsewhere*'s originality, *Business Insider*'s Carrie Wittmer writes, "'St. Elsewhere' was one of the first truly ground-breaking dramas that experimented with the episodic format and wasn't afraid to take narrative risks."[22] However, Wittmer does go on to critique the series finale, which in her opinion "tried way too hard to outdo its incredible self in its finale."[23]

As well as a positive response from critics then and now, during its six-season run on NBC, *St. Elsewhere* was recognized by the academy, garnering sixty-three Emmy nominations and winning thirteen awards, despite finishing in forty-ninth position or lower in ratings tables during the broadcast of each passing season. In 1984, *St. Elsewhere* earned what is possibly its biggest accolade, the Peabody Award. Named after American businessman and philanthropist George Foster Peabody (1852–1938), the Peabody Award "exist[s] to recognize when storytelling is done well; when stories matter." It celebrates stories "that engage viewers as citizens as well as consumers [and] demonstrate how media can defend the public interest, encourage empathy with others, and teach us to expand our understanding of the world around us." In their rationale for awarding *St. Elsewhere*, the Peabody committee wrote,

> From Young Dr. Kildare to Marcus Welby, from Janet Dean, R.N. to Trapper John, M.D., medical programs have been a staple of American popular entertainment. Unfortunately, most portrayals treat doctors as heroic archetypes, and their tools and procedures as the ultimate tri-

umph of technology over human frailty. St. Elsewhere is a glorious exception to this trend. Each week, this outstanding series examines the complexities of life in a Boston hospital—from personal pressures to professional rivalries, from the chaos of the emergency room to the solace of the chapel. St. Elsewhere is distinguished television, set apart from other dramatic series by its depth of characterization, crisp and believable dialogue, and unusual variety in lighting, staging and photography. The only regularly-scheduled dramatic series to be so recognized, a 1984 Peabody Award to NBC and MTM Enterprises for St. Elsewhere.[24]

St. Elsewhere would mark the first of three Peabody Awards awarded to television series created by Brand and Falsey.

Traditionally in the television industry, positive critical reception and recognition in the form of awards are seldom enough to keep a series on air. The reason *St. Elsewhere* was kept on air for so long rested in the fact that the series was fruitful to advertisers. With its stylistic conventions, daring narratives, and sometimes morally ambiguous characters aside—which earned the series a place in critical and scholarly discussions about so-called "quality TV" since[25] —*St. Elsewhere,* in the opinion of Van-DerWerff, "deserves to be remembered as the show that led to an idea that's essentially taken over television: keeping a program on the air because it appeals to a younger demographic."[26] According to VanDer-Werff, *St. Elsewhere* was kept on air exclusively because of its appeal to a specific demographic: namely young adults. In *MTM: "Quality TV,"* Jane Feuer highlights the significance of the "quality TV" demographic to the television industry. The "quality TV" demographic—or what Feuer describes as the "young, urban adult viewer"—is a significant group in the television industry, especially since the advent of cable and, more recently, on demand.[27] For advertisers in particular, capturing the attention of the "young, urban adult viewer" presents a prime commercial opportunity to advertisers to tailor their adverts and the products they sell—which includes television technologies and services themselves—in order to exploit the disposable income of an upwardly mobile generation. Moreover, for each specific network television station (whether CBS, NBC, ABC, or HBO), appealing to this demographic is seen as a victory, in that they have essentially succeeded in persuading them—at least for that particular time slot—away from the allure of the offerings of other cable television channels.[28] This was as true in the 1980s as it is today.

The younger demographic is still what the industry depends on today in the era of "quality" and "prestige" offerings from the likes of networks such as HBO, FX, and AMC, who, like the competing networks of the 1980s (NBC, CBS, and ABC), today compete with the likes of on –demand services such as Netflix, Hulu, Amazon Prime Instant Video, and Disney+. For this reason, among many others, *St. Elsewhere* is a series with a long-reaching cultural legacy that is still felt today. As Robert J. Thompson writes in the *Washington Post*,

> "*St. Elsewhere*" did to medical dramas what "*Hill Street Blues*" did to police shows: It crowded the screen with a large ensemble cast, padded the script with a bewildering number of ongoing stories and introduced human flaws to a breed of professionals that television previously had presented as super-human. The personal lives of the doctors were as important as the jobs they were doing. They were flawed, they made mistakes and their patients didn't always get better. "*St. Elsewhere*" was a literary achievement, filled with sophisticated dialogue, complex stories and an attention to narrative detail never before seen in a TV series. Although critics loved the show, it never achieved real ratings success over its six-year run.[29]

From *ER* to *Grey's Anatomy*, from *The Good Doctor* to *New Amsterdam*, it is impossible to consider the medical drama today without first considering *St. Elsewhere*.

Despite only being involved with its first two seasons, leaving due to creative differences and going on to work on other television projects, with *St. Elsewhere*, Brand and Falsey had revolutionized both the medical drama and arguably television in the 1980s and beyond. In his call for audiences to revisit *St. Elsewhere*, Sepinwall lauds the "morally complicated drama" for its profound complexity in regard to characters; its responsiveness to contemporary issues; its intertextual relationship with itself, its genre, and television; and its willingness to take risks that paved the way for the television that followed it.[30] With the exception of *Hill Street Blues*, *St. Elsewhere* had perhaps the most impact on the landscape of American television, influencing a host of contemporary medical dramas and arguably television series more broadly ever since.

A YEAR IN THE LIFE

For Joshua Brand, "never say no" became something of a mantra. While a dangerous prospect, given that it could lead to all kinds of creative catastrophes, for Brand it is a mantra that has only led to good things. Brand and John Falsey's follow-up to *St. Elsewhere*, *A Year in the Life*, is a perfect illustration of this.

A Year in the Life was a television event. The first of its three feature-length episodes, a total of six hours, aired on NBC on 15 December 1986 and ran consecutively until 17 December. *A Year in the Life* retreads familiar territory, for Falsey specifically. With echoes of the plot of his *New Yorker* short story "The Bachelor," *A Year in the Life* is a melodrama that provides a snapshot of the lives of a Seattle-based family, the Gardeners, a year after the death of the matriarch, from Christmas season to Christmas season. The Gardener family consists of a father, Joe (played by Richard Kiley), and his four adult children: daughters Anne (played by Wendy Phillips) and Lindley (played by Jayne Atkinson) and sons Jack (played by Morgan Stevens) and Sam (played by David Oliver).

When it aired, *A Year in the Life* opened to rave reviews, particularly from John J. O'Connor of the *New York Times*, who praised its achievements, especially given that it was a drama restricted to the television miniseries template. Furthermore, O'Connor's review recognizes the series's ambitions to challenge and transcend the boundaries of storytelling in the soap opera genre:

> There are soap operas—the most visible being television's so-called daytime dramas—and there are soap operas—the tonier efforts such as British series "*Upstairs, Downstairs*" and the films "*Terms of Endearment*" or "*Kramer vs Kramer.*" Somewhere in the middle is "*A Year in the Life.*" . . . At first glance, the Gardeners might have stepped out of some glossy magazine ad as they cheerfully exude warmth and togetherness. Up close, of course, they are mired in enough problems to keep a typical domestic drama at a vigorous simmer. [31]

The formula of taking something familiar, or even tired, and giving it a fresh spin, as O'Connor recognizes in his review of *A Year in the Life*, seems to come naturally to Brand and Falsey. It could be suggested that it is their creative signature, as arguable auteurs of television, and their stamp on television history. *The White Shadow*, for example, added a complexity to the high school narrative, granting its cast of young adult characters a fresh voice, treating them and their issues with respect, and maturing the format of the teen drama, just as film had done in the 1950s with Nicolas Ray's 1955 classic *Rebel without a Cause*, for example. Similarly, with *St. Elsewhere*, Brand and Falsey self-consciously re-worked the genre of the television medical drama (at least while they were attached to the series), reconfiguring its conventions and expanding its narrative to both reflect everyday events while equally subverting viewer expectations. This time mobilizing the melodrama genre, Brand and Falsey used *A Year in the Life* to elevate the soap opera. They began by carefully casting for the roles of the Gardener family, pulling in a mix of experienced actors from the stage and from the screen. Doing so brought both confidence and depth to the performances. Meanwhile, the combination of excellent direction by Thomas Carter and Brand and writing, in the form of a fine-tuned script developed by Brand, Falsey, and Stu Krieger, added levels of complexity to what is, or what could be interpreted as, a fairly generic dramatic premise. As O'Connor rightly points out, rather than overcomplicating the narrative of a family working through their individual dramas and collective grief, *A Year in the Life*'s true strength was its focus on the finer details and events in life that have significance. As O'Connor writes, "at its best, 'A Year in the Life' captures the essence of small moments that can have enormous meaning."[32]

While skillfully executed in the end, *A Year in the Life* was not a smooth production. Brand and Falsey were brought onto the project in August 1986. Unlike the situation where creatives first join a television series and have a reasonable amount of time to spend on development and preproduction, filming, and postproduction, on day one, Brand and Falsey were told by the executives at NBC that the series had to air on Christmas that same year. In light of this rapid, and quite frankly seemingly impossible, turnaround, they would have to start shooting in October for the project to be ready in time. And if that wasn't enough, there was one more surprise in store for Brand and Falsey: there was no script. Governed not by rationale but by a mantra ("never say no"), Brand and Falsey, rather than quit on the spot, instead embraced the challenge.

Brand openly admits that family dramas were not his thing, but they were of interest to Falsey: "He always loved the family stuff. He would have been happy to continue doing the family stuff. I got bored."[33] Fortunately, Brand stuck it out. As well as high praise from critics, *A Year in the Life* was well received by audiences, achieving the third-highest ratings between 1986 and 1987. Furthermore, it was recognized at annual award ceremonies with top prizes: the drama won a Primetime Emmy Award for Outstanding Limited Series (1987); meanwhile, for actor Richard Kiley, he was awarded a Primetime Emmy for Outstanding Lead Actor in a Drama Series (1988) and a Golden Globe for Best Performance by an Actor in a Television Series—Drama (1988).

"NOT KNOWING ENOUGH OR NOT KNOWING TOO MUCH"

With their collaborations *The White Shadow*, *St. Elsewhere*, and *A Year in the Life*, Joshua Brand and John Falsey helped define "television's second golden age."[34] Moreover, the combined experience of working together on these series helped establish Brand and Falsey's creative collaborative process. Brand and Falsey had cracked the code, had figured out their dynamic as creatives, and had defined a particular style of television series in the process: their series were experimental; they contained complicated characters; they had a playful approach to genre; they were both self-referential and self-reflexive; and, most importantly, they were willing to take risks. Such risks had led them in the first place to enter an industry with no prior knowledge. Such risks caused them to say yes to projects rather than no. Such risks put them in the same room where they had to learn to collaborate. But, fundamentally, such risks allowed them to commit to trying new things with a *fuck it* mentality—a philosophy even, one that comes from "not knowing enough or not knowing too much."[35]

Brand and Falsey's imprint on the American television landscape is profound, despite only working together on a handful of projects. As Christopher Keyser, the president of the Writers Guild of America West (WGAW), writes, their collaboration—which has garnered, in total, over fifty Emmy Award nominations—has led to "some of TV's most enduring, memorable series that have both entertained and moved a generation of viewers."[36] He continues, "Defined by an expert blend of sharp observation, dry wit, and honest emotion, their work is, like a singer with a five-octave range, breathtaking in its scope and its power. Together,

Brand and Falsey have created an enviable legacy that both veteran and up-and-coming writers can aspire to match."[37] Along with the critical praise and the cultural currency of their names in the television industry as the creators of "one of the first truly ground-breaking dramas,"[38] it was only natural that when the time came to pitch *Northern Exposure* to Universal Television and CBS (under the alias of "Dr. Snow"), Brand and Falsey banked on their previous success and celebrity as creators who could execute concept.

NORTHERN EXPOSURE

The fish-out-of-water premise of *Northern Exposure*—the outsider thrust into a new place and a strange way of life—is not a new one, nor was it in 1990. However, the influences that inspired the series, both its basis and its characteristic nature, are rooted in a unique blend of filmic references and cocreator Joshua Brand's personal biography. In an interview with the Writers Guild Foundation, Brand is up front about these influences. Brand is a fan of Scottish film director Bill Forsyth, who is best known for writing and directing *That Sinking Feeling*, *Gregory's Girl*, and *Comfort and Joy*. When it came to conceiving *Northern Exposure*, Brand found quite a bit of inspiration in another of Forsyth's films: his understated 1983 film *Local Hero*.[39] *Local Hero* depicts the journey of MacIntyre (Peter Riegert), a Houston-based oil executive of the Knox company who is sent by his boss, the eccentric Felix Happer (Burt Lancaster), to the remote Scottish village of Ferness to buy the town for the development of an oil refinery. Ferness, complete with its rural stereotypes and folkloric traditions, alienates Mac at first. However, as business and pleasure begin to mix, "Mac finds himself enchanted by both the picturesque community and its oddball denizens."[40] *Local Hero* is a unique blend of both drama and comedy—a combination that is perfectly embodied and conveyed in Riegert's performance as Mac as he navigates everyday life in the remote village. Likewise, it is a careful balance that surfaces in the equally dramatic and witty script delivered by the eccentric locals and supporting cast and characters. These include the Scottish Knox representative Danny Oldsen, played by *The Thick of It* and *Doctor Who*'s Peter Capaldi (who played the twelfth incarnation of the titular character between 2014 and 2017); the hotelier-cum-waiter-cum-lawyer-cum-barman Gordon Urquhart, played by Denis Lawson; a visiting Russian named Victor, portrayed by Christopher Rozycki; and the stubborn beachcomber Ben Knox, played by Fulton Mackay, who will not sell Mac his land. As Criterion writes of Forsyth's film,

> Packed with a near nonstop stream of droll one-liners and deadpan gags, this enchanting cult hit finds Forsyth surveying the idiosyncrasies of small-town life with the satirical verve of a latter-day Preston Sturges, arriving at a sly commentary on conservation, corporate greed, and the legacies we leave behind.[41]

Local Hero is the blueprint for *Northern Exposure*. Tonally, it is like-for-like. In terms of its cast of characters, the television series shares striking similarities, from the barman-cum-mayor-cum-hotelier with a young partner, which Holling and Shelley are a near carbon copy of, to a visiting Russian to Ferness who speaks poetry and sings, such like season 2's Nikolai. And Riegert's performance could be viewed as a blueprint for Rob Morrow's Dr. Joel Fleischman. Not only does Morrow's Joel share a general physical resemblance to fellow New Yorker Riegert in terms of appearance and styling, but in his posture and accent too. It is tempting to imply that this similarity is in no way a coincidence, given Brand's professed love of *Local Hero*.

The second influence on Brand came from another film, coincidentally released in 1983. The film was Disney's *Never Cry Wolf*—Disney's first feature film to be released under the label "Walt Disney Pictures." Sourced from Farley Mowat's autobiographical novel, *Never Cry Wolf*, directed by Carroll Ballard, tells the story of Tyler (Charles Martin Smith), a biologist who embarks on a solo government-sponsored mission to research arctic wolves. Lauded for its "compassion, commitment, and unexpected humor,"[42] for Brand, Ballard's film was revelatory for another reason. Aside from its depiction of nature at its rawest in the frozen wilds of the Canadian Arctic—a climate that Tyler struggles to adapt to much in the same way that Joel struggles to adapt to remote Alaska—*Never Cry Wolf* profoundly influenced Brand with its depiction of indigenous peoples. As Brand reflects, "I'd never seen them [indigenous people and their culture] depicted like that in anything. They were real."[43]

Both *Local Hero* and *Never Cry Wolf* are seminal films for understanding the story of *Northern Exposure*. Both films offer a distinct take on culture-clash story lines, a staple of the fish-out-of-water narrative. The sense of alienation of their protagonists, both MacIntyre and Tyler, can quite easily be traced to Joel as he adapts to small-town life in Cicely. Both films—but especially *Local Hero*, with its blend of drama and comedy—set the tone for the writing, direction, and general nature and pace of *Northern Exposure*. Moreover, and perhaps most importantly, *Never Cry Wolf* would ensure that the writers of *Northern Exposure* aspired to a higher standard for respectfully representing its extensive Native American cast.

As mentioned, there was a third influence on Brand that would cement his vision for *Northern Exposure*, and once again it was found in his friend, Lance Luria, who had previously inspired the idea for *St. Elsewhere*. Though he was not exactly like Joel, at the point when Brand was first circling the idea of *Northern Exposure*, Luria himself was living and had his own practice in the middle of nowhere in Upstate New York.[44] Therefore, Luria's story and situation, combined with the cinematic palette of *Local Hero* and *Never Cry Wolf*, crystallized into the idea that Brand eventually developed with Falsey and pitched to the networks.

While the idea began to germinate in Brand's mind about a new series that focused on a young New York doctor sent to Alaska, he was apprehensive about pursuing it. Brand wrestled with the idea of doing another medical drama after his experience on *St. Elsewhere*. "I did not want to do another doctor show. I wasn't going to do that," Brand said.[45] However, as it developed further, it gradually became clearer to Brand that *Northern Exposure* was not just another "doctor show." Following this realization, Brand was convinced. Also, it was an opportunity for him to create something so closely inspired by his own filmic tastes and personal connections that it was clear that only he could make it. Despite initial apprehensions, Brand found himself enthusiastic about the material. *Northern Exposure* was no longer just another television series for Brand. Instead, it had become a personal ambition. Brand goes as far as confessing his love for the material, the script, in his interview with the Writers Guild Foundation, adding that the series was the closest thing to who he was as a person. Furthermore, through the perspective of Joel, he had both access to and the opportunity to experience the world of a rural American small town through an outsider's perspective, much in the same way that MacIntyre's journey in *Local Hero* granted us access to the people and way of life in Ferness, and Tyler's research expedition in

Never Cry Wolf allowed us to encounter life on the extreme fringes of the Arctic.

With the premise set, all *Northern Exposure* needed was a location. Early on, Brand was adamant on setting the series in Alaska, "the final frontier."[46] Often in interviews he is asked the question, why Alaska? It is an unsurprising question. On reflection, to many it might appear a strange location to set the series when so many American dramas and comedies with a similar premise to *Northern Exposure* opt for either sending a rural person to New York or California (think *Big Business*) or, alternatively, sending their urban characters to smaller locales in the Midwest or the Deep South (from *Doc Hollywood* to *Hart of Dixie*). For Brand, Alaska was a no-brainer. Ideologically, the state represented "the final frontier, where everybody goes to recreate themselves; everything that's loose, that isn't tied down, so it was going to be a fun place." Not only were Brand's sights set on Alaska as the setting for *Northern Exposure* from the start, but he had also settled on the name of the small town in which the dramedy would be set: Cicely. As already established in the introduction, when canvassing locations for the "Dr. Snow" shoot, the preproduction crew searched high and low for the perfect setting. They considered both Colorado and Seattle before eventually settling on Roslyn, Washington, whose location and likeness to rural Alaska was an influential factor. The search, however, was a long one, and before they visited Roslyn, it was not going too well. Recalling this period in an interview, Brand remembers all but giving up on finding the ideal location when, at the eleventh hour, his location manager mentioned having one more location to show him. Brand accepted the invite and took a tour of Roslyn. As Brand describes, generally he was convinced by the town. However, it was not until near the end of his tour, when the car turned down Roslyn's main street, Pennsylvania Avenue, and he first read the word "Roslyn" on the mural on the side of the café, that Brand had an epiphany. Not only was he immediately set on Roslyn, but, on the spot, upon seeing the mural, he conceived the story of the town of Cicely, and the rest, like the backstory of Cicely and Roslyn, the town's founders, which is documented in "Cicely,"[47] wrote itself. *Northern Exposure* was born, in the creative imagination at least.

When production started in Roslyn in 1989, it soon became clear to the creators, the crew, and all those involved that—based on its traditional premise but its creator's storytelling daring—the series was not going to be what Brand and Falsey had originally pitched to the network. It was not going to be formulaic and rule abiding. In sum, it was not "Dr. Snow." There is no clearer demonstration of this than the pilot episode that was produced in Roslyn that year and was eventually screened to the network. The pilot that Brand and Falsey had created, and which the producers watched, is not what we recognize as *Northern Exposure*'s "Pilot" today.[48] Instead, it is the episode "Aurora Borealis: A Fairy Tale for Big People,"[49] which explores the strange effect that the northern lights have on the denizens of Cicely, creative and confusing. For the network, it was feared that the episode, which bore no allegiance to the medical drama genre formula, would alienate first-time viewers. After some negotiation with the producers, the episode became the season 1 finale, where it perhaps worked better. Subverting the expectations that Brand and Falsey had created around "Dr. Snow," *Northern Exposure* (and the episode "Aurora Borealis" specifically) was not the standard television medical drama. Instead, it was a series that subverted narrative and generic expectations at every turn. It was, as Lazic describes, "a show where a doctor is sent to a remote, cold place but rarely saves lives; where many people die yet there is no murder mystery; where simple small-town life and literature naturally coexist; and where not everything is explained but everything is well."[50] What Brand and Falsey had delivered was not a medical drama in the typical sense. Instead, the series was a generic oddity, a small-town dramedy that courted high- and low-brow culture without prejudice. Little to Brand and Falsey's surprise, the producers did not like what they saw. "The network didn't understand the show," said Brand. "When [they] saw it, they thought it was too weird and odd and they didn't want to air it."[51] And, honestly, who can blame them? After all, as Brand jokes, "they thought it was a medical show [in which] Rob [Morrow] would get on his sled and carry the serum to the sick people." Oddly enough, while for the majority of episodes this is not the case, in the matter of the episode that was screened for the producers—"Aurora Borealis: A Fairy Tale for Big People"—this is exactly the plot, which leads Dr. Fleischman away from Cicely, into the woods, bringing him into direct contact with the fabled man of the wild, Adam (Adam Arkin). Producers feared that *Northern Exposure* would alienate viewers with its off-the-wall plot and tone, and they negotiated with Brand and Falsey to air the episode as the season 1 finale. Au contraire, as we once again know from hindsight, the episode has since become a firm favorite among fans. "Aurora Borealis: A Fairy Tale for Big People" is the episode that was chosen to be screened at the special reunion events at the ATX Television Festival 2017, where it was met with great excitement from the vocal audience.

The network would continue to struggle to understand what *Northern Exposure* was, what it could be, and what it would become. Regardless of the low expectations set by the producers, who thought no one would watch it, to their surprise, as much as to the surprise of the writer-creator duo, people did. Audiences loved what they saw in those early years, as did the television critics, who lauded the series for its uniqueness and diverse representations and championed it for its simplicity, intelligence, and the respect it showed for its audience. However, as the following chapters will illustrate, this success was not immediate. Nevertheless, as the chapters will also show, *Northern Exposure*'s success owed nothing to its critical and cultural status as a cult favorite.

Unlike many other cult television series or films, whose preproductions are riddled with conflicts and complications—problems such as funding, pitch, script development, or tensions between studios and creatives—the story of *Northern Exposure*, from its conception to its production, is relatively uncomplicated, at least at the start. But what if Brand and Falsey had not tricked the producers into making the series they wanted to make? It pains one to think.

3

"THE PARIS OF THE NORTH"

The Characters, Setting, and Stories

What makes a "cult" television series a hit? What makes a "cult" television series, full stop? This is a question that the late television scholar David Lavery pondered to great lengths in the introduction to *The Essential Cult TV Reader*.[1] Off the backs of other scholars such as Steven Peacock, Lavery evokes the "notoriously slippery" nature of the term "cult."[2] Unable to immediately pinpoint a definition, like all television scholars and critics, Lavery revisits the work of Sara Gwenllian-Jones and Roberta E. Pearson, whose notes on "cult" television's appeal to viewers do not necessarily help to understand what "cult" television is but rather how it operates. As Gwenllian-Jones and Roberta E. Pearson write, "Cult television's imaginary universes support an *inexhaustible range of narrative possibilities*, inviting, supporting and rewarding close textual analysis, interpretations, and inventive reformulations."[3] Lavery enhances our understanding of "cult" television by evoking the work of Matt Hills, which first distinguishes "cult" television by its "'hyperdiegesis': the creation of a vast and detailed narrative space, only a fraction of which is ever directly seen or encountered within the text,"[4] before situating "cult" content—be it television, film, or digital games—within a wider context: "rather than simply 'celebrating cult texts for their supposed uniqueness,' we should focus on 'analyzing and defining cult TV as a part of broader patterns within changing TV industries.'"[5]

When approaching *Northern Exposure*, one can do so in a myriad of ways. This chapter and the next does so through the ideas presented by Lavery, Gwenllian-Jones and Pearson, and Hills. This chapter recognizes *Northern Exposure*'s "hyperdiegesis," or how it creates a small world and asks its viewers to engage with an even smaller slice of it. Meanwhile, the final chapter of this book, which focuses on the series's cultural legacy, zooms out to consider the position of the series within the wider television industry of the 1990s and since.

Northern Exposure exists in its own universe. Cicely is that world. It is the "Paris of the North,"[6] the "Alaskan Riviera."[7] And while some characters on the rare occasion leave the limits of the small town, only to feel its magnetic pull, or some character appears unable to leave, most characters find solace in its microcosm. This chapter will take you into the world of *Northern Exposure*, and through the microcosm that is Cicely, via a selection of the town's eclectic, eccentric denizens—characters that television viewers at home were first introduced to via the point of view of Cicely's newest resident, Dr. Joel Fleischman, in the first episode.[8]

DR. JOEL FLEISCHMAN

In the vein of classic literature and myth, the premise of *Northern Exposure* is that of the hero's journey. Proposed by Joseph Campbell in *The Hero with a Thousand Faces*, the hero's journey is a storytelling structure that explains the various stages of a protagonist's adventure. The hero's journey, or the "monomyth," as it is alternatively referred to, adheres to a three-part formula: separation, initiation, and return.[9] Simply put, in the first instance, the main character answers the call to adventure, where they are separated from their everyday world, life, and routines and thrust into an unknown—a new place, a new culture, sometimes even a supernatural world. Philosopher Mikhail Bakhtin refers to this other place—this other world—as "adventure time,"[10] which is not only a physical space but a temporal plane (the adventure takes place outside of real time).[11] In "adventure time," the hero encounters obstacles that they must overcome. Usually these come in the form of battles, both internal (mental) and external (physical), or puzzles to solve—stages that the hero has to progress through in order to return to their everyday life. Only after the

NEW YORK
IS A
STATE OF MIND //
Love,
Joel //

Maggie O'Connell
P.O. Box 86
Cicely, AK
99729

hero has overcome these obstacles—has been victorious in battle, has passed the test, has solved the puzzle, has found their path, and, fundamentally, has met their objective—can they return to their previous world, changed.[12] As Campbell illustrates with reference to a selection of myths,

> Prometheus ascended to the heavens, stole fire from the gods, and descended. Jason sailed through the Clashing Rocks into a sea of marvels, circumvented the dragon that guarded the Golden Fleece, and returned with the fleece and the power to wrest his rightful throne from a usurper. Aeneas went down into the underworld, crossed the dreadful river of the dead, threw a sop to the three-headed watchdog Cerberus, and conversed, at least, with the shade of his dead father. All things were unfolded to him: the destiny of souls, the destiny of Rome, which he was about to found. . . . He returned through the ivory gate to his work in the world.[13]

The hero's journey is a popular trope in narrative storytelling, deployed not only in literature but also in film, television, and digital games. It can be found in film adaptations of Greco-Roman mythology, such as Don

Chaffey's 1963 classic *Jason and the Argonauts*, Desmond Davis's 1981 film *Clash of the Titans*, and even the Disney animated film *Hercules*. Likewise, it can be found in films inspired by Greco-Roman mythology, such as the Coen brothers' Great Depression–set drama-comedy-musical *O Brother, Where Art Thou?*, which is loosely inspired by Homer's *Odyssey*, or the young adult adventure series *Percy Jackson and the Olympians* (comprising *Percy Jackson and the Lightning Thief* and *Percy Jackson: Sea of Monsters*), which repositions characters from ancient mythology in a contemporary narrative. As well as narratives rooted in, adapted from, or inspired by ancient myths, the hero's journey is present across major film narratives, from classic Hollywood titles such as Preston Sturges's *Sullivan's Travels* to Peter Jackson's modern epics, *The Lord of the Rings* and *The Hobbit* trilogies.

Likewise, the hero's journey can be found in the majority of television series. Though the three-act structure of the hero's journey is perhaps obscured by the extended narrative form of an entire season or series, the key elements are usually identifiable. This is true of certain television genres in particular, perhaps most evidently in the sitcom. Consider *Frasier* as a prime example. As Joseph J. Darowski and Kate Darowski outline in their introduction to Frasier: *A Cultural History*, the premise of this classic sitcom is as follows:

> Frasier Crane is a pompous psychiatrist who moves back to his hometown Seattle as the host of a radio advice show. His father, Martin, is a gruff cop who was shot in the hip in the line of duty. He can't live on his own anymore because of his injury, so Frasier takes him into his home, even though their relationship has never been great. Throw in an uptight brother, an eccentric home health care worker, and a sassy producer for the radio show and you have all the ingredients for a good sitcom.[14]

Frasier Crane's (played by Kelsey Grammer) backstory and "call to adventure" is absent in *Frasier*'s pilot, purposely left out as it has already been established in the earlier television series *Cheers*, in which Frasier Crane was a supporting character. The sitcom depicts Frasier's journey in the "adventure time" of Seattle. In this location, over the course of eleven seasons and a total of 263 episodes, we see Frasier being constantly tested by his close family members (especially by his father, Martin, played by the late John Mahoney); his job and colleagues at his workplace; across various aspects of his new life in Seattle (for instance, grievances with his neighbors); and by his many romantic relationships. After enduring these trials and tribulations and fundamentally growing in character, in the final season of *Frasier*, rather than return to the tavern in Boston—his former everyday setting—Frasier accepts a new "call to adventure," following his girlfriend Charlotte (played by Laura Linney) to Chicago in the series finale, "Goodnight Seattle."[15]

From Prometheus's ascent to the heavens to steal fire from the gods and Jason's voyage to retrieve the guarded Golden Fleece, to Frodo Baggins setting out from the Shire to destroy the ring, to Frasier leaving Boston for Seattle, the hero's journey of *Northern Exposure*'s protagonist, Dr. Joel Fleischman, begins on the red-eye from JFK to Anchorage (in a scene described in chapter 1).

As is immediately established in the opening scene of "Pilot,"[16] Joel is a newly qualified physician fresh out of Columbia Medical School, Manhattan, New York. Born in Flushing, Queens, to Herb and Nadine Fleischman, played by David Margulies and Joanna Merlin, respectively, who are first introduced in the episode "Birds of a Feather,"[17] Joel has enjoyed the career path of many young medical professionals. Furthermore, he has become accustomed to the exciting pace and all that life in New York City has to offer an upwardly mobile twenty-something. He is climbing the career ladder and working toward the promises of the renewed American Dream, an ideology left over from Ronald Reagan's administration (1981–1989).[18]

Joel is played by actor Rob Morrow, for whom *Northern Exposure* was really a career starting role. Since *Northern Exposure*, Morrow has had a consistent presence on-screen. Immediately after *Northern Exposure*, Morrow starred in Robert Redford's 1994 film *Quiz Show*. Based on a true story (Richard Goodwin's 1988 memoir *Remembering America: A Voice from the Sixties*), in *Quiz Show*, starring opposite John Turturro and Ralph Fiennes, Morrow plays the lead character, Richard Goodwin, a young and ambitious lawyer who investigates a potentially fixed game show. The film was critically lauded, its adapted screenplay earning Paul Attanasio a British Academy Film Award (BAFTA). Moreover, with Morrow cast as the lead character, the actor was as exposed as ever. He appeared in several other films shortly after *Quiz Show*, but since the turn of the 2000s, he has made a return to television, appearing in various recurring character roles: as Kevin Hunter in *Street Time*, Don Eppes in

Numb3rs, and Jimmy Brogan in *The Whole Truth*, and more recently in supporting roles in *The People v. O. J. Simpson: American Crime Story* and on Netflix in the original animated series *BoJack Horseman*, as well as *Designated Survivor* and *Billions*.

At the start of *Northern Exposure*, Joel has already left behind his life in New York City. Recently graduated, he is traveling to Anchorage to practice medicine in the city for four years, as per his contractual agreement with the state of Alaska, who sponsored his medical education at Columbia University. His scholarship application to Alaska was something of a last resort. As he tells his fellow passenger, it was his only successful application following seventy-five prior rejections. Joel's journey to Anchorage is diverted, however. Just as he arrives at the Alaskan embassy, Joel finds out that Anchorage is not his final destination. Rather, it is a stop-off. At the Alaskan embassy, Joel is greeted by representative and liaison Peter Gilliam (played by Robert Nadir). After exchanging pleasantries, Gilliam informs Joel that he is no longer needed in Anchorage. "What are you talking about?" asks a baffled Joel. "You're expendable, Joel. You're superfluous." Gilliam explains that the state has overfunded the training of young medical students and as a result has more doctors than they need. To his relief, Joel is under the impression that he is spared his commitment to the state and is no longer required to fulfill his four-year term in Alaska. However, Gilliam is quick to break it to him that this is not the case. He explains that instead of Anchorage, Joel is to be redirected to another part of Alaska. "So, what we've decided to do is set you up in Cicely. An area that we Alaskans refer to as the Alaskan Riviera. Ideal weather, breathtaking scenery, shopping, dining. Aspen has got nothing on this place." Joel is suspicious but feels reassured enough by Gilliam, who informs him that if he does not like Cicely he can "absolutely" leave. Satisfied by these terms, Joel agrees to give it a try.

A short montage on the 152 bus depicts Joel embarking on another major leg of his hero's journey, this time to his new base of Cicely. Before his arrival, though, he is dropped off on the side of the road. Here he waits to be met by his personal driver, Ed Chigliak (played by Darren Burrows), who, sure enough, arrives in a pickup wearing his signature black leather jacket and a Neil Young T-shirt—a recurring outfit and something of a trademark costume that distinguishes Ed. In the short but revealing conversation that takes place between Joel and Ed, Joel is introduced to his first Cicelean, who quickly becomes his lasting friend and something of a guide, facilitating his journey in Cicely. Furthermore, Ed demonstrates to Joel his curious nature and his intense relationship with the screen, which more often than not results in Ed inserting film and television trivia into conversations. For example, in this scene, upon hearing that Joel is a doctor, Ed randomly blurts out medical terms. This prompts Joel to respond with a curious expression. Before Joel has the opportunity to ask how he knows such things, Ed declares his love for *St. Elsewhere*, a tongue-in-cheek nod to Joshua Brand and John Falsey's earlier medical drama. It is a moment of self-referentiality, a common characteristic in the series.

After the brief exchange between Joel and Ed, Ed brings the truck to a halt in the middle of the road, gets out, and provides Fleischman with directions for the rest of his journey before disappearing into the forest. This comes much to Joel's surprise. Baffled, Joel follows Ed's directions, which bring him to the driveway of Maurice J. Minnifield, who, after sighting Joel from his rooftop as he steps out of the truck and walks toward his lodge, rappels down to greet him. After a humorous and somewhat bigoted conversation, Maurice drives Joel into town and gives him a tour of the town center of Cicely along Pennsylvania Avenue, where Joel's adventure will play out.

CICELY

Like the town of Roslyn, Washington, in which *Northern Exposure* was shot, the fictional outpost of Cicely is also a frontier settlement established in the latter part of the nineteenth century that succumbed to hardship during the industrial age at the turn of the twentieth. However, different from Roslyn, Cicely's past is steeped in its own mythology and heritage.

Before becoming a tourist destination in 1990—the product of a thirty-year project of reinvention by ex-astronaut and entrepreneur Maurice J. Minnifield—Cicely experienced something of a cultural renaissance in the first decade of the 1900s when a liberal, freethinking pioneer named Cicely (played by Yvonne Suhor) and her partner Roslyn (played by Jo Anderson) arrived in the then unnamed settlement in 1908. A 108-year-old man named Ned Svenborg (played by Roberts Blossom) passing through town informs us in the series's famous episode "Cicely"[19] that the town as we know it today was founded in 1909 by Cicely and Roslyn (however, this date is disputed by Maurice, who argues that it was founded in the early 1890s). Before the arrival of Cicely and Roslyn, the unnamed settlement was lawless. Run by outlaws, the town resembled the settlement of Deadwood in the television series of the same name, more than that which we are introduced to in the 1990s.

Cicely's move north was motivated by her declining health and her ambitions to establish a creative community of artists and freethinkers—a dream that she shared with her partner, Roslyn. From their arrival in the unnamed town in a Ford Model T automobile, their presence—as a same-sex couple, as independent women, as drivers of new technologies with freethinking ideas about art and culture—marked progress. Corresponding with Joshua Brand's assertion that Alaska represented a place in which people are free to reinvent themselves, the town represented a space in which Cicely and Roslyn could do just that, while also turning their dream of establishing "a thriving, bohemian artist's commune on the frontier away from society's conservative eyes" into a reality (*Northern Exposure* wiki entry for "Cicely, Alaska"). As Svenborg remembers, in a short time Cicely and Roslyn's dream became a reality. "One person can have a profound effect on another," Svenborg says. "And two people . . . well, two people can work miracles. They can change a whole town. They can change the world."[20]

Cicely and Roslyn certainly changed the town, which by 1908 had quickly transformed from a slum to a bohemian mecca. Fondly, Svenborg recalls the town as a thriving cultural epicenter, calling it "the Paris of the North," in which a creative educational program was established, which taught Svenborg how to read; salons were started for intellectual exchange; performances and talent shows took place; and new opportunities were created for disenfranchised members of society. It is revealed in Svenborg's story that the town was host to blocked writer and thinker Franz Kafka (visually depicted as Joel in the imagined flashback), who, based on his experiences in Cicely and conversations with Mary O'Keefe (played by Maggie O'Connell), conceptualized his 1915 career-defining story, *Metamorphosis*. "In this tiny corner of Alaska," the character Cicely can be quoted as saying in the episode, "the human spirit has triumphed. We hold in our hands, the most precious gift of all: freedom. The freedom to express our art . . . our love; the freedom to be who we want to be. We are not going to give that freedom away, and no one shall take it from us!"

Cicely and Roslyn's project was brought to a screeching halt, however, with the death of Cicely. In a standoff between Mace Mowbry (Maurice J. Minnifield) and his outlaw gang, a fellow gunman nervously fires at Roslyn. Seconds before, Cicely spots the gunman and instinctively dives in front of the bullet to protect her. Cicely's death, her sacrifice, earned the town its name. But after Cicely's death, Roslyn, alone, lost the drive to keep their vision alive. Withdrawing to the point of absence from public view, Roslyn left town one night, never to return.

Before knowing the story of the town, a story full of promise, ambition, and, sadly, tragedy, Cicely for Joel has a less than romantic first impression in the pilot episode. "Is this it? Is this the town?" Joel asks Maurice as he steps out of Maurice's 1960 Cadillac Eldorado Biarritz 6467E. "This is it. This is Cicely," Maurice proudly confirms, his chest pushed out. A camera pan from left to right establishes the fictional small town of Cicely in its entirety to both Joel and the audience at home, who has only glimpsed its various local attractions in the opening credit sequence as Morty the moose ambled through it. After the high street, the next stop on Maurice's introduction to Cicely is Joel's practice, located in the blue "Northwestern Mining Co." building. To Joel's disappointment and Maurice's frustration, the establishment has long been left empty and is in a state of disrepair. The site is also bittersweet in that it is here that Joel first encounters the mostly monosyllabic Marilyn Whirlwind (Elaine Miles), who has turned up to interview for the job as his secretary.

Joel's arrival in Cicely signifies the conclusion of the initial part of his hero's journey, the "call to adventure," which, after some protest, takes the hero out of their everyday life (in this case Joel's life in New York City) and drops them into their temporary new world (Cicely). The next stage is often referred to as the "ordeal" or the "initiation," and true to the promise of this stage, Joel's first impression of Cicely is predictable. He hates it.

Following Maurice's tour of the downtown area of Cicely, the less than welcoming introduction to his new workplace, and the strange encounter with Marilyn, Joel is sent into a panicked frenzy. He bursts out of the Northwestern Mining Co. building and rushes across the street to the Brick, Cicely's tavern, to make a phone call to Peter Gilligan at the

Alaskan embassy. When he connects, Joel demands to leave Cicely immediately:

> Yeah, I'm in Cicely. I've taken a look around, I've checked the place
> out, and I've thought about it long and hard and I want out. No, I don't
> have my contract with me. I'm at a bar in the middle of nowhere.
> What? What! No, no, no, no, no. You told me, you said if I didn't like
> it, I could leave. No, I don't like it, I hate it! And I demand to
> leave! . . . Well, that is because you are not the one who is supposed to
> spend the next four years of his life in this godforsaken hole-in-the-
> wall pigsty with a bunch of dirty, psychotic rednecks!

Despite his protests on the phone at the Brick, Joel did stay in Cicely for
five years, and Morrow, despite tensions with the studio, stuck with the
series for a total of 102 episodes, over which he gradually succumbs to
Cicely. For Joel, his relationship with Cicely and its population has its
ups and downs, going from strained to comfortable and back again. For
audiences, though, Cicely proves nothing but charming. As Frank
McConnell writes,

> Cicely . . . like all great pastorals, is a myth that knows it's a myth and
> invites us, every week, to share the secret that the lies of our innocence
> are our innocence. It's a consensual hallucination of the primal Gar-
> den, and without the skeptical Fleischman it would fall apart just be-
> cause Joel's skepticism, like that of Shakespeare's fools, keeps re-
> minding us that this ideal little place can't be real: and, by the same
> token, must be real, because we all dream it so desperately.[21]

From its pilot, and from Joel's perspective as the outsider that suddenly
finds himself in a strange new world, *Northern Exposure* "immediately
dropped viewers into a space that felt both alien and warmly inviting."[22]
And while we can acknowledge that, despite its harsh conditions, Cicely
has much to offer in the way of outstanding natural beauty, much of this
warm invite is down to the Ciceleans themselves. So, let's meet them.

MAURICE J. MINNIFIELD

Maurice J. Minnifield is a walking contradiction. He is stuck in the past
yet forward thinking. He surrounds himself with a diverse community

and yet is, at first, very closed minded. He performs the role of a "man's man"[23] but has a deeply sensitive side. In sum, to use the words of Joshua Brand, "Maurice really embodies the best and the worst qualities of what it means to be an American."[24] You need not look any further than the first season of *Northern Exposure* to understand the layers that define Maurice.

Maurice is played by Barry Corbin, a trained Shakespearian actor, whose career before and after *Northern Exposure* is long and rich, despite being sometimes narrowly cast. More often than not, Corbin can be seen in authoritative roles, his characters regularly donning the titles "General," "Lieutenant," "Colonel," or "Sheriff." Before securing his legacy as Maurice J. Minnifield, Corbin enjoyed a consistent career on the small screen. He appeared in several classic television series, including episodes of *M*A*S*H*, *Hill Street Blues*, *The Waltons*, and *Matlock*, and he enjoyed several recurring roles on *Dallas* as Sheriff Fenton Washburn, *The Thorn Birds* as Pete, and *Boone* as Merit Sawyer. However, outside of his performance as Maurice, Corbin is perhaps best remembered (in the opinion of this author) for his role as General Berringer in the 1983 cult classic *WarGames* directed by John Badham. Following his Emmy Award nomination for his performance as Maurice, Corbin has enjoyed consistent work, especially in television. He guest starred in episodes of *Murphy Brown*, *Ellen*, *Columbo*, *Spin City*, *King of the Hill*, *Godless*, and *Parenthood*, to name but a few, and had recurring roles in television dramas and comedies, including *One Tree Hill*, *Modern Family*, *Anger Management*, *Blood & Oil*, *The Ranch*, and the *Breaking Bad* spin-off *Better Call Saul*.

The character Maurice was born in Tulsa, Oklahoma, and is the older of two boys. His younger brother, Malcolm, is introduced to us via the flashbacks of a grieving Maurice after the news of Malcolm's death reaches Cicely in "A Kodiak Moment."[25] Before becoming an astronaut for NASA's Mercury program, Maurice served in Korea as a fighter pilot and was even imprisoned in a prisoner of war camp. After his mission to space, Maurice left behind life in Tulsa. Northbound to Alaska, he was filled with pioneering ambition. Arriving in Cicely, Maurice poured a large amount of his accumulated wealth into the town with the vision of transforming the rural, postindustrial outback into a thriving tourist attraction: the "Alaskan Riviera." He started by establishing a small media empire, the Minnifield Communications Network, comprising the KBHR radio station, where he employs Chris Stevens as the resident DJ, and the *Cicely News and World Telegram* newspaper.

Although scenes in the pilot episode grant audiences a comic introduction to Maurice early on, his complexities as a character are truly revealed for the first time in the subsequent episode: "Brains, Know-How, & Native Intelligence."[26] In the episode, Maurice fires Chris from his morning show spot on KBHR because of his references to the homosexual undertones in the poetry of Walt Whitman. With Stevens out of work, Maurice temporarily assumes the role of disk jockey, flooding the airwaves with opinionated rants and Broadway show tunes. However, his time in front of the microphone is short-lived as he is voted off the air by the residents of Cicely in an impassioned town hall meeting—one reminiscent of a Western, and staple of small-town dramas and comedies since. Before handing the role back to Chris, Maurice, with his tail between his legs, takes to the microphone one last time, opening with a declaration of admiration for the American screen icon John Wayne.

> When I was a boy growing up in Oklahoma City, I'd go to the show on Saturday. My favorite was John Wayne. It didn't matter what kind of movie it was—cowboy picture, war movie—I was with him all the way. Except for *The Quiet Man*. That one bored the hell out of me.

Maurice goes on to explain how Wayne's masculinity on-screen shaped his own: "By the time I was nine years old, I was walking and talking like the Duke." Typical of Maurice, his citation of Wayne's oeuvre, of course, comes with the exception of John Ford's 1952 film *The Quiet Man*, a romantic comedy in which Wayne played retired American boxer Sean Thornton who returns to his birthplace in a small village in Ireland where he finds love in the form of Mary Kate Danaher (played by Maureen O'Hara). The complexity of Maurice's relationship with his childhood screen idol, and moreover his relationship with his own perception of masculinity and sexuality, is shaken when Maurice heard a troubling piece of information about John Wayne:

> Then one day the walls came crashin' down. I was playin' army with the Marshall boys, Jed and Jeff, in Bailey's woods, and Jeff said kind of offhandedly that John Wayne didn't do his own fighting, didn't throw his own punches, didn't take his own hits or his own falls. Well, I kicked the hell out of the Marshall boys, and then I ran all the way home and asked my daddy if it was true that John Wayne didn't do his own fighting. And he said yes.

Maurice reflects:

> John Wayne was my hero, and the Marshall boys gave him feet of clay. Now, I don't give a damn if Walt Whitman kicked with his right foot or his left foot, or that J. Edgar Hoover took it better than he gave it, or that Ike [Dwight D. Eisenhower] was true-blue to Mamie, or that God-knows-who had trouble with the ponies or with the bottle. We need our heroes! We need men we can look up to, believe in; men who walk tall. We cannot chop 'em off at the knees just to prove that they're like the rest of us!

Maurice's message comes to an end with his signature line of bigotry, but his sentiment is laced with a contradictory defense:

> Now, Walt Whitman was a pervert, but he was the best poet that America ever produced. And if he was standing here today, and somebody called him a fruit or a queer behind his back, or to his face, or over these airwaves, that person would have to answer to me. Sure, we're all human. But there's damn few of us that have the right stuff to be called heroes. That closes the book on that subject.

The contradictions embedded in Maurice's radio broadcast signal a more nuanced character than the comic bigot the pilot portrays, or that which Maurice is commonly associated with in popular cultural memory. It signifies a man defined by conflict: his masculinity shaped by icons and heroes of the big screen but undermined by their performative betrayal; his tastes in cooking, fine wine, and Broadway musicals leading to his sexuality being mistakenly interpreted by the couple Ron (played by Don McManus) and Eric (played by Doug Ballard) later in the series. Maurice is vulnerable—his legacy in the air, his world lonely.

For his stubbornness and sometimes selfish pursuits, Maurice is a giving person. After all, he has poured a vast amount of his fortune into the improvement of Cicely, allowing it to achieve its potential (or at least the potential he envisions for it). He provides for the local economy. He is a father figure to the likes of Chris and Ed, employing them and mentoring them at times. And he is inviting, hosting communal events at his home during holiday seasons.

For all that he is set in his ways, Maurice is also adaptable. He grows, albeit resistantly at times, gradually coming to accept change. He overcomes his heartbreak from the loss of Shelly, finding admiration and eventually love with Officer Barbara Semanski (played by Diane Delano). He restores his personal relationships with friends. He accepts his Korean-born son, Duk Won (played by James Song), whom he first finds out about in "Seoul Mates."[27] He finds points to admire about Ron and Eric. And, in the finale, he asks Officer Semanski to marry him. Lastly, Maurice is a catalyst. Maurice brought life back to Cicely and arguably brought Cicely back to life. He is the very reason that Joel—and, by extension, we, through Joel's perspective—is brought to Cicely in the first place, the result of him acquiring Joel's contract from the Alaskan state. He would, of course, repeat this move later in the series, bringing another doctor and his journalist wife, the Capras, to Cicely in season 6 (but more on them later in the book). Not only is Maurice significant in the history of Cicely and intrinsic to the fabric of the series, but he is important for bringing another beloved character, Shelly, to Cicely and in the process upsetting his bond with his best friend.

SHELLY MARIE TAMBO AND HOLLING VINCOEUR

While guest judging the Miss Northwest Passage beauty pageant in 1988, Maurice J. Minnifield became enamored with contestant and crowned winner Shelly Marie Tambo. Born in Saskatoon, Canada, Shelly, who is played by Cynthia Geary, is defined by her "somewhat 'surfer dude' shallow-but-sweet personality."[28] Geary's performance earned her two consecutive Emmy Award nominations in 1992 and 1993. Head over heels in love, Maurice swept Shelly off her feet. Despite already being married to her high school love, Wayne Jones (played by Brandon Douglas), whom we are introduced to in "Sex, Lies and Ed's Tape,"[29] Shelly agreed to jump in the car with Maurice and travel with him to Cicely to become his wife. But on her arrival in Cicely, things did not go as planned. On her first visit to the Brick, Shelly fell in love with landlord Holling Vincoeur, a man forty-four years her senior, at first sight. (The

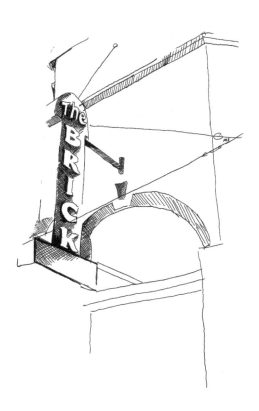

meeting of Shelly and Holling at the Brick is played out *Rashomon*-style in three ways in flashbacks in the episode "Only You."[30]) Quickly she becomes the catalyst for a friendship rivalry between Maurice and Holling.

Holling is played by the Tony Award–winning actor John Cullum, a veteran of the Broadway scene. He made his debut as Sir Dinadan in *Camelot* in 1960 before going on to play Laertes in *Hamlet* opposite none other than Richard Burton. (Cullum would star opposite Burton almost two decades later in *Private Lives* from the eminent playwright Noël Coward.) Cullum earned his first Tony Award nomination for *On a Clear Day You Can See Forever* and was later awarded a Tony Award for Best Actor in a Musical for *Shenandoah* and again for *On the Twentieth Century*. He has since graced the stage in countless other productions, recently starring in *August: Osage County* and *Waitress*. Alongside his stage appearances, Cullum is a consistent presence in film, from *Hamlet* to *Kill Your Darlings* and *Love Is Strange*, and in modern television series, including *ER*, *Mad Men*, *Madam Secretary*, and *The Middle*. Cullum's diversity as an actor of both stage and screen lends itself to the performance of the complex character that is Holling.

Holling is a former rugged man of the wild who, through his utter devotion to his partner Shelly, undergoes several personal transformations. As stated on the website Moosechick Notes, "having exchanged his days of big-game hunting to become the proprietor of Cicely's only tavern . . . Holling's main concerns in life now are keeping the townspeople well fed and keeping Shelly happy."

While endearing (and somewhat uncomfortable), the relationship between Holling and Shelly has its moments of tension. The age difference between Holling and Shelly sometimes leaves one or the other feeling alienated by a lack of shared history or by Shelly's references to modern popular culture. When they decide to marry, Holling's heritage, composed of men he characterizes as "despicable human beings," leads to him standing Shelly up at the altar. Confronted with domesticity, Holling, despite being in his mid-sixties, experiences a midlife crisis. This is explained by the longevity of Vincoeur men; Holling's father and grandfather were centenarians. The two concerns—marrying Shelly and age—converge, as Holling, protective of Shelly, becomes paranoid that if he marries her, she will die young, just as his mother and grandmother had.

While the unit of Holling and Shelly comes with its difficulties, including age and cultural differences and Holling's familial anxieties, throughout the series it is mostly endearing, with each utterly devoted to the other. For example, when Holling decides to come out of retirement and return to hunting to slay the fabled Jessie the bear, Shelly insists on accompanying him, stating, "Whether you shoot Jessie or he mauls you, I want to be there by your side."[31] And in regard to their cultural reference points, while they mostly go unregistered by the other, that matters not in the end. As Shelly says to Holling in "Dreams, Schemes and Putting Greens," "You may think that because you're so much older than me you know more about the world. Well, in some cases that may be. But I read magazines! I watch TV! I know how people are supposed to treat each other."[32]

CHRIS STEVENS

Whereas episodes of *Northern Exposure* can sometimes seem abstract, their themes are often framed or curated by the series narrator, the voice of Cicely. This voice comes in the form of convict–turned–radio DJ at KBHR and philosopher of the airwaves Chris Stevens. Like other DJs in film—and here I am thinking about those in cult classics, such as Richard C. Sarafian's *Vanishing Point*, Robert Altman's *Nashville*, Walter Hill's *The Warriors*, and Barry Levingson's much-loved 1987 film, *Good Morning, Vietnam*—Chris fulfills the narrative obligation of the Greek chorus, commenting on the collective experience in the dramatic action. Chris is played by John Corbett, who has been a consistent presence on big and small screens alike. Prior to *Northern Exposure*, Corbett made his small-screen debut in 1988 in *The Wonder Years*, in which he played Karen's (played by Olivia d'Abo) boyfriend, a hippie named Louis. However, with *Northern Exposure* really putting him in the spotlight in the early 1990s, Corbett's face would become a more prominent one in American films and television series, playing supporting characters in movies such as *Volcano*, *Serendipity*, and *Raising Helen*; as Ian Miller in *My Big Fat Greek Wedding* and its sequel; and in *To All the Boys I've Loved Before* and *To All the Boys: P.S. I Still Love You*, and appearing in recurring roles in the television series *Sex and the City* as Aidan Shaw

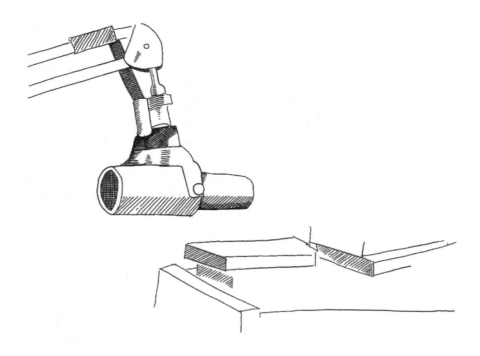

(for which he also reunited with the cast for the second film), *United States of Tara*, and *Parenthood*.

While absent from the first episode of *Northern Exposure*, Chris quickly became a series regular, not only musing on the philosophy of everyday life and the existential woes and themes that present themselves in Cicely with each episode (particularly in the early seasons), but also taking on the roles of the community news anchor; a public artist (of public art and performance pieces); a mentor to his friends who seek his advice in confidence; and an ordained minister, officiating at the weddings of Holling and Shelly and of Ron and Eric.

The early seasons of *Northern Exposure* granted Corbett a meaty, dense script, often composed of deep thoughts or long excerpts from classic literature—perhaps a reflection of the influence of Joshua Brand and John Falsey before they left the series. In particular, the series was keen to develop Chris quickly, introducing a half brother in the form of Bernard (played by Richard Cummings Jr.), prompting Chris to confront his familial heritage; putting Chris through the trials of the creative process in several episodes in which he is committed, but struggles, to create artworks; and even his own personal crisis of character. Corbett's portrayal of Chris in these earlier seasons earned him a Golden Globe Award nomination for Best Supporting Actor in a Series or Miniseries or Television Film, and a Primetime Emmy Award for Outstanding Supporting Actor in a Drama Series. However, after Brand and Falsey's exit, Chris's scripts fell into the realm of pastiche, even caricature.

ED CHIGLIAK

As Brian Doan articulates in his 2015 article, Ed Chigliak is "the soul" of *Northern Exposure*: "his quizzical eyes and pursed lips staring out at a universe both unsettling and rich with opportunity," his point of view (in the early seasons particularly) framed through the lens of the camera and supplemented by his voice-over, as in the documentary film he makes about Cicely.[33] Ed is "the conduit for the show's spirit of generosity."[34]

For Ed, cinema is everything. He as a person and his view on the world are shaped by the films of his cinema idols, the likes of Martin

Scorsese, Ingmar Bergman, Steven Spielberg, Federico Fellini, and Woody Allen, to name but a few. Beyond cinema, Ed is searching. An orphan, he is searching for a sense of history and of heritage and, ultimately, for meaning in his life. It is a journey that over the course of the series reveals his childhood, from birth and abandonment to adoption, a journey that informs his perspective as a filmmaker and later in the series directs him toward his calling as a shaman.

Ed is played by Darren E. Burrows. In addition to playing the much-loved existential twenty-something cinephile-turned-shaman Ed, actor Burrows, son of the actor Billy Drago,[35] has demonstrated his range, playing supporting characters in notable films and television series. His comic timing can be found in his role as Milton Hackett—Hatchet Face's devoted boyfriend in John Waters's 1990 satire of *Grease*, *Cry-Baby*—while his supporting performances in Brian De Palma's *Casualties of War* in 1989, Steven Spielberg's *Amistad* in 1997, and Ira Sachs's *Love Is Strange* (in which he was reunited with fellow *Northern Exposure* actor John Cullum) demonstrate his ability to deliver emotional depth in drama. Following *Northern Exposure*, Burrows's career in television has been less consistent than some of his costars, but nonetheless his appearances—in the likes of *NYPD Blue*, *The X-Files*, and *CSI: Crime Scene Investigation*—are always welcome. Beyond the screen, Burrows has been instrumental in continuing the legacy of *Northern Exposure*. As the final section of this book will explore more, his book *Northern Exposed* (2014) and his supplementary documentary *Return to Cicely* (2014)—both the product of a deep passion for the series and a successful online fund-raising campaign—reignited interest in the series, leading to the development of a revival script.

MAGGIE O'CONNELL

Like Maurice Minnifield, perhaps no other character in *Northern Exposure* is as conflicted as Maggie O'Connell. Originally from Grosse Point, Michigan, Maggie came to Cicely with her boyfriend Dave, a writer who was researching and writing a book on climbing. While Dave's journey came to an end when he fell asleep during an expedition and froze to death, Maggie continued to live in Cicely, where like Maurice she is something of a jill-of-all-trades. First and foremost, Maggie is a bush

pilot, earning her money working as an air taxi and courier. But, as the "Pilot" also established—in her initial meeting with Joel at the phone in the Brick, where Joel mistakes her as a prostitute—Maggie is also a landlady. Outside of these duties, over the course of the series, we also see her assume mayorship over the town, regularly working as a mechanic or handywoman, and venture out as an entrepreneur, developing her portfolio with the acquisition of the local movie theater.

Maggie is portrayed by Janine Turner, whose acting career is headlined by several high-profile television series and films. Prior to *Northern Exposure*, Turner had appeared in a three-episode arc in *Dallas* before making her name as Laura Templeton in *General Hospital*. Following her breakout on *General Hospital*, Turner juggled a television and film career, appearing in episodes of *The A-Team*, *Knight Rider*, and *Quantum Leap*, as well as the hit film *Steel Magnolias*. After finding success with her role as Maggie O'Connell in *Northern Exposure*, Turner was cast as the female lead, Jessie Deighan, in *Cliffhanger*, starring opposite Sylvester Stallone, and she has enjoyed a range of television roles since, including the role of Dr. Dana Stowe in Lifetime's *Strong Medicine* and as Katie McCoy in *Friday Night Lights*.

While a headstrong independent woman and hardened feminist, *Northern Exposure* gradually reveals Maggie's deeply sensitive side. This is exposed through her insecurities, especially concerning her fatal record with men (her "boyfriend curse"), her longing for a romantic partner, and her genuine compassion for Joel and her sympathy with his situation of having to adapt to life in rural Alaska being a city dweller (once she is able to get beyond her irritation with his *ways*).

Originally Maggie was introduced as a romantic partner for Joel, and for a while the series teased the "will they/won't they?" television trope. However, as the series went on, *Northern Exposure* resisted the impulse to bring them together, rejected it even, and instead committed to focusing on their close friendship. It is Maggie who helps Joel complete his hero's journey in "The Quest" (6.15), and after Joel's (and Morrow's) departure from the series, it is in Chris that Maggie completes her own.

RUTH-ANNE, MARILYN, AND SOME OF THE OTHER SERIES REGULARS

While Joel, Maurice, Chris, Ed, and Maggie are perhaps the key characters in *Northern Exposure*, the series is unique for its prioritization of developing the arcs of the series's supporting characters and long-lasting favorites. These include general store owner Ruth-Anne Miller (played by Peg Phillips). Originally from Portland, Oregon, like many other characters in the series, Ruth-Anne ups sticks and moved to Cicely following a life-changing personal event: in Ruth-Anne's case, she moved to Cicely shortly after the death of her husband, her decision to move to Alaska made by a familial connection to the state, namely her grandfather, who had move to, lived in, and sadly died in Alaska during a blizzard. Ruth-Anne is a free spirit, her past defined by an affair with an English officer during World War II and by her entrepreneurial instinct and self-sustaining business as the proprietor of Cicely's general store, which is also a library, a video rental store, an archive, and a post office. It is this free spirit and romantic nature that manifests in her feeling of unapologetic apathy toward her son Matthew, an investment banker, and celebration in the life of her poet son, Rudy. Ruth-Anne plays to her own tune. Marilyn Whirlwind, Joel's secretary and assistant nurse, is the second of *Northern Exposure*'s beloved characters. A consistent character from the pilot episode, Marilyn, played by Elaine Miles, is characterized by her contemplative nature, her silence, and, when she does speak, her mostly monosyllabic wisdom. As the series progresses, Marilyn's character evolves. We see her move out of her mother's house and become romantically entangled, at first with Enrico Bellati, the "flying man," who visits Cicely with a traveling circus, and later with Ted, an Alaskan Native. Then there is the fabled man of the wild, Adam (played by Adam Arkin), a recluse with a mysterious past that hints toward a history with the CIA, and his hypochondriac wife Eve (played by Valerie Mahaffey), who make the occasional appearance in *Northern Exposure*.

CONCLUSION

Northern Exposure exists in its own universe, and its universe, Cicely, Alaska, is both Joel's adventure space, where his hero's journey will play out, and home to an eclectic mix of characters. *Northern Exposure* is defined by such characters. Audiences relate to or recognize the frustrated New Yorker (Joel), the patriotic American (Maurice), the freethinking existentialist (Chris), the curious creative (Ed), and the headstrong woman (Maggie). Likewise, they might even remember the quirky jumper-wearing, chain-smoking general store owner who prefers her one son to the other and rides a Harley-Davidson (Ruth-Anne); the monosyllabic secretary and ostrich farmer who dates a mute flying man (Marilyn); or the enigmatic paranoid hermit (Adam) and his hypochondriac wife (Eve). Cult television always traffics in such quirkiness, and *Northern Exposure* has well and truly earned its place in the pantheon of "cult" television series. However, while it was celebrated at the time, and today is fondly remembered, for its diverse cast of oddballs, over time this praise has faded, as the series fell out of favor and, arguably, faded away.

4

FROM CRITICALLY ACCLAIMED TO CANCELED

Thirty years after it originally aired on CBS, *Northern Exposure* is still widely considered a "cult" classic. From the moment *Northern Exposure*'s first season aired, gradually generating much buzz and anticipation for its second season, critics, journalists, scholars, and audiences have been quick to group it alongside other "cult" favorites such as David Lynch and Mark Frost's *Twin Peaks*. However, like many so-called cult favorites, while immediately exciting and novel, *Northern Exposure*'s fate was equally sealed just a few seasons in: a dwindling audience resulted in the series's eventual cancellation by CBS in 1995. This chapter is committed to tracing the arc of the series, as both the title and this introduction suggest, from its initial critical acclaim and recognition by the industry in terms of awards to its inevitable cancellation.

SERIES OVERVIEW

Communicating the story of *Northern Exposure* over the course of its six seasons is not an easy task. It is a series in which, for use of a better word, nothing happens. It is a hangout show, whereby we, the audience, are allowed to spend time with characters without the usual pressures of time and the need to progress the plot. One thing each season reveals, however, is a relationship between the writers' vision, characters, and select themes. The following therefore traces the journey of *Northern Exposure* season by season, theme by theme.

As Ashlie D. Stevens writes in her *Salon* retrospective, season 1 of *Northern Exposure* is a typical fish-out-of-water story. As Stevens writes, "The culture shock narrative helps drive the show's first season—the man just wants to know where to get a good bagel!—and guides Joel's interactions with the town members, all of whom vary in their eccentricities."[1] From its pilot episode, audiences are introduced to the series hero, Dr. Joel Fleischman, whom we meet in the first phase of his hero's journey, where he has left behind his everyday life in New York City to move to Anchorage.[2] Immediately, Joel is challenged. The first of these challenges comes when his journey is diverted (he finds out that he is being sent to the outpost of Cicely instead of Anchorage). Accepting this alteration, the second challenge comes upon seeing the town of Cicely, immediately hating it, and being unnerved by the strange locals he encounters. Joel quickly finds out that he is contractually obliged to stay there for four years, the stipulation of his contract from the Alaskan state in return for funding his medical education.

From the start, the series embraces, or rather establishes, its stance in opposition to most television series. Television is often pressured by time constraints and increasing audience appetites for plot progression, leading to the sacrifice of character development in favor of action to fulfill audiences' narrative expectations. This is especially true in network television, where episodes are strictly limited and series are obligated to the external pressures of sponsors and advertisers. As the first season establishes, the tone of *Northern Exposure* is immediately different from other series. Nothing really happens, that is, in terms of plot. However, the strength of this freshman season lies in its immediate commitment to character relationships. Often shifting focus from Joel's assimilation in Cicely and his romantically strained relationship with the headstrong bush pilot Maggie O'Connell, the season spends considerable time on the lovable burgeoning filmmaking career of Ed, the "soul" of the series;[3] the relationship between Holling and Shelly, which is not only tested by their considerable age gap but by Holling's family heritage; Maurice's fragility, especially in terms of his sense of self and masculinity, as well as his loneliness and legacy; and Chris's spiritual journey, which is developed in part through the arrival of his half brother Bernard at the end of season 1.

For lack of a better word to characterize it, season 1 of *Northern Exposure* is uneven. This could be because it only really gets off to a good start—that is, its tone and characters click into gear—in episode 3, "Soapy Sanderson," when Joel and Maggie are forced together following the death of a professor living a hermit existence. The season finale, "Aurora Borealis: A Fairy Tale for Big People,"[4] an experimental episode that revolves around Chris wrestling with his creative demons while coming to terms with the existence of a half brother, provides a dose of *Northern Exposure* to come.

Building on the ambitions of the season 1 finale, season 2 of *Northern Exposure* begins to find its confidence. This is in part due to its growing popularity among television critics and audiences. There is no better illustration of this than the final scene of the episode "War and Peace,"[5] in which Joel interrupts a duel between Maurice and visiting Russian Nikolai (played by Elya Baskin), breaking the fourth wall to address the higher expectations that the "highly sophisticated" audience holds for the series. One episode shorter than season 1, season 2's seven-episode arc allows for characters to really grow beyond the awkward initial introduction stage, in which they seem to be suspended in many episodes belonging to season 1. Moreover, season 2 intimately probes the anxieties and flaws of key members of Cicely's population—so intimately, in fact, that the series begins to build on the surrealist dimension explored in "Aurora Borealis," with Chris and Bernard's shared consciousness.[6] By delving into the subconscious of multiple characters, the series is gradually allowed to realize its magic realist ambitions.[7]

In terms of its narrative themes, season 2 is bookended by the theme of loss. A "Dear John" letter from Elaine to Joel sets up this theme in *Northern Exposure*'s second season.[8] She is leaving him for an older man. The letter and the breakup further sever our hero's ties to his former life in New York City. Joel's depression and lack of closure inspires Ed to take action. Ed stages a scene outside the Brick in which Maggie volunteers to play Elaine in the scenario and Joel is invited to talk to *her* in order to gain closure and begin to heal. It is a real bonding experience between Joel and Ed, and, importantly, it stirs romantic interests between Joel and Maggie, despite her being committed to Rick (played by Grant Goodeve). Whereas Joel's loss of Elaine sets the stage for season 2, Rick accidentally being killed by a falling satellite—a fate sealed by Maggie's boyfriend curse—brings the season to a poetic close.

In addition to the losses experienced by Joel and Maggie, respectively, many of the secondary narratives of season 2 also center on connection and love. A string of petty crimes in Cicely, committed by Chris, sees the town visited by Officer Semanski, with whom Maurice becomes besotted. Holling's love for Shelly, and his sensitivity toward her feelings, sees him grapple with the decision to get circumcised. Tense and relaxed, tragic and optimistic, nostalgic and forward looking, season 2 is full of tensions that come to a halt with the breaking of the ice in the season finale. Taking a swallow of whiskey, the men of Cicely, Joel included, disrobe for Cicely's annual "running of the bulls" custom. Arms raised in the air, one by one they burst through the doors of the Brick and run naked, confident, into the streets—the series, and season 2, demonstrating its own confidence in having found itself and running headstrong into season 3.

Following two shorter seasons, season 3 was the first season in which *Northern Exposure* had an extended run of episodes (a total of twenty-three), each episode contained but also connected by the common theme of history. History catching up with characters is a recurring subject in season 3. Elaine visits Joel after the death of the man she left him for back in New York City between seasons 1 and 2, finally offering Joel closure; Maggie has the opportunity to come to terms with Rick's death and his unfaithfulness through a stray dog that arrives on her doorstep, which she is convinced is Rick reincarnate; Maurice discovers that he fathered a son during his exploits in Korea in the award-winning episode "Seoul Mates";[9] Holling and Maurice's good friend passes away, which sends them into the wild to bury him;[10] Shelly divorces Wayne when her best friend, Cindy (Christine Elise), visits Cicely and asks her to make it official so that they can marry;[11] and Chris's criminal past prevents him from voting in "Democracy in America."[12]

While season 3 starts with the town of Cicely coming together to remember the recently departed Rick,[13] honoring him in the form of a statue, it concludes with everyone coming together to honor the town and its history in the award-winning episode "Cicely,"[14] as they pay tribute to the oral history of the town as told by a 108-year-old man—a former resident whom Joel almost runs over when driving at night. Season 3 is as much about Cicely as it is about its characters, their eccentric qualities, communal bonds, and petty squabbles all contextualized as cyclical in the town's larger history.

Not only were the characters and narratives in *Northern Exposure* confronting their past, but so were the writers. Joshua Brand and John Falsey, for example, were encountering the same tensions with producers behind the scenes of *Northern Exposure* that they had experienced on their earlier television series, *St. Elsewhere*—tensions that formerly caused them to exit the hospital drama in its third season. Whereas with seasons 1 and 2, Brand and Falsey were able to fly under the radar and thus experiment with *Northern Exposure*'s form and narratives, the growing popularity of the series among audiences and critics meant that the producers were developing a more vested interest in their property. According to the Associated Press, *Northern Exposure* achieved an AM-Nielsen-Season rating score of 15.5, earning it a place in the top listed television series in 1991 and 1992. This had earned *Northern Exposure* another short season (season 2) in 1990–1991, and the series didn't air again until the following spring. But as fans awaited its small-screen return, word of mouth generated buzz and anticipation. Audiences' appetites had been whetted. In March 1991, a month before the start of its second season, *Northern Exposure* was honored at the Museum of Television and Radio's annual TV Festival (now known as PaleyFest). While most episodes might have caused producers to notice the degree to which *Northern Exposure* was challenging the television landscape and industry, others, such as "War and Peace,"[15] made them nervous. While the aforementioned breaking of the fourth wall in "War and Peace" earned the series notoriety with fans and critics alike, it landed its cocreator Brand in a whole heap of trouble with the studios. Before they were aware of how the episode would be received, the producers feared that such a stunt would lose the audience if the episode aired. This was not a feeling Brand shared. To put it frankly, Brand couldn't care less: "I don't care. It's great. It's funny. It's terrific," he can be quoted as saying in response.[16] After the episode aired, Brand was flown to New York City to be confronted by a tested Jeff Sagansky. "Where are all the medical stories? There's no medical stories in this show," he would ask Brand, still under the impression that the series was going to deliver on the promise of "Dr. Snow." As established from the start, Brand and Falsey were against the idea of the series being a medical show. Sagansky would take a moment before asking Brand, "Are you going to be a good boy?" to which Brand, according to his interview with Matz, agreed to play by the rules: "I kissed the ring."[17] However, Brand thought about his agreement to such conditions beyond his meeting with Sagansky and would eventually change his mind. He approached Falsey and said, "I can't do this. I'm not doing this. I'm sorry. I wasn't negotiating or being a wise guy," he explained. "I just didn't want to do it. I loved it. I loved what I was doing." Falsey understood. Brand took his decision to exit the series to his agent, who was never keen on the series to begin with. "Fuck it," his agent replied, "we're out."[18]

All of this happened at the end of season 2. When Brand told the studio the following day, after reaching the conclusion with his agent, the studio backed off, granting Brand carte blanche, as long as he didn't ask for more money. "You've got a deal," replied Brand.[19] This permitted Brand and Falsey to do what they wanted with the series, which they did for a few more years, upholding their promise to the studio to never ask for more money. A wise decision, as their daring resulted in some of the finest episodes of *Northern Exposure* that, in the opinion of this writer, make seasons 3 and 4 stand out as the strongest seasons. However, having explored all of their ideas with the series, Brand later decided, more organically this time, that he had run his course as the series writer-creator. He was convinced it was the right time to leave the series. Brand had decided that he had achieved all he wanted to with *Northern Exposure*. When he told Falsey, Falsey agreed. They took their decision to the studio, and with that, without negotiation or aggravation, Brand and Falsey were out, free to explore other possibilities. As we know, they partnered once again in 1993 on *I'll Fly Away: Then and Now*, and until Falsey's sudden and tragic death in January 2019, both were set to reprise their former roles on the temporarily green-lit *Northern Exposure* revival.

By the end of season 3, it was clear that the creative direction of Brand and Falsey with *Northern Exposure* was working with audiences and critics alike. When it came to award seasons, *Northern Exposure* was highly recognized by the entertainment industry. The first wave of award nominations came in 1991, just after *Northern Exposure*'s first season, when the series was included in multiple major categories. These included the Primetime Emmy Award for Outstanding Drama Series and Outstanding Writing in a Drama Series (for Joshua Brand and John Falsey); the Creative Arts Emmy Award for Outstanding Sound Mixing for a Drama Series; three Golden Globe nominations for Best Television Series Drama and Best Actor and Actress in a Television Drama Series for Rob Morrow and Janine Turner, respectively; and three Television Critics

Association Awards for Program of the Year, Outstanding Achievement in Comedy and Drama. In 1991, *Northern Exposure* only had one win, the award for Outstanding Production of Television Award for Brand and Falsey, awarded by the Producers Council of America. However, 1992 was a much greater success story for the series. By 1992, *Northern Exposure* led with nominations in many of the most important categories during that year's award season. *Northern Exposure* won three 1992 Primetime Emmy Awards for Outstanding Drama Series, Outstanding Individual Achievements in Writing in a Drama Series for Diane Frolov and Andrew Schneider for the episode "Seoul Mates,"[20] and Outstanding Supporting Actress for Valerie Mahaffey's portrayal of Eve in "Lost and Found."[21] That same year it was nominated for six other awards at the same ceremony. Additionally, the series earned an award from the Directors Guild of America for Outstanding Directorial Achievement in a Drama Series for the season 3 finale "Cicely,"[22] directed by Rob Thompson; a Creative Arts Emmy Award for Outstanding Individual Achievement in Art Direction for a Series and Outstanding Individual Achievement in Cinematography for a Series, both again for "Cicely"; the 1992 Golden Globe Award for Best Television Series—Drama; and the Television Critics Association award for Program of the Year.

The years 1991 and 1992 are also important to consider in terms of awards, as in both years *Northern Exposure* and its producers were awarded the prestigious Peabody Award—a prize that acknowledges excellent and important storytelling in the service of people across media, not just in television. In 1991, Brand and Falsey Productions were recognized for the second time by the Peabody Awards committee for their contributions to storytelling on television over the course of their career, the first time being for *St. Elsewhere* in 1984. In 1991, the award was for both *I'll Fly Away* and *Northern Exposure*. In recognition of Brand and Falsey's contribution, the committee released the following statement:

> Perhaps the most collaborative of the visual arts, the soul of successful series television resides in the producer. In the past decade, the producing and writing team of Joshua Brand and John Falsey have brought renewed vigor, innovation, intelligence and a sense of style to one of TV's most moribund forms—evening serial drama. Previously recognized with the Peabody in 1984 for *St. Elsewhere*, two vastly different but equally deserving programs from this outstanding creative team are hereby honored. *I'll Fly Away*, from Lorimar Television and pre-

sented on NBC, is a vivid, compelling tableaux of a small Southern town in the midst of the civil rights struggle of the late 1950's. *Northern Exposure*, from Pipeline Productions, Universal Studios and presented on CBS, depicts in a comedic and often poetic way, the cultural clash between a transplanted New York doctor and the townspeople of fictional Cicely, Alaska. Though wildly diverse, each show is marked by the "Brand-Falsey touch"—strong characterization, deft narrative, and compelling subject matter. For creating intelligent and unusual series television, a Peabody Award to Brand-Falsey Productions for *I'll Fly Away* and *Northern Exposure*.

The second of *Northern Exposure*'s Peabody Awards was awarded not to the series but to a specific episode, the already highly decorated "Cicely," for which the committee released the following statement:

> It is a rare occasion when a television entertainment series is recognized with a Peabody Award in two consecutive years. Yet this particular episode of a popular series moved the show to an even higher standard. The thrust of *Northern Exposure* each week concerns the means by which people of diverse backgrounds and experiences strive to accept their differences and co-exist in the community. In *Cicely*, this theme is given its strongest and most effective treatment. Roslyn and Cicely arrive in 1909 and encounter a town characterized by intolerance and immorality. By the close of the episode, Cicely has been transformed to a place where differences are universally accepted. To writers Andrew Schneider and Diane Frolov, director Rob Thompson, executive producers, Joshua Brand and John Falsey, and an ensemble cast of true excellence and diversity, a Peabody to *Northern Exposure: Cicely*.

Season 3 represents the pinnacle for *Northern Exposure* being awarded by the entertainment industry, and deservedly so. The top spot is a tough gig to sustain, though, but season 4 does so admirably.

The town of Cicely is constantly in dialogue with itself and with its past. History is explicitly established as a theme in season 3, and it is a theme that continues to play out in season 4 as each character's past continues to greet, influence, and in some instances confront them in the present. For Ed, a pressing concern is his heritage. For Maurice, the return of his South Korean son, Duk Won, sees their father-son dynamic get lost in translation.[23] Adam and Eve grace the town with their presence yet again, this time with child in tow,[24] whereas for Marilyn, an ex-boyfriend, the flying man, whom we were first introduced to in "Get Real,"[25] makes a surprise visit.[26] Holling is visited by a daughter, whom he knew nothing about.[27] And the arrival of Officer Barbara Semanski is a pleasurable visit for some, though for Chris it is not so, as she comes to arrest him and put him on trial for his former crimes.[28]

As well as the past catching up to the present, the lives of the Cice-leans in season 4 are also developed. In the case of Joel, their situations are prolonged. While Ruth-Anne achieves independence, purchasing the general store from Maurice;[29] Shelly falls pregnant;[30] and Ed struggles to come to terms with his arranged marriage,[31] for Joel and Maggie their agony is somewhat prolonged. Sexual tensions mount, only to amount to nothing, leaving Maggie to pursue her quest for a romantic other against the odds of the curse that appears to be following her with men. She briefly finds romance with Mike Monroe (Anthony Edwards), an environmentalist confined to a bubbled existence due to his paranoia about exposure to germs from the outside world. For Joel, his four-year stint in Cicely, which comes to an end in this series, is prolonged by a year based on the value of the dollar, which has fluctuated due to the economy and inflation.

Season 4 was well nominated at the 1993 award ceremonies. In partic-ular, the directors, writers, and cast involved in "Kaddish for Uncle Man-ny" were widely recognized by the likes of the Directors Guild of Ameri-ca, the Primetime Emmys, the Creative Arts Emmys, and the Q Awards.[32] But the series only took home a handful of wins. These in-cluded an ACE Eddie Award for editing (awarded to Briana London for "Kaddish for Uncle Manny"); a BMI Music Award for David Schwartz's score, one of the series's three awards that *Northern Exposure* and Schwartz earned in this category (in 1992, 1993, and 1994); and an Envi-ronmental Media Award for TV Drama.

"Seasons change but somehow not the scenery," read the lyrics of the song "What We've Won" by the band Blue States released in 2002. This is very much the case for season 5 of *Northern Exposure*, in which we see a number of narratives and themes, in the opinion of this writer, careless-ly recycled. As with most television series, their mid-late seasons can often be awkward; accused of being "samey" or "too familiar," they are forced to confront themselves, their tropes, and to grow in order to sur-vive the cull. Fortunately, *Northern Exposure* appeared to be somewhat self-aware of these trappings. First and foremost, it confronts at least one of them, putting an end to Joel and Maggie's "will they/won't they" relationship by testing them as a couple before accepting their fate. However, the end of the romantic relationship comes at the expense of the tension they had built up over the years—which holds much of our interest in Joel and Maggie in the first place. Likewise, the series' magical quality, which had enchanted audiences for four seasons, is all but absent from this more bitter, realist season (perhaps the influence of David Chase, creator of *The Sopranos*, as the executive producer).

One thing that is clear in this season—in which the most positive moments come from the birth of Miranda, Holling and Shelly's daughter,[33] and Ed's pursuit of the meaning of life as a shaman[34]—is that Joel and Maggie are no longer the central focus. As a result, *Northern Exposure* loses its focal point, its perspective, that of its hero, which until this season had been Joel. Reflecting the tensions between Morrow and the studio, one cannot help but feel that season 5 is the beginning of the series's farewell to Joel—only we, the audience, and the series itself are just not ready to say good-bye.

The series's distancing from Joel hardly came as a surprise. Rumors of Morrow's departure from *Northern Exposure* began to circulate in the fourth and fifth seasons when Morrow's disputes with the studio over his contract and pay were well publicized in the news. A 1992 *Los Angeles Times* article, for example, reported that Universal Television had raised a breach of contract suit against the actor for his refusal to attend a shoot on-set. The article details that, despite their commitment to a seven-year contract with built-in salary bumps, the actor was demanding double his $30,000 per episode salary.[35] While refusing to comment on the specifics, coproducer Falsey acknowledged the on-set tensions that hung over the production of the series, hoping that they could be resolved promptly. However, what he also signaled was that if Morrow's disputes couldn't be resolved, he would be forced to play his hand and create a new character to be written into the series to take his place (as opposed to casting another actor to play him). And while the news media was plagued with idle gossip that painted a portrait of strained working relationships between Morrow and other cast members and crew, others chose to express sadness and solidarity with Morrow's professional choice to leave. Esteemed writer Diane Frolov (who served as producer on fifty-five episodes, writer of twenty-five) was one of these people. In an interview with the *Chicago Tribune*, Frolov commends Morrow's agreement to return for thirteen episodes in season 6 (though he was due to leave after season 5) so that the writers—chiefly Frolov and her longtime collaborator Andrew Schneider—had the chance to ensure that "Fleischman's farewell could be handled creatively."[36] Frolov continues:

> We all value Rob. We don't want to see him go. . . . There is no war going on (with Morrow). . . . There's nothing like that. Rob wants to leave the show. He's been unhappy, and this is going to make him happy. . . . Just say we are parting on good terms, and let Rob speak to his own behavior.[37]

What would *Northern Exposure* look like without its central character, Dr. Joel Fleischman? This question hung over *Northern Exposure* as early as news first broke about Rob Morrow's contractual disputes, and around season 5, after it was announced that Morrow was exiting the series, audiences awaited season 6 to see what the answer would be. Following Joel and Maggie's argument in "Full Upright Position,"[38] Joel takes off, leaving Cicely to live with a remote tribe in "Up River."[39] Joel's absence from Cicely, and indeed the series, is blatant in the subsequent episodes. Its impact, on both the viewer and the characters, is severe. In Joel's place, the writers introduced two new characters, Phil and Michelle Capra, introduced in "Sons of the Tundra,"[40] a doctor and a journalist from Los Angeles, to fill the void, banking on the same fish-out-of-water tropes that Joel was subjected to in season 1.

The entrance of the Capras from Los Angeles signaled a narrative loop—a repetitive one at that. Of course, life in Cicely does not begin and end with Joel. While episodes such as "Cicely" provide us with a contextual history of the town and its former residents, and while the series itself documents the lives of its current residents (Maurice, Maggie, Chris, Ed, etc.) as it plays out, season 6 marks the entrance of its future residents in the form of the Capras. Dr. Phil Capra is played by Bronx-born stage and screen actor, filmmaker, producer, and comedian Paul Provenza. After a stint in New York's theater circuit and studies abroad, Provenza enjoyed a run on television. He appeared in the series *Kids' Court* and *Empty Nest* before *Northern Exposure* and went on to enjoy roles in *Sabrina the Teenage Witch* and *The West Wing* before turning to stand-up, radio, podcasting, directing, and writing. Meanwhile, Michelle Capra is played by Teri Polo, an actress who first appeared in the miniseries *The Phantom of the Opera* before *Northern Exposure*. Like Provenza, Polo also had a prime role in the highly popular series *The West Wing*, famously playing the role of Helen Santos, the wife of presidential candidate Matt Santos (Jimmy Smits). Polo's television career is broad, ranging from *Frasier*, *Chicago Hope*, and *Numb3rs* to *Medium* and *Criminal Minds*. Aside from television, Polo is perhaps more recognized for her role in *Meet the Parents* and its sequels, in which she plays Pam Byrnes, wife to Greg Focker (played by Ben Stiller).

In addition to the Capras, season 6 also treads water with some secondary narratives. Perhaps the biggest is the attempt to fill the Joel and Maggie–sized romantic hole with another Maggie romance, this time with Chris, who first notices his feelings toward her when she is elected mayor in "Realpolitik"[41] and again in "Balls."[42] However, with Joel mostly absent from the narrative or, when present, subjected to hostility by the other characters, *Northern Exposure* seemed lost and bitter.

It is my opinion, and the opinion of quite a few fans that I have met along the way, that the final season, and indeed the series as a whole, ends with one of season 6's best episodes, "The Quest,"[43] which truly gives Joel the sendoff he deserves, returning him to New York City, bringing closure to his relationship and friendship with Maggie, and thus concluding the hero's journey around which *Northern Exposure*, the series, is constructed.

Not only did Joel and Morrow's exit from *Northern Exposure* mark the end of Joel's hero's journey, but it would be the final nail in the coffin for the series as a whole. On Wednesday, 24 May 1995, CBS announced that *Northern Exposure* was canceled. As the title of Jerry Crowe's article in the *Los Angeles Times* reads, "The Lights Slowly Dim on '*Northern Exposure*': Television: The loss of a main character and its time slot were the beginning of the end for one of CBS' most popular prime-time programs."[44] Crowe's article continues: "Six months later, the show had all but disappeared into the Alaskan wilderness, its audience having dropped by half and its star, Rob Morrow, having left to pursue a movie career."[45] Aside from the departure of Joel and Morrow, the executives felt that *Northern Exposure* "was showing its age."[46] As executive producer David Chase said in an interview, CBS felt that "they needed to invest in the future."[47] "They needed to rebuild their Monday night with something that was all upswing and all future, as opposed to mostly past. So, they put their chips on 'Chicago Hope.'"[48] Swapping broadcast slots, *Chicago*

Hope "thrived," according to Crowe, whereas *Northern Exposure* "went south."[49] Crowe's article also quotes Jeff Melvoin, another of *Northern Exposure*'s executive producers, who speaks to the disappointing way in which the series disappeared from public attention: "One has to be realistic: Every show comes to an end. . . . But rather than sail off into the sunset to some sort of grand farewell, [this show] just slipped under the waves."[50] The opinion that the series could have gone out on a high, resisting the temptation to prolong or even extend its intended lifespan, is shared by Morrow's costar Janine Turner: "In a perfect world, we could have ended the show when Fleischman left and it could have been a beautiful, wonderful ending. . . . We can just throw the last nine [episodes] away, as far as I'm concerned."[51]

Whether, in your opinion, *Northern Exposure* ended with "The Quest"[52] or with "Tranquility Base (Our Town),"[53] it ended. Early in season 1, in the episode "Soapy Sanderson," a depressed Joel confides in Chris about his contractual obligation to the state of Alaska and his feeling of entrapment in Cicely, to which Chris responds,

> Well, you know, the way I see it, if you're here for four more years or four more weeks, you're here right now. You know? And I think when you're somewhere you ought to be there, and because it's not about how long you stay in a place. It's about what you do while you're there, and when you go is that place any better for you having been there?[54]

Joel, played by Morrow, as we know spent a total of six seasons, or five years, on the series before leaving in "The Quest." And while life went on for the people of Cicely after his departure, he nevertheless—like all those who pass through Cicely—left an impression. *Northern Exposure* lasted six seasons on CBS before its curtains closed. Just as Joel had left an impression on Cicely after he returned to New York City, *Northern Exposure* had, without a doubt, left an impression on television beyond its cancellation. Like many so-called cult favorites or classics of the late 1980s and 1990s—such as the aforementioned *Twin Peaks*, but also *Thirtysomething*, *Picket Fences*, *My So-Called Life*, and *Freaks and Geeks*, to name but a few—*Northern Exposure* did not live out its years on broadcast television for the multitude of reasons explored in this chapter. However, with VHS tapes, DVDs, and more recently Blu-ray, the series has enjoyed a life of its own beyond the schedule. The next chapter explores

Northern Exposure's cultural legacy, examining the invested fan culture the series has inspired and the efforts to revive *Northern Exposure*, with the aim of bringing its six seasons to contemporary streaming platforms and expanding its reach to new audiences, as well as looking back on the less than positive aspects of the series through a contemporary critical lens.

5

NORTHERN EXPOSURE
A Cultural Legacy

When *Northern Exposure* emerged onto the landscape of American television at the beginning of the 1990s, not only did it immediately find a place alongside other series belonging to "television's second golden age,"[1] but despite its awkward midseason slot, it also found an audience "willing to go on any ride [its creators, Joshua Brand and John Falsey] wanted to take them."[2] This final chapter reflects on both of these factors—the context of television in the 1990s and *Northern Exposure*'s audience—as it examines the legacy of the series, which turned thirty years old in 2020. It asks in what ways *Northern Exposure* was a product of the television landscape of the late 1980s and early 1990 and to what extent it contributed to television of and beyond its time. Moreover, being a series from the 1990s, it considers the problematic aspects of *Northern Exposure* when analyzing it through a contemporary lens. And finally, focusing on the fans, this cultural legacy also reflects on the impact of the series beyond the screen.

NORTHERN EXPOSURE AND TELEVISION'S SECOND GOLDEN AGE

Television's "second golden age" is unlike television's "first golden age" of the 1950s. Defined by studio-produced variety shows or plays adapted for the screen, television's "first golden age" is described by Robert J. Thompson as being "a golden age of mass-distributed theatre" that came in tension with the ambitions of television as a storytelling medium.[3] As Thompson goes on to write,

> Adaptations of established plays made especially for television fell more into the traditions of the stage than that of the small screen. Broadcast live from small studios, these shows were not yet able to take advantage of the medium's unique ability to play fast and easy with time and space, an ability television now shares with film.[4]

As television branched out into other genres and formats, it drew criticism as a medium and form of entertainment. No criticism of television is perhaps more scathing than that of President John F. Kennedy's Federal Communications Commission chair, Newton Minow, who famously declared television "a vast wasteland" at the National Association of Broadcasters in Washington, DC, on 9 May 1961. Minow's speech was not entirely a critique of television, however, but also appeals to the medium's potential. In full, Minow can be quoted as saying:

> When television is good, nothing—not the theatre, not the magazines or newspapers—nothing is better. But when television is bad, nothing is worse. I invite each of you to sit down in front of your television set when your station goes on air and stay there, for a day, without a book, without a magazine, without a newspaper, without a profit or loss sheet or a rating book to distract you. Keep your eyes glued to that set until the station goes off. I can assure you that what you will observe is a vast wasteland. You will see a procession of game shows, formula comedies about totally unbelievable families, blood and thunder, mayhem, violence, sadism, murder, western bad men, western good men, private eyes, gangsters, more violence, and cartoons. And endlessly, commercials—many screaming, cajoling, and offending. And most of all, boredom. True, you'll see a few things you will enjoy. But they will be very, very few. And if you think I exaggerate, I only ask you to try it.[5]

Television's "second golden age," and the ambitions of the production studios that were pioneering its content (such as the aforementioned MTM Enterprises), can be understood as a corrective to this. As explored in relation to *Hill Street Blues* and *St. Elsewhere*, part of this ambition was realized through the maturity of television's content, but perhaps even more so, it was established in the embrace of its form (episodic narratives, seasonal arcs). Whereas the programming of television's "first golden age" had borrowed from a cacophony of other earlier entertainment forms—most notably theater, film, and advertising—television, especially from the 1970s, grew increasingly interested in longer narrative forms. Capitalizing on the potential of its extended form—the potential for stories that could be told over a number of episodes or seasons—television began to exact its literary ambitions. As Horace Newcomb writes,

> [Television's] real relationship with other media lies not in movies or radio, but in the novel. Television, like the literary form, can offer a far greater sense of density. Details take on importance slowly, and within repeated patterns of action, rather than with the immediacy of other visual forms. It is this sense of density, built over a continued period of time, that offers us a fuller sense of a world fully created by the artist. [6]

As Thompson adds to Newcomb's early understanding of television's form, specifically the series,

> The series is, indeed, broadcasting's unique aesthetic contribution to Western art. Unlike any other medium but old-time radio and the comic strip, television presents stories that can go on forever. In soap operas and long-running series, we can see characters age and develop both physically and narratively in a way that even Wagner's longest operas or Dickens's most extended novels didn't allow. [7]

To return to Newcomb's assertion of a sense of artistry in television, and both Newcomb and Thompson's recognition of television's unique relationship to the novel, *Northern Exposure*, in the opinion of this writer, has a strict sense of belonging to an author: as this book stresses time and time again, and as bodies such as the Peabody Award committee recognize, *Northern Exposure* is a Joshua Brand and John Falsey series. The following section reflects on *Northern Exposure*'s form and its creators' signature, while also exploring how the series went on to make a profound impact on the landscape of American television.

In his article for *The A.V. Club*, writer Noel Murray reflects on *Northern Exposure*'s "Thanksgiving" episode. [8] Murray starts his article by establishing *Northern Exposure*'s context, the stage that the series shared with other television series when it was first broadcast in 1990: "In 1990, *The Simpsons'* first half-season arrived, along with a four-episode summer tryout for *Seinfeld* and the stunning first eight installments of *Twin Peaks*. All of these shows had become surprise hits in the months before *Northern Exposure* began its own eight-episode summer run."[9] *Northern Exposure* is often regarded alongside *Twin Peaks*, David Lynch and Mark Frost's offbeat, cult, small-town noir. And once it was in *Twin Peaks*'s shadow, *Northern Exposure* never really stepped out of it. As the website *Outcryer* reported, "critically, [*Northern Exposure*] has often been cast as a soft alternative to David Lynch's groundbreaking and bizarre *Twin Peaks*. Both shows aired at more or less the same time and were concerned with the eccentric residents of rural small towns in the Northwestern United States with a supernatural bent."[10] However, as the review continues, "where *Peaks* was unsettling and sinister, *Northern Exposure* was thoughtful and charming. While the struggling-for-ratings *Peaks* developed a legacy as a critical darling and cult object, *Northern Exposure* was for years one of the most popular series on television, but rapidly faded from the public eye."[11] Similarly, in his praise for *Northern Exposure* in the *Guardian* online, journalist Phil Harrison, in addition to calling the series "sprawling, ambitious and open-ended," drew the same comparison to Lynch and Frost's cult favorite as a way of defining *Northern Exposure*: "Think *Twin Peaks*, with the surreal horror replaced by meditative, down-home philosophy, and you are somewhere near."[12]

Rather than compare the two series, as many critics often do, this book instead regards *Twin Peaks* as useful in situating *Northern Exposure* in a specific cycle of television series released in the early 1990s. On several occasions this book refers to *Northern Exposure* as a Joshua Brand and John Falsey series. The reason we speak of television as we would a film or a book, in terms of its author (or auteur)—an Orson Welles film or a Jane Austen novel—is arguably because of series like *Twin Peaks* and other earlier series, especially those created by Steven Bochco (*Hill Street Blues*, *NYPD Blue*). *Twin Peaks* elevated television to almost the status of the art film or the auteur film. It is Frost and Lynch's vision of life in the small Pacific Northwest town of Twin Peaks. Likewise, its formal elements (its visual aesthetics, score, editing, ambiguous plot) are emblematic of the visionary director and writer's style or signature. Filmed just a stone's throw from the set of *Northern Exposure* at the same time the latter was being filmed, *Twin Peaks* compelled and mystified audiences with its bizarre characters and at times almost-impossible-to-follow narrative based around solving the crime of who killed Laura Palmer (played by Sheryl Lee). (Who killed Laura Palmer is a narrative mystery that is completed in Lynch's 1992 film *Twin Peaks: Fire Walk with Me* and whose story is continued in 2017's *Twin Peaks: The Return*).

Twin Peaks, like the other series that Murray draws contextual connections with (*The Simpsons* and *Seinfeld*) is significant for another reason: its self-referentiality and self-reflexivity. Specifically, *Twin Peaks* has a self-referential relationship with Lynch's oeuvre, which included, prior to *Twin Peaks*, the likes of *Blue Velvet, Dune, The Elephant Man*, and *Eraserhead*. *Twin Peaks*'s foregrounding of a clearly self-referential and self-reflexive mode—referencing and playing with the conventions of Lynch's early work, as well as other films and cinematic genres (crime and film noir in particular)—is characteristic of television in the 1980s and 1990s. For example, *The Simpsons* engaged with the earlier nuclear family sitcoms of the 1960s and 1970s, with Homer being an Archie Bunker–like patriarch, referencing Carroll O'Connor's character in *All in the Family*. *Seinfeld* consciously dismissed the tropes that had come to define the friendship-based sitcom—a mission set out in the comedian and creator Jerry Seinfeld's manifesto for the series, which stated, "no hugging, no learning," thus effectively suspending characters in stasis and rendering the allusion of a "series about nothing," as *Seinfeld* is often thought of. And both *My So-Called Life* and *Buffy the Vampire Slayer* are essentially systematic breakdowns of the high school paradigm enforced by the likes of earlier television series, such as *Happy Days*.

Northern Exposure can be viewed as another iteration of this self-referential and self-reflexive *kind* of television. As Brian Doan writes, *Northern Exposure* is heavily influenced, if not by the plots, then by the mood of earlier television series:

> "*Northern Exposure*" took a stylistic playfulness pioneered by "*Thirty-something*," "*Moonlighting*" and other '80s shows, and made it more organic to the program's usual mise-en-scène. Falsey and Brand's imagery was no less surreal or playful, but was more fully integrated into the program's ongoing camera and color schemes, so the line between fantasy and reality wasn't as clear or self-conscious; this confusion of space only intensified the show's richness. [13]

As both Doan and Murray also point out, *Northern Exposure*'s "integrated" self-consciousness even resulted in the series gently parodying *Twin Peaks* in its first season. In the episode "Russian Flu,"[14] Holling takes Joel and his fiancée Elaine on a sightseeing expedition. Staring down the sight of his binoculars, he makes reference to a character in *Twin Peaks*, such as Margaret Lanterman, who is better known as the Log Lady (played by Catherine E. Coulson), while the score echoes the infamous original soundtrack by Angelo Badalamenti. The scene is dreamlike, coated in a mist with hues of green and brown, akin to *Twin Peaks*'s visual aesthetic—a dreamlike quality that, as Doan comments, *Northern Exposure*'s later showrunner, David Chase, would transpose to his pioneering HBO gangster melodrama, *The Sopranos*.[15]

Such criticism and comparison affirm *Northern Exposure*'s place in the pantheon of television series belonging to the medium's so-called second golden age, while Doan's suggestion illustrates *Northern Exposure*'s reach beyond, claiming its influence on later television series such as *The Sopranos*. *Northern Exposure* was ahead of its time. Returning to Harrison, *Northern Exposure* is the "prototype modern television series."[16] The following explores some of the ways in which it was groundbreaking.

NORTHERN EXPOSURE AND GENRE

Try to imagine a small-town dramedy such as *Gilmore Girls*, *Schitt's Creek*, or *The Good Place* without first considering *Northern Exposure*. It is difficult. *Northern Exposure* not only had a profound influence on the subgenre of the small-town dramedy but also helped pioneer the television subcategory that is "quirky television."[17] Thompson helps us to understand *Northern Exposure*'s place as a "quirky" television series by situating it alongside *Twin Peaks* and *Picket Fences*. All three, Thompson writes, form the basis of what he calls "quirky" television series. Seen as an extension of the emergent "quality" label, championed by earlier series such as *Hill Street Blues* and *St. Elsewhere*, which had elevated the position of television to the likes of the novel, the goal of "quirky" television is to purposely subvert expectations and exploit the weird. As Thompson writes (with reference to the *New York Times*'s Jeff MacGregor),

Quirky, the word many viewers and critics enlisted to describe these shows, "became not just an adjective but an objective, a goal that producers sought when writing and designing (and most especially pitching) new shows." . . . Once television began trying to keep ahead of the cutting edge, its discovery of the truly bizarre couldn't be far behind.[18]

While, for Thompson, *Northern Exposure* championed a "quirkiness" shared with a handful of other series at the time that he, along with critics like MacGregor, coined "quirky" television, for David Scott Diffrient and David Lavery, *Northern Exposure* fits better under the headline "screwball television," sharing the slot with the likes of *Gilmore Girls*.[19]

Being labeled "quirky" or "screwball" can be detrimental to the reception of a television series and its lasting legacy. Reviewers at the time of *Northern Exposure*'s broadcast seem to have failed to recognize the importance of the series. Or, rather, in their defense, they were not in the position of hindsight that we view the series from today. At the time of its release and duration on CBS, *Northern Exposure* sustained and even elevated the position of a particularly higher caliber of dramedy. However, it is worth recognizing that with time, and with hindsight, critics have come to appreciate the impact *Northern Exposure* had, and arguably continues to have, on the television that succeeded it. Doan's writing on the series is a prime example of this. In his article, he traces the influence of *Northern Exposure* to the likes of *Buffy the Vampire Slayer*, *Parks and Recreation*, and, again, *Gilmore Girls*, "whose small-town quirk, screwball-meets-melodrama tone, and character archetypes owe almost everything to 'Exposure.'"[20] Furthermore, describing *Northern Exposure* as "an early example of a dramedy without a laugh track," Doan commends the series's playfulness with mood and champions the respect it showed for its audience. *Northern Exposure*, writes Doan, "respected its audience's intelligence, wisely ignoring 'high/low' divisions of culture and assuming viewers would appreciate references to both Voltaire and *Aliens*, Walt Whitman and the Home Shopping Network."[21] Doan's opinion affirms that of the *Guardian*'s Phil Harrison. Harrison similarly speaks to the complexities of the series and its sophistication in terms of its pitch and reach, while also demonstrating its capacity to find its audience, whom the writer-creator duo (Brand and Falsey) had full confidence in from the start.

NORTHERN EXPOSURE AND ON-SCREEN REPRESENTATION

In 2019, PBS premiered an animated series titled *Molly of Denali*, a television series aimed at children between the ages of four and eight. The show focuses on a ten-year-old girl named Molly Mabray (voiced by an Alaskan Native called Sovereign Bill), each episode revolving around Molly producing a video blog about rural Alaskan life in the fictional village of Qyah, with each blog entry filled with stories of eccentric family members and friends and accounts of adventure and discovery had by her and her malamute, Suki. *Molly of Denali* is significant for two reasons: first, it is "the first nationally distributed children's series with a Native American lead,"[22] and second, both the children's series and the network, PBS, were lauded for their "most ambitious effort yet to educate its young viewers about a distinct cultural group, while investing in making sure that members of that group are involved at every level of production."[23]

Similarly, in another medium, that of digital games, the 2014 game *Never Alone* tells the story of the adventure of an Iñupiaq girl named Nuna and her arctic fox. As Nathan Shafer writes in *Augmented Reality in Education*, both *Never Alone* and *Molly of Denali* are key examples of progressive representations of Alaskan Natives in popular culture in the twenty-first century, with "most aspects of its culture . . . manifesting in new media formats."[24] It is impossible to consider the possibility of Alaskan Native cultural heritage featuring on contemporary American popular television or in a digital game distributed globally without considering *Northern Exposure*, which, in the opinion of Clint E. Wilson II and his colleagues, provided a "unique twist . . . to Native American television portrayals" in the 1990s.[25]

In addition to paving the way for a respectable representation of Native Americans, and specifically Alaskan Natives, on television, *Northern Exposure* was instrumental for foregrounding other narratives and representations on-screen. Through characters such as Maggie O'Connell and the town's founders, Cicely and Roslyn, *Northern Exposure* offered at times a strong feminist discourse on gender; *Northern Exposure* pushed the boundaries of sex and gender, featuring the first same-sex wedding in prime-time programming with its broadcast of the wedding of Ron and Eric; and, coinciding with attitudes toward the environment particularly prevalent in the early 1990s, *Northern Exposure* had a part to play in platforming discussions about the environment and global warming in mainstream television narratives (perhaps a subject taken for granted on television today). As Jennifer Gatzke suggests, perhaps *Northern Exposure* owes some of its success, and its ability to feature such narratives around race, gender, and the climate crisis, because it aired during a time in history, and particularly American history, when many social movements were at their peak. As Gatzke writes, this era saw

> the revival of Earth Day and the Environmental Movement, the eruption of New Age Spirituality and "political correctness," a move toward global awareness, and the collapse of communism. It was a time in America's history for reevaluation, and social change seemed possible. A Republican administration was in office when the show was formulated. The global events combined with the political framework for its historical production indicates a possible need for a competing ideology. Evidence of this need for a shift in political power was the election of a Democratic President in 1992, mid-series for *Northern Exposure*. The television industry recognized that the American audience was becoming more diversified and saw an opportunity to target a fragmented population. The producers of *Northern Exposure* used political fads as character traits and challenged "political correctness" and stereotypes, all with a cross-cultural and global perspective.[26]

Given our current climate, amid cross-cultural and global discussions about race, sex, power, political allegiances, and global warming, there is certainly a place on television schedules and on-demand platforms today that remains empty for *Northern Exposure*.

LOOKING BACK THROUGH A CONTEMPORARY LENS

It is not always easy to address the problematic areas of one of your favorite television series, or to shine a spotlight on and challenge your own position as a viewer, for that matter. While *Northern Exposure* is pioneering in a myriad of ways—for its depictions of Alaskan Native culture on-screen; for its daring to foreground debates around gender, race, and sex in America; and for its diverse cast (at least more diverse than a lot of series, then and now, occupying the prime-time slot)—one has to acknowledge some of the ways in which the series has aged badly. In researching this book, it was vital to gather the opinions of fans on various aspects of the series and their engagement with it. Thus, a questionnaire was designed to gather opinions of *Northern Exposure* (see a summary of all the responses to the questionnaire in appendix B of this book). And while most of the questions invited fans to reminisce about the series and reflect on its broader cultural influence, particularly the fan culture that surrounds the series, one question was included with the aim of provoking *Northern Exposure* fans to confront the series's politics. That question was, "Are there any aspects about Northern Exposure that you find problematic today (i.e., representations of gender, race, sexuality, identity, culture, and heritage)?" The responses to this question were fascinating. While a slight majority of those who took part in the questionnaire answered "no" to this question, others took the time to list some really interesting readings of the series from a contemporary perspective. With the permission of all those who took part in the questionnaire, I have gathered their responses together and will summarize some of these points here.

As expected, Maurice's dialogue attracted a lot of attention, especially for his attitude toward same-sex couples, which we see play out time and time again in the series: his firing of Chris out of rage born of his response to Chris exploring the homosexual undertones of the poetry of Walt Whitman; his reluctant denial of the romance of the town's founders, Cicely and Roslyn; and his vocal unacceptance of Ron and Eric. For one person who answered the questionnaire, they found Maurice to be "bluntly homophobic," and for another, a gay person, they register Maurice's offensive attitude toward Ron and Eric but also recognized it as part of the lesson of the series—to objectively highlight competing attitudes by integrating them within the series discourse.

Meanwhile, for all its pioneering representations of peoples of color, race representation formed a critical part of some of the responses. While one writer recognized their own position of privilege, lauding the series for its inclusive and broad representations of a cross-section of American identities and cultural story lines, another took aim at some of the portrayals, situating them alongside Native American stereotypes in popular culture, as well as *Northern Exposure*'s casting choices at times, with "Native Americans played by non–Native Americans."

For all of Maurice's brazen masculinity, it is Maggie's feminism that really came under criticism in the questionnaire responses, and two aspects in particular. First, there is her sense that she will find fulfillment in a man, a pursuit that she is willing to change herself for. As one person responded, "Maggie's feminism, such as it is: she wants a man, changes herself for Mike, gets on a high horse about the artifacts in her yard, and she was violent to Joel (throwing things, punching him)." Second, her sexual politics are pulled into question after the events of "It Happened in Juneau" (3.21), when she and Joel are away at a conference and come close to having sex. Only, the act is not carried out by Joel when he finds Maggie asleep. One person wrote, "Maggie being enraged by Joel not having sex with her while she was asleep in Juneau was creepy as hell," while another wrote, "Maggie being upset that Joel did not rape her did *not* age well at all—that plotline always made me cringe, but it's worse now than ever."

Northern Exposure is highlighted by some of the fans for the series's blatant sexism. In addition to one fan taking aim at the series's overemphasis on the importance of women getting married, the dynamic between men and women, with hindsight, really highlights a serious flaw in the series. One person's response stood out and, I think, hit the nail on the head, emphasizing the many times the series simply got it wrong. They wrote,

> It's sexist, unfortunately, and it isn't so much a question of aging well or badly. The show doesn't even attempt to tackle the feminist issues of the time (bearing in mind this was the political atmosphere of the time). Instead, any insecurities that a female character (i.e., Maggie) might face are addressed with a mocking eye roll. Women are presented as hot tempered, irrational, and emotive. The show continuously pushes the idea that male and female differences are a biological fact. Somehow, Chris, a fairly adolescent and surfaced character, has the final word on any feminist issues. Many episodes are aimed around the premise of tricking female characters into sex. See season 3, episodes 4, 5, 20, and 21 (where Joel enjoys fooling Maggie into thinking they had sex while she was sleeping). The relationship between Holling and Shelley is frighteningly inappropriate. The question of their age would be less glaring if it weren't for Holling's constant infantilizing of Shelley, e.g., season 4, episodes 1 and 7.

There are some hard truths in the above that we *Northern Exposure* fans must confront and some wrongdoings that we must hold the series creatives accountable for. *Northern Exposure*—a show we all think of fondly for its easygoing nature—is complicated as a result of some of the issues highlighted above (and not always in a good way). Here, I do not speak of complication in terms of the series content, but rather—and I speak for myself—they force me to interrogate my relationship with the series as a result. While we can still love and value some aspects of a series, one must acknowledge that there are areas that are just ugly, mishandled, or neglected. We can all excuse it as being "of its time," but when a series wears its ambition to do better on its sleeve, one cannot help but feel sometimes that the series really could have done just that: better.

CICELY 2.0—*NORTHERN EXPOSURE* AND FANDOM

On 1 August 2015, a day after the twenty-fifth anniversary Moosefest came to a close in Roslyn, work began on dismantling the KBHR radio studio set from which resident DJ Chris Stevens broadcast his daily morning show. The KBHR radio studio had been installed on-site since the first episode was filmed twenty-five years earlier. However, having remained stationary for that time, serving as a landmark, a prop, and a photo opportunity for many a fan-tourist who made their annual pilgrimage to Roslyn, it was time for the station to be dismantled. It was not to be disposed of entirely, however. But its pieces were to be transported and reassembled in the adjacent space in the same building. For one *Northern Exposure* pilgrim, Corey Davorin, who happened to be attending Moosefest that year, he was able to capture the dismantling of the studio on video, later publishing the footage as a time-lapse online.[27] KBHR's transfer was, however, problematic. Not all of the equipment and furniture was going to fit in the new space. Whatever had to be left behind was tragically destined for the trash. Distressed by the prospect of a landmark of prime-time television heritage being discarded, Davorin claimed it for himself, repurposing the equipment. As he explained in our correspondence, "It turned out that only around two-thirds of the original KBHR was going to fit in the new space, so instead of the rest going into the trash pile, we loaded it up in our truck and drove two thousand miles with the tailgate down back to Texas the following day. We were excited to get home and start putting it together to say the least."

Jump ahead to 21 December 2016, when Davorin and his close friend, actor William J. White, who played the Brick's burger chef, Dave, in the series, were ready to unveil their project publicly. "KBHR South" was its name. KBHR South was modeled on the *Chris in the Morning* broadcasts in the series. But rather than the show's reach being limited to the local population of Cicely and the surrounding counties, KBHR South, broadcast over the internet, is able to reach fans the world over with an internet connection. Davorin assumes the role of DJ in KBHR South broadcasts, often accompanied by White. In terms of the series, to use Davorin's own words, "KBHR South doesn't have a list of rules, and the outcasts," as Davorin affectionately refers to his loyal listeners, "have joined and can discuss freely." So, what motivated Davorin to go to such lengths to save a television landmark from being destroyed and to then transport said equipment two thousand miles from Washington to Texas and revive the studio from a quarter of its original set to a fully operational online radio station from which Davorin and his committed partners broadcast to the world? As Davorin explained in our correspondence, "In the beginning I was just a fan seeking other fans and through these unfortunate events [the dismantling of the original KBHR film set] inadvertently created a more lax group, with the real KBHR being the foundation, out of necessity." In Davorin's response we find the answer to the questions posed earlier. He, like us, is a fan of the series hoping to connect to others. His project was more than a personal interest. It was a necessity.

Davorin's personal story is just one of many illustrating the extent to which some fans have gone to express their appreciation of the series and to connect with other fans globally through the series. Davorin's story has, in the opinion of this author, a metaphorical quality when it comes to thinking about *Northern Exposure* and its legacy three decades after its original television broadcast. Perhaps not as epic in scale, but like abandoned sets from Hollywood's studio system—from its so-called golden age—the leftover KBHR studio, which sat stationary for twenty-five years before having to be dismantled and relocated, paints a portrait of a piece of television history and the memory of a series in popular culture. In the same way that Hollywood tour companies capitalized on the skeletal remains of the sets of D. W. Griffith's 1916 *Intolerance* or Joseph L. Mankiewicz's 1963 *Cleopatra*, for example, granting fans the opportunity to witness a slice of Hollywood's "golden age," fans of *Northern Exposure* could take a photo with the set during their pilgrimages to Roslyn. However, also like the Hollywood sets, the *Northern Exposure* KBHR studio set sat dormant, save for an annual broadcast. Thus, through Davorin's repossession of the discarded set, it was reclaimed like a forgotten memory, and through its current form—rebuilt in a new setting (Texas) and operated by a new DJ (Davorin)—not only is that memory, and the series, kept alive, but so too is its unifying message or purpose (just as KBHR functions in the series itself). Davorin, like many fans, embodies the spirit of *Northern Exposure* and continues its legacy decades after it went off air. It is a metaphor for the passing of the torch from one era to the next, from one source and one community (*Northern Exposure* and Cicely) to another (KBHR South and a new generation of *Northern Exposure* fans online today). Through such ventures, *Northern Exposure* is reborn, or is at least revived, and we can consider this period as the next phase or incarnation. It is a life beyond the script and screen, placed in the hands of a globally connected community of fans online: Cicely 2.0.

While annual *Northern Exposure*–inspired footfall to Roslyn dwindled over the years, from the thousands to the hundreds since the late 1990s, fan investment and involvement in the series—beyond tourism—has done anything but diminish. This investment is particularly visible online. Take, for example, the "Moosechick Notes" website, an online archive of everything *Northern Exposure.* Interviewing the website's creator, Jerrilyn, who has over the years tirelessly populated and updated the website, she explained that the site "started as just an episode guide and kept growing. . . . It became a way for [her] to keep the show alive and in front of people." In addition to dedicated websites like Moosechick Notes, fan communities on various social media sites continue to pop up and grow in terms of followers in the wake of the series. Facebook groups and accounts on Twitter and Instagram flourish with activity, including posts about episodes, favorite quotes, personal memories of the series production, visits to Roslyn, and annual Moosefests. Others use the virtual spaces to broadcast live streams, to post and share the latest *Northern Exposure* news, and to take quizzes and participate in questionnaires. Online, thousands of fans contribute daily to preserving the series memory and, more importantly, to calcifying its legacy in the process. Such sites and digital social media spaces provide fans with a sanctuary where they can be themselves. It is where older fans share memories of the series and newer fans ask questions. Moreover, on occasion, it is a space where even the stars of the series reach out, respond, connect. As Darren Burrows who plays Ed said in an interview on *HuffPost*,[28] "Our fans are like the Trekkies of Alaska. . . . I think it [the fandom] is larger now than it was when it [the series] first aired."[29]

Fan activity is not limited to interactions via posts on Facebook walls or the liking of photos on Instagram. As Davorin's KBHR South project proves, fans are active in preserving the legacy of the series in the twenty-first century. Another, Erik Kalinski, combined his love for the series with his personal passion for creating model railways. Kalinski shared his diorama of Cicely, complete with a model railway that runs through Pennsylvania Avenue. Kalinski's work demonstrates countless hours of dedication and was even recognized in *Model Railroader* magazine in 2011. For others, their love of the series has resulted in fan wikis and websites (such as Moosechick Notes) and podcasts (two such examples are *The Alaskan Riviera* and *Northern Overexposure*) that provide alternative ways of revisiting the series.

Fan activities such as those mentioned above have not only kept the memory of *Northern Exposure* alive over the years but have been instrumental in ensuring the series's continuation. Fan investment online goes beyond just sharing content. Perhaps the most explicit indicator of this is the fans' literal financial investment in the series, with hundreds generously donating to online crowd-funding campaigns with the goal of raising enough money to sponsor projects related to and with the ambition of reviving the series. An example of this is the successfully funded Indiegogo project "Northern Exposed." Launched by Darren Burrows, Northern Exposed aimed to raise the money to support the writing and publishing costs of Burrows's book, *Northern Exposed*, and the supplementary documentary, *Return to Cicely*. Both the book and the documentary contained behind-the-scenes information, including accounts and insight into the production of the series from the likes of Burrows and other cast members that Burrows interviewed. Another example of fans' financial investment in the series was the "More NX Now" campaign, which raised $97,530 to go toward the development of the first script for season 7 to pitch to the studios.

REVIVAL

On 9 June 2017, there was a *Northern Exposure* cast reunion at the ATX Television Festival in Austin, Texas. The event was attended by cocreator Joshua Brand; cast members Rob Morrow, Janine Turner, Cynthia Geary, and Adam Arkin; and executive producers Mitchell Burgess and Robin Green. Chaired by television critic Maureen Ryan, their panel discussion explored shared experiences of producing, writing, and starring in the series and, as the ATX team described in their promotional copy for the event, sought to answer the question of "why we are still thinking about that damned moose more than twenty years later." While insightful and nostalgic, the main takeaway from the event came in the form of a universal commitment on behalf of the producers and cast to the revival of the series if the opportunity were ever to arise. This caught the attention of the media. However, it was not until November 2018 that *Hollywood Reporter* journalist Rick Porter formally announced that the *Northern Exposure* revival had been green-lit by CBS and was indeed in the works. Capitalizing on the contemporary popular cultural phenomenon of reviving television series, particularly those from the 1980s and 1990s, *Northern Exposure*'s revival was to join a long queue of resurrected television series. These included the likes of *90210* (2008–2013), which originally aired between 1990 and 2000; *Fuller House* (2016–2019), Netflix's reboot of *Full House* (1987–1995); *The X-Files* (2016–2018), bringing to a close Agent Mulder and Agent Scully's (played by David Duchovny and Gillian Anderson, respectively) story, which enthralled audiences from 1993 to 2001; *Will and Grace* (2017–2018), which ran on NBC between 1998 and 2005; *Murphy Brown* (2018), which originally aired between 1988 and 1998; *Rosanne* (2018), a reboot of the sitcom that ran from 1988 to 1996 (rebranded *The Connors* in 2019 due to the firing of Rosanne Barr after a series of racist tweets she posted on Twitter); *Roswell: New Mexico* (2019–), a continuation of the young adult series *Roswell* (originally released in 1999–2002); and of course *Twin Peaks: The Return*, which reimmersed audiences in the nightmarish Pacific Northwest town as depicted in its original short-term run in 1990–1991.

Just as quickly as the reignited excitement for *Northern Exposure* heightened in response to the news of a potential revival, the sudden death of John Falsey in January 2019 appears to have stopped it in its tracks, and understandably so. There is still hope for its revival, though, for fans and cast members alike. Actor Rob Morrow, for example, often publicly expresses his hope for a return to Cicely on his various social media pages and in a recent interview, as does David Schwartz, the series composer. Journalist Brittany Frederik of *Hidden Remote* asked Schwartz, "There have been rumors of *Northern Exposure* being revived for years now. If it does come back, would we hear David Schwartz composing the music again?" To which Schwartz replied,

> Yes, the buzz has been coming and going. I hope that there is still a chance of it coming back. *Northern Exposure* was my first show, and I was really learning how to compose, flying by the seat of my pants. It would be interesting composing for *Northern Exposure* now that I have a great deal of experience. Fingers crossed. [30]

CONCLUSION

Just as Morty the moose had wandered onto and continued to amble through the streets of the fictional town of Cicely, Alaska, in the series's opening credit sequence, *Northern Exposure* "itself [had] wandered onto the schedule unassumingly,"[31] and arguably since has left a deep imprint on popular culture. Despite the series's positive critical reception, acclaim, and arguable status as a "prototype modern television series,"[32] beyond its run on broadcast television, *Northern Exposure* has endured many challenges in terms of access to the series (for its original audience, keen to rewatch the series, and new audiences). As Harrison's review highlights, despite being a series made for television audiences today, television audiences today have limited options available to them in order to access the series. *Northern Exposure*—at the time of writing this book—is not available online or on demand. Instead, the only way to view the series is on DVD or, as of 2019, on Blu-ray in the UK. *Northern Exposure* on DVD, however, comes with its own compromises, namely the bastardized version of its "immaculately selected soundtrack," which, as Harrison explains, replaced its carefully curated audio tracks with "muzak mulch."[33] This is a problem as, for those familiar with the series, music regularly plays a key narrative function, with resident disc jockey Chris Stevens "usually bookend[ing] the show with a thematically appropriate song."[34]

From a "midseason slot-filler" to a popular television series,[35] from cult favorite to being relegated to television history, in its six seasons, *Northern Exposure* "transformed from the story of a big city doctor in a small town to a magical, charming, and engaging series that dared to be smarter and sweeter than anything else on television."[36] As Jim McKairnes of *USA Today* writes,

> "Exposure" shook up the formulaic prime-time world with what might be called TV's first holistic series, catering to viewers' emotional and spiritual well-beings. . . . It mined material few other dramas of the time had, from Native American mysticism to lesbian partnership to Jungian debates. Equal parts philosophical and cartoonish, it was Plato meets Pluto.[37]

As Frank McConnell proposes, *Northern Exposure* provides a "special place—the Secret Garden . . . where you can take all your everyday cares and, by playing at a simpler, more natural life, have them clarified and healed."[38] Lavery and Cain, on the other hand, provide a more interactive portrait of the dynamic between the series and the viewer: "Northern Exposure was always at play, always in play, and it required us to play with it."[39]

At its simplest, *Northern Exposure* gives us a smart, experimental, self-referential, and self-reflexive series that is willing to take risks. At its best, however—as illustrated by its fandom—*Northern Exposure* can teach us that, despite our differences, unity is possible, or it at least presents an image of unity that one can aspire to.

In what many fans consider to be the final episode of *Northern Exposure*, titled "The Quest,"[40] Joel returns to Cicely, having spent several weeks (several episodes in the series) at a reservation upriver. On his return, Joel enlists Maggie to undertake a final adventure with him to find the "Jeweled City of the North." Typical of the final stage of the hero's journey, "The Quest" sees Joel and Maggie solve a series of puzzles that, upon completion, promise to deliver Joel to his Jeweled City of the North, depicted in the final scene of the episode as a mirage of the Manhattan skyline. Here, he says his good-byes to Maggie before parting and dissolving into the darkness. The scene is symbolic of his return to the upper world, to his previous life from which he set off on his journey at the start of the series. Weeks later, Maggie receives a postcard, on the back of which Joel has written the words, "New York is a state of mind." She smiles.

For Joel, New York is a state of mind. For Maggie, and for the extensive cast of characters in the series, Cicely is a state of mind. And— regardless of whether you know the series as *Doctor en Alaska* (Spain), *Bienvenue en Alaska* (France), *Ausgerechnet Alaska* (Germany), *Un medico fra gli orsi* (Italy), たどりつけばアラスカ (Japan), *Przystanek Alaska* (Poland), *Det ljuva livet i Alaska* (Sweden), *Det gode liv i Alaska* (Norway), *Villi pohjola* (Finland) or *Северная сторона* (Russia)— *Northern Exposure*, for audiences the world over, is a state of mind.

EPILOGUE

I finished writing this book while living in Birmingham, England, during the winter of 2020. As I finished the final part of the book, which examines the cultural legacy of *Northern Exposure*, exploring the series's online fandom, it quickly became obvious that I have one final reflection to make. The year 2020 marked the thirtieth anniversary of *Northern Exposure*. All formal celebrations in and informal trips to the town of Roslyn, Washington, were canceled due to the outbreak of the global coronavirus pandemic (COVID-19) and the ensuing periods of lockdown. While disappointing for many, the tragic pandemic and the prolonged periods of lockdown globally have affirmed everything I have thought and written about the fans of *Northern Exposure*. Throughout 2020 to present, the online spaces still function in their usual way, with people sharing their favorite *Northern Exposure* memories or news items celebrating the series's legacy. However, overwhelmingly, these online spaces—what I dubbed in the final part of this book "Cicely 2.0"—have exceeded being just hangouts for people with a common interest: a television series broadcast in the first half of the 1990s. Instead, they have become spaces for positivity, support, and kindness. In her article looking back at the series thirty years later, *Salon*'s Ashlie D. Stevens nailed it when she wrote, "Thirty years after its premiere, it's a balm for social isolation, with its gentle interrogation of the ways in which myth, folklore and fantasy inform our internal lives—and what happens when we eventually take those parts of ourselves out into public again."[1] While it is often easy for writers, like myself, to measure the success of a television show according to its critical reception, its audience esteem, its fan following, and so forth, we can sometimes lose sight of its true value, and especially what it offers us, the audience, in times of need. I tapped into this in my opening to the book (see the prologue, "On a Personal Note"), explaining what *Northern Exposure* offered me during my time away from home when I was first attending university. During COVID-19, the series has exceeded my expectations: on one hand, rewatching the series gave me a brilliant way to spend my time at home. Whereas on the other hand, watching the series in lockdown provided me, like many thousands in the world online, with a sense of community during a period of intense isolation.

APPENDIX A

Episode Summaries

Northern Exposure ran for a total of six seasons, with 110 episodes. Below is a short summary of each of those episodes, including its director(s), writer(s), and original date of broadcast on CBS in the United States. Along with each episode summary is a favorite quote. Furthermore, out of the 110 episode summaries, ten contain an episode recap. Some of these selected episode recaps from *Northern Exposure* are my personal favorites, while others were chosen by the fans.[1] They are inspired by television critic Matt Zoller Seitz's approach to recapping episodes of *Mad Men* in *Carousel: The Complete Critical Companion*. In that book, Seitz explains that his *Mad Men* recaps were inspired by those of Andrew Johnson, television critic of *Time Out New York* and *The Observer*. Rather than simply rewording the synopsis of each episode, each recap instead reflects on key details within. These could be items, themes, moments, motifs, figures, or scenes that define each episode of *Northern Exposure*. These recaps are marked with an asterisk (*). If you're keen to jump ahead, they include the following episodes (in order of appearance, not preference): "Soapy Sanderson" (1.3); "A Kodiak Moment" (1.7); "Aurora Borealis: A Fairy Tale for Big People" (1.8); "War and Peace" (2.6); "Burning Down the House" (3.14); "Three Amigos" (3.16); "Nothing's Perfect" (4.3); "Homesick" (4.20); "Kaddish for Uncle Manny" (4.22); and "The Quest" (6.15).

SEASON 1 (1990)

1.1 "Pilot"

Directed by Joshua Brand and John Falsey
Written by Joshua Brand and John Falsey
Broadcast: 12 July 1990

> I don't like it—I hate it! And I demand to leave! . . . Well that is
> because you are not the one who is supposed to spend the next four
> years of his life in this godforsaken hole-in-the-wall pigsty with a
> bunch of dirty, psychotic rednecks!—Joel

Twenty-seven-year-old Columbia Medical School graduate Dr. Joel
Fleischman arrives in Alaska to begin his term as a general practitioner in
Anchorage. However, due to an oversubscription of medical professions,
he soon finds out that his journey is diverted to the remote outpost of
Cicely. There, over the course of this first episode, he meets, and offends,
almost all of Cicely's quirky denizens.

1.2 "Brains, Know-How, & Native Intelligence"

Directed by Peter O'Fallon
Written by Stuart Stevens
Broadcast: 19 July 1990

> Indians don't knock. It's rude.—Ed

Joel continues to wrestle with the inevitable fate of his immediate future
in Cicely, and this journey starts at his home. After his shower fails to
work on the icy morning after his arrival in Cicely, he needs to make
amends with Cicely's plumber. The only problem is, it is Maggie, also his
landlady, whom he offended just the day before at the Brick by assuming
that she was a prostitute. Joel attempts to smooth things over with Maggie, while also attending to his first patient, Ed's uncle, Anku, a medicine
man who refuses modern medicine. Meanwhile, Chris is fired from
KBHR after exploring the homosexual undertones of the poetry of Walt
Whitman, offending his boss, Maurice.

1.3 "Soapy Sanderson"*

Directed by Stephen Cragg
Written by Karen Hall and Jerry Stahl
Broadcast: 26 July 1990

> I did not get off the plane and say that I am Marcus Welby, kindly physician, and all around swell guy! Okay! I was fully prepared to do my time in Anchorage, but I am contractually bound to this tundra under false pretenses and against my will. So if I resort to some unscrupulous practices to right a greater wrong . . . look, where's Amnesty International when it comes to Joel Fleischman?—Joel

> Well, you know, the way I see it, if you're here for four more years or four more weeks, you're here right now. You know, and I think when you're somewhere, you ought to be there, and because it's not about how long you stay in a place. It's about what you do while you're there, and when you go, is that place any better for you having been there?—Chris

The suicide of Dr. Soapy Sanderson, an ex–college professor living a hermit existence, rocks a depressed Joel after he names him and Maggie as executors of his estate. The suicide captures the attention of a film crew, made up of ex-students of Sanderson, the presence of which entices and ignites the creative ambitions of cinephile Ed.

Recap

In "Soapy Sanderson," death and legacy are used as a catalyst. While Soapy's journey has come to an end, for Joel, Maggie, and Ed, their journeys are just beginning. Bequeathing his estate to Joel and Maggie, Soapy attempts to orchestrate their relationship, for their dynamic reminds him of his own marriage: his late wife is a headstrong woman, and he is a stubborn man. Beyond Joel and Maggie, the legacy of Soapy's estate, and the transaction of the land from Joel to the Native Alaskans, righting the wrongs of early American settlers, attracts a documentary crew to Cicely made up of film students from Soapy's alma mater. They have come to respect their university's former professor but are also on the quest to discover the "real Alaska"—a quest that is all but ended by Holling's reflection of what Soapy used to say: "Alaska is not a state but a state of mind." While the filmmakers' quest comes to a halt, another begins, as the somewhat existential Ed, who, after seeing the production of a film and gaining hands-on experience with the camera, realizes a potential future as a filmmaker, driven by the ambition to become "the Bergman of the North."

1.4 "Dreams, Schemes and Putting Greens"

Directed by Dan Lerner
Written by Patrick Sean Clark (credited: Sean Clark)
Broadcast: 2 August 1990

> You may think that because you're so much older than me you know more about the world. Well, in some cases that may be. But I read magazines! I watch TV! I know how people are supposed to treat each other.—Shelly

News of Shelly's pregnancy sparks Holling to propose, and hastily their wedding is arranged. The wedding stirs Holling's fears over Shelly's safety—his anxieties rooted in the fact that the wives of the male Vincoeur centenarians all died young. Meanwhile, the entrepreneurial Maurice entertains a group of Japanese businessmen and fellow venture capitalists looking to invest in the development of a luxury resort in Cicely, bringing Joel on board to sell the vision of a complete professional golf course.

1.5 "The Russian Flu"

Directed by David Carson
Written by David Assael
Broadcast: 9 August 1990

> G-O-O-O-O-D MORNING, CICELY!—Ed

Bad luck has it that when Joel's fiancée Elaine comes to visit him, Cicely falls prone to a case of the "Russian flu," and both the Russians and their resident doctor, Joel, are caught in the town's delirious crosshairs. While a perplexed Joel searches high and low for a cure in modern medicine journals, Marilyn prescribes a secret native remedy that gradually cures the town. Coming around to the prospects of alternative medicine, Joel attempts to appeal to Marilyn to share the recipe to what could be, for him and the Western world, a medical breakthrough.

1.6 "Sex, Lies and Ed's Tape"

Directed by Sandy Smolan
Written by Joshua Brand and John Falsey
Broadcast: 16 August 1990

> Let me tell you something, buster. You might not be dying, but you're gone.—Maggie

Committed to making a film, Ed struggles with the age-old dilemma of creative block, failing to find inspiration in the everyday. Meanwhile at the Brick, Holling and Shelly's relationship is complicated when Wayne, Shelly's secret husband from back home, turns up in Cicely requesting a divorce. While attempting to treat Rick's paranoia about Maggie's "boy-friend curse" after a visit from Rick regarding a growth on his chest, Joel advises Ed to seek inspiration in the quotidian, like many of his auteur heroes. Ed takes Joel's advice, eventually settling on the subject of everyday life in Cicely for a documentary.

1.7 "A Kodiak Moment"*

Directed by Max Tash
Written by Steve Wasserman and Jessica Klein
Broadcast: 23 August 1990

> There are four words you need to know to adequately prepare yourself for childbirth. Take notes here, ladies: I. Want. My. Epidural.—Joel

The death of Malcolm Minnifield, brother of Maurice, prompts him to contemplate his own mortality and legacy. This is a recurring concern for Maurice. Temporarily, he lines up Chris to inherit his estate as the son he never had (or at least thought he never had). His own father issues considered, this provides a burden for Chris, who respectfully eventually declines the responsibility. Meanwhile, Holling and Ed, with Shelly in tow, attempt to track down Jesse the bear, and Joel (accompanied by Maggie) teaches a child-birthing class in another part of Alaska.

Recap

Symbolically, the bagels transported hundreds of miles by Maggie to Joel's office in the opening scene signify the pervading theme in this episode: circles. Maurice's news of his brother's death forces him to confront the cycle of time and legacy. When Shelly joins Holling and Ed on their hunting expedition on the trail of Jessie the bear, it results in the two lovers coupling up in the tent, leaving an awkward Ed third-wheeling beside the campfire. Holling misses his chance to confront the past with Jessie, whereas for Ed, Jessie is caught through the circular lens of Holling's camera. Lastly, Joel and Maggie's final prenatal class sees a student going into labor. The event not only affirms Joel's earlier witty remark when the student immediately yells, "I want my epidural," but more poignantly, it brings the narrative to a poetic close. As Maurice gently puts it when he visits Fleischman in the closing scene: "Man dies. Baby is born. Cycle continues."

1.8 "Aurora Borealis: A Fairy Tale for Big People"*

Directed by Peter O'Fallon
Written by Charles Rosin
Broadcast: 30 August 1990

> I finally figured out we are somewhere between the end of the line and the middle of nowhere.—Joel

> Jung says that dreams are the woofer and tweeter of the total sound system.—Chris

While Joel is confronted with Cicely's Bigfoot, spending the night in a cabin in the middle of the woods with the fabled Adam, Chris is motivated by the northern lights to create a public work of art. However, he has a problem: he is creatively blocked. Fortunately, this block is temporary, as Chris is visited by Bernard, who turns out to be his long-lost brother—secret sons of their traveling adulterous father.

Recap

The moon is the focal point of this season 1 finale. Curated in the sound-track to the episode with songs such as "Moonlight Sonata," "Moon River," and "Blue Moon," the moon physically disrupts the sleep and behavior of Cicely's residents. It inspires Chris to create a sculpture. It causes an employee of the IRS (Inland Revenue Service) named Bernard to randomly quit his job and follow the trail north from Portland to Cicely on his motorcycle. Bernard is instinctively drawn to Cicely and cosmically linked to Chris, who, as we find out by the end of the episode, is his half brother. And it is in the moonlight that Joel, stranded in the middle of nowhere after visiting a patient, first encounters the fabled Adam, with whom he spends the night eating the most delicious dim sum noodles and drinking a bottle of fine red wine.

SEASON 2 (1991)

2.1 "Goodbye to All That"

Directed by Stuart Margolin
Written by Robin Green
Broadcast: 8 April 1991

> Sex should be wild, unfettered, and free. We're animals, aren't we? And, basically, we're all wolves in sheep's fur. I always wanted more. Not frequency—I am not talking about frequency, although that would have been great, too. I wanted more intensity. I wanted to be out there, outside myself, outside my skin. I wanted sex to be like robbing life out of the jaws of death!—Joel

The outside world intruding on the everyday lives of Cicely—in particular those of Holling and Joel—is the key theme of this episode. Upon receiving a Dear John letter from Elaine, who has left him for a mature man in the city, Joel is depressed. Ed and Maggie concoct a plan to cheer Joel up, which includes re-creating a typical New York City scene so that Joel can achieve closure. Meanwhile, Holling installs a satellite disk outside the Brick, delivering hundreds of channels to its customers. While united by live sports and international soap operas, for Shelly the technology is isolating, as she succumbs to an addiction to its endless flow of content.

2.2 "The Big Kiss"

Directed by Sandy Smolan
Written by Henry Bromwell
Broadcast: 15 April 1991

> There's an old saying that if you come back to the place where you became a man, you will remember all those things you need to be happy. . . . That saying never made sense to me, but I thought it was worth a try.—One-Who-Waits

At the heart of "The Big Kiss" is not a kiss at all, but a search. While a mute Chris searches for his voice—his expressive tool and professional attribute—which has been stolen by a beautiful woman passing through town, Ed undertakes a spiritual quest with his spiritual shaman, One-Who-Waits, a 256-year-old Indian spirit, to locate his parents. For Chris, the search is a success; for Ed, it continues.

2.3 "All Is Vanity"

Directed by Nick Marck
Written by Diane Frolov and Andrew Schneider
Broadcast: 22 April 1991

> "Vanitas vanitatum, et omnia vanitas," says the preacher. "All is vanity." I think that's a pretty good epitaph for all of us. When we're stripped of all our worldly possessions and all our fame, family, friends, we all face death alone. But it's that solitude in death that's our common bond in life. I know it's ironic, but that's just the way things are. "Vanitas vanitatum, et omnia vanitas." Only when we understand all is vanity, only then, it isn't.—Chris

Against the backdrop of identifying an unknown man who is found dead in Joel's waiting room, Holling wrestles with the idea of getting a circumcision after Shelly makes a personal comment, and Maggie pretends Joel is her boyfriend to please her father after he turns up in Cicely unexpected.

2.4 "What I Did for Love"

Directed by Steven Robman
Written by Ellen Herman
Broadcast: 29 April 1991

> Trapped as we are on that merry-go-round of time, we've circled
> around once again to the annual Cicely, Alaska, birthday bash extrava-
> ganza.—Chris

While Maurice entertains a married astronaut groupie for their annual
passionate affair, Chris prepares for Cicely's anniversary. Meanwhile,
Maggie has Joel spooked about his forthcoming vacation to New York
after she shares her nightmare in which Joel is killed in a plane crash.
Like James Stewart's George Bailey in *It's a Wonderful Life* (Frank
Capra 1946), Joel contemplates life in Cicely without him as he witnesses
the townsfolk bond with temporary physician, David Ginsberg (Leo Get-
er), brought in from New York, who is every part his opposite.

2.5 "Spring Break"

Directed by Rob Thompson
Written by David Assael
Broadcast: 6 May 1991

> Wildness, Ed. We're running out of it, even up here in Alaska. People
> need to be reminded that the world is unsafe and unpredictable, and at
> a moment's notice, they could lose everything, like that. I do it to
> remind them that chaos is always out there, lurking beyond the hori-
> zon. That, plus, sometimes, Ed, sometimes you have to do something
> bad, just to know you're alive.—Chris

> White people. They get crazy.—Marilyn

The changing of the seasons affects each person in Cicely in different
ways. For Holling, the arrival of spring makes him aggravated, picking a

fight with everyone he sees; for Chris, the changing season results in him resorting to his former ways, causing a string of car radio thefts in Cicely, before being caught by the cinephile–turned–hard-boiled detective Ed; and the changing climate results in Maggie and Joel experiencing shared dreams.

2.6 "War and Peace"*

Directed by Bill D'Elia
Written by Henry Bromell and Robin Green
Broadcast: 13 May 1991

> Hold it, hold it, hold it! This is ridiculous! Hey, we play to a very sophisticated television audience. They know Maurice is not going to kill Nikolai, and they definitely know that Nikolai is not going to kill Maurice.—Joel

All of Cicely welcomes visiting Russian celebrity Nikolai to town, with the exception of Maurice, for whom his visit revives Cold War tensions. Meanwhile, Holling's sleep is disrupted by constant nightmares, and Ed's fantasies come true as he enters a sexual relationship with Lightfeather Duncan—a passion sparked by romantic letters written by Chris on his behalf.

Recap

Beyond the distraction of Nikolai and Maurice's tense relationship, Holling's intense nightmares, and Ed's affair with Lightfeather Duncan, the most talked about element of this episode is the fourth wall—the wall between the characters, the set, and us, which Joel infamously breaks when he disrupts a potentially fatal gun duel between the visiting Russian, Nikolai, and hardened patriot, Maurice. It is a moment that registers the audience. Time and narrative are suspended. Actors break from character momentarily, confronting and challenging the script, before resuming the episode's alternative ending, a sing-along at the Brick to Irving Berlin's "What'll I Do." It is in this scene that *Northern Exposure* winks to the viewer beyond, it lets them in, it treats them with respect, and it demonstrates early on the series's flexibility.

2.7 "Slow Dance"

Directed by David Carson
Written by Diane Frolov and Andrew Schneider
Broadcast: 20 May 1991

> Calling you a moron is an insult to morons. Broccoli has more brain
> power than you. Cauliflower!—Maggie

Just as Maurice feels the victim when same-sex couple Ron and Eric, two
budding entrepreneurs, come to town to purchase a property from him,
challenging his conservative politics, Maggie's "boyfriend curse" claims
another victim, this time the unfortunate Rick, who is struck by a falling
satellite.

SEASON 3 (1991–1992)

3.1 "The Bumpy Road to Love"

Directed by Nick Marck
Written by Martin Sage and Sybil Adelman
Broadcast: 23 September 1991

> Men can only think of one thing. The joystick. Is it big enough, and
> where can they put it?—Maggie

While Rick's body, melded with the metal of the fallen satellite, is committed to the ground at the end of season 2, season 3 starts with the
erection and unveiling of a bronze statue of Maggie's latest above
ground, which brings to town a strange woman (one of many) with whom
Rick was having an affair. The arrival complicates Maggie's grieving
process.

3.2 "Only You"

Directed by Bill D'Elia
Written by Ellen Herman
Broadcast: 30 September 1991

That's the movies, Ed. Try reality—Joel
No thanks.—Ed

Self-image plays a significant role in this episode: Chris grapples with his own conceit, unable to convince a woman he is attracted to to go out with him; Maurice gets upset with Holling over what he believes to be an unflattering photograph that he took of him; and Maggie fears that her degrading eyesight is a sign of aging.

3.3 "Oy, Wilderness"

Directed by Miles Watkins
Written by Robin Green
Broadcast: 7 October 1991

What are wolverines, anyway? Are they little wolves that swarm all over you and nibble you to death?—Joel

For the first time, Joel and Maggie are forced to spend an extended amount of time with each other when Maggie is pushed to make an emergency landing in the middle of nowhere. While Maggie adapts, survival instinct switched on and her rifle in hand, Joel, desperate, chooses to apply his medical knowledge to fixing her light airplane.

3.4 "Animals R Us"

Directed by Nick Marck
Written by Robin Green
Broadcast: 14 October 1991

Because all we are, basically, are monkeys with car keys.—Grandma Woody (Allen)

A stray dog with a taste for beer, beef jerky, and Maggie's company convinces a bereaved Maggie that it is Rick reincarnate. Meanwhile, upon discovering Marilyn's gigantic ostrich eggs, produced at her home farm, Maurice struggles to convince her to go into business with him with the aid of a personal brand and a life-size cardboard cutout replica of her.

3.5 "Jules et Joel"

Directed by James Hayman
Written by Stuart Stevens
Broadcast: 28 October 1991

> There's a dark side to each and every human soul. We wish we were
> Obi-Wan Kenobi and, for the most part we are, but there's a little
> Darth Vader in all of us. Thing is, this ain't no either/or proposition.
> We're talking about dialectics, the good and the bad merging into us.
> You can run but you can't hide. My experience? Face the darkness,
> stare it down. Own it. As brother Nietzsche said, being human is a
> complicated gig. Give that old dark night of the soul a hug! Howl the
> eternal yes!—Chris

A fall and a bump on the head causes Joel to fantasize about having an
identical twin brother named Jules, every part his opposite.

3.6 "The Body in Question"

Directed by David Carson
Written by Henry Bromell
Broadcast: 4 November 1991

> History is powerful stuff. One day your world is fine. The next day it's
> knocked for a metaphysical loop. Was Napoleon really at Waterloo?
> Would that change what I had for breakfast? Thoughts turn to our
> refrigerated friend Pierre Le Moulin, Pierre the Windmill, stepchild of
> history. If those chapped lips could speak, what would they say? Bon-
> jour? Mes amis, j'ai faim?—Chris

Historical integrity is on trial in this episode, in which the body of a
Frenchman, believed to be Napoleon, washes up in Cicely. For Joel, the
arrival of the cadaver raises fears about the ramifications of rewriting
history. Meanwhile for Holling, given his French heritage, its discovery
resurfaces his anxieties over genetics, and for Shelly, the whole incident
sparks worries about fertility.

3.7 "Roots"

Directed by Sandy Smolan
Written by Dennis Koenig
Broadcast: 11 November 1991

> Einstein said, "God doesn't play dice with the universe," but I don't
> know . . . maybe not as a whole, but I think he gets a pretty big kick out
> of messing in peoples' backyards.—Chris

While Joel's day-to-day is disrupted by the arrival of Elaine in town,
reigniting old feelings, a vivid but fragmented dream, accompanied by
the soundtrack and ritual of African dance, awakens and confuses Chris.
It is only after a visit from his half brother Bernard that the duo come to
the realization that their subconsciouses are entwined and that Chris's
dream is a calling to Bernard to connect with his African heritage.

3.8 "A-Hunting We Will Go"

Directed by Bill D'Elia
Written by Craig Volk
Broadcast: 18 November 1991

> You bought me a grave for my birthday?—Ruth-Anne
> Do you like it?—Ed
> Yes . . . yes, I do, Ed. It's a great spot to spend eternity.—Ruth-Anne

Ruth-Anne quietly turns seventy-five and suffers from an accidental fall,
prompting a concerned Ed to ruminate on the topic of age and aging. The
caring Ed automatically switches into an overprotective and overbearing
mode around Ruth-Anne, causing her great frustration. Meanwhile, pro-
voked by Maggie in the street outside, Joel's hunting instincts are awoken
when he accompanies Chris and Holling on a hunting trip: Chris loaded
for bear (or in this case, game) and Holling with his SLR camera.

3.9 "Get Real"

Directed by Michael Katleman
Written by Diane Frolov and Andrew Schneider

Broadcast: 9 December 1991

> When I finally complete this indentured servitude, no one's even gonna remember who Joel Fleischman is.—Joel

While Joel is locked away in his office, studying with Ed for a medical exam, the circus comes to town after their bus breaks down nearby. Cicely becomes the stage for both a love story, as one of the circus performers—Enrico Ballati, "the flying man" (played by Bill Irwin)—falls for Marilyn, and trouble in paradise, as Shelly leaves Holling after he judges her large feet. All the while a romantically lost Maggie, feeling the absence of a partner, ponders her love life.

3.10 "Seoul Mates"

Directed by Jack Bender
Written by Diane Frolov and Andrew Schneider
Broadcast: 16 December 1991

> A long time ago, the raven looked down from the sky and saw that the people of the world were living in darkness. The ball of light was kept hidden by a selfish old chief. So the raven turned itself into a spruce needle and floated on the river where the chief's daughter came for water. She drank the spruce needle. She became pregnant and gave birth to a boy which was the raven in disguise. The baby cried and cried until the chief gave him the ball of light to play with. As soon as he had the light, the raven turned back into himself and carried the light into the sky. From then on, we no longer lived in darkness.—Marilyn

History, myth, heritage, and tradition all collide in this Emmy Award–winning episode. Maurice is brought face-to-face with an old flame from his time served in Korea during the Korean War, along with a surprise son, Duk Won; the town prepares for its annual Raven pageant, starring Marilyn; Maggie finds herself emotionally confused as her family cancels their Christmas plans in favor of a Caribbean holiday; Joel, a person of the Jewish faith, develops festive feelings, purchasing his first Christmas tree; and Shelly mourns her traditional Catholic seasonal traditions.

3.11 "Dateline: Cicely"

Directed by Michael Fresco
Written by Jeff Melvoin
Broadcast: 6 January 1992

> Happiness doesn't come from having things; happiness comes from being a part of things.—Chris

"Trees talk" is the latest headline on the front page of Maurice's local newspaper, penned by a concealed source (which is eventually identified as Adam). The implication has Maggie convinced but Joel in doubt. Meanwhile, Holling's tax dodging on the Brick catches up with him, bringing with it a significant deficit that he cannot afford. It is a debt that forces him to partner with Chris at the Brick, who has recently come into some money. Their partnership proves tense.

3.12 "Our Tribe"

Directed by Lee Shallat Chemel
Written by David Assael
Broadcast: 13 January 1992

> She says you look unhappy. . . . I told her you always look like that.— Marilyn (to Joel)

While Holling closes the Brick all of a sudden and sends Shelly to Saskatoon to visit her family, causing a suspicious Maggie to investigate, Joel is adopted into a local tribe after curing an elder.

3.13 "Things Become Extinct"

Directed by Dean Parisot
Written by Robin Green
Broadcast: 20 January 1992

> Every alder branch contains a flute; your job is to find it.—Ira

As the title of this episode implies, endangered identity is the core theme. Ed spends some time with Ira Wingfeather, documenting his process of crafting unique traditional flutes, with the aim of cultural preservation; Joel's sense of isolation only grows as he comes to the realization that he is the only Jew in Cicely, perhaps even Alaska; and Holling is catapulted into his own midlife crisis with news that his uncle has died, leaving him to carry the torch for the Vincoeur men.

3.14 "Burning Down the House"*

Directed by Rob Thompson
Written by Robin Green
Broadcast: 3 February 1992

> The thing I learned, folks, this is absolutely key: It's not the thing you fling. It's the fling itself.—Chris

Artistic inspiration takes center stage in this memorable (and highly quoted) episode, in which Chris, after Ed spoils his original idea, searches for a new thing to fling in his purpose-built trebuchet. Fortunately for Chris, Maggie's visiting mother, after breaking it to Maggie that she is divorcing her husband, Maggie's father, accidentally burns down her house, leaving only a piano standing.

Recap

The dialogue between destruction and creation collides with the absurd in this episode. The realization of creative ambition, the parting of ways with beloved objects, and the coming to terms with family issues are all emphasized, yet muted, in the final transcendental scene in which Chris launches Maggie's piano through the air.

3.15 "Democracy in America"

Directed by Michael Katleman
Written by Jeff Melvoin
Broadcast: 24 February 1992

My friends, today when I look out over Cicely, I see not a town, but a nation's history written in miniature, inscribed in the cracked pavement, reverberating from every passing flatbed. Today, every runny nose I see says "America" to me.—Chris

A contest from Edna, a disgruntled denizen of Cicely, sees Holling's role as mayor being challenged as Cicely takes to the polls. A fierce running mate, Holling's power, while it does not deter Edna, turns Shelly on. Meanwhile for Chris, he gets off on a patriotic high brought about by the democratic process, while for Ed, it forces him to contemplate the weight of his first vote.

3.16 "Three Amigos"*

Directed by Matthew Nodella
Written by Mitchell Burgess and Robin Green
Broadcast: 2 March 1992

As Bill used to say, "You don't get cold in the bush. Either you're warm or you're dead."—Holling

No-Name Point is the end destination for Holling and Maurice as they venture out on horseback to bury an old friend.

Recap

The bond between the past and the present, the wild and the domestic, simmers throughout this episode, in which Maurice and Holling venture to No-Name Point to bury their friend—the nature of their enduring friendship coming into focus when their adventure is juxtaposed with Chris's reading of *The Call of the Wild*, Jack London's 1903 novel about power, dominance, and loyalty among sled dogs.

3.17 "Lost and Found"

Directed by Steven Robman
Written by Diane Frolov and Andrew Schneider
Broadcast: 9 March 1992

It changes everything. The ego falls away, and you stop worrying about yourself; you just focus on the baby. You think: this person inside me, what will she be like? . . . Will she be asthmatic? Will she pronate? Will she have her father's malocclusion? It's all such a glorious mystery.—Eve (about pregnancy)

The perceived voice of the ghost of a man who committed suicide in his cabin haunts Joel, who becomes obsessed. Meanwhile, Joel is visited by hypochondriac Eve, wife of Adam, who is under the impression that she is suffering from an exotic illness, and Maurice's impression of his former commanding officer from the Korean War is shattered when he asks Maurice for a loan.

3.18 "My Mother, My Sister"

Directed by Rob Thompson
Written by Kate Boutilier and Mitchell Burgess
Broadcast: 16 March 1992

You're just going to leave me with a baby? What am I supposed to do with a baby?—Joel
Feed her.—Marilyn

With Adam experiencing a sympathetic pregnancy following the news that Eve is with child, an abandoned baby in Joel's office is temporarily adopted by the town. Meanwhile, Shelly's mother and her young U.S. Army husband turn up in Cicely unexpectedly, putting the nature of Shelly and her mother's relationship into perspective.

3.19 "Wake Up Call"

Directed by Nick Marck
Written by Diane Frolov and Andrew Schneider
Broadcast: 23 March 1992

Shelly seems pretty well adjusted. She makes good eye contact. How does she get along with animals?—Leonard

The seasonal cycle is once again having a profound impact on Cicely, as the town is once again hit by spring fever. The change of season causes Shelly to break out in a skin rash; Joel to take under his wing a new mentor, in the form of Leonard, Marilyn's cousin; and Maggie to fall in love with a mysterious stranger who also happens to be a mythic bear.

3.20 "The Final Frontier"

Directed by Tom Moore
Written by Jeffrey Vlaming
Broadcast: 27 April 1992

> Fleischman, you are just not human! Humans have inquiring minds and a thirst to know! You're just a thing! A rock! A shoe! A 2×4! A person with absolutely no imagination and curiosity!—Maggie

In addition to a mysterious package arriving at Ruth-Anne's general store with stamps showing that it has traveled the world, Cicely is also swamped with visitors from Japan who have ventured north to Alaska to copulate under the northern lights at Ron and Eric's themed bed and breakfast, much to Maurice's shock.

3.21 "It Happened in Juneau"

Directed by Michael Katleman
Written by David Assael and Robert Rabinowitz
Broadcast: 4 May 1992

> Be open to your dreams, people. Embrace that distant shore. Because our mortal journey is over all too soon. "Those cloud-capped towers, the gorgeous palaces, the solemn temples. The great globe itself. Yea, all which you inherit shall dissolve and, like this insubstantial pageant faded, leave not a rack behind. We are such stuff as dreams are made on, and our little life is rounded with a sleep."—Chris (quoting William Shakespeare's *The Tempest*)

Joel's plans for a naughty weekend at a conference in Juneau are dashed—first, when the overpopulated hotel forces him to share his suite with Maggie, and second, when the aggressive approach of a promiscuous New York doctor at the conference intimidates his masculinity. Meanwhile, in Cicely, Chris and Bernard, who has recently returned from Africa, discover that they are out of sync.

3.22 "Our Wedding"

Directed by Nick Marck
Written by Diane Frolov and Andrew Schneider
Broadcast: 11 May 1992

> Marriage. It's a hard term to define. Especially for me; I've ducked it like a root canal. Still, there's no denying the fact that marriage ranks right up there with birth and death as one of the three biggies in the human safari. It's the only one, though, that we'll celebrate with a conscious awareness.—Chris

An embarrassed Maggie avoids Joel after their return from Juneau, under the impression that they slept together. Meanwhile, a distracted Eve avoids getting in the spirit of her wedding to Adam due to a secret that she carries hidden: that she is aristocratic and rich.

3.23 "Cicely"

Directed by Rob Thompson
Written by Diane Frolov and Andrew Schneider
Broadcast: 18 May 1992

> One person can have a profound effect on another. And two people . . . well, two people can work miracles. They can change a whole town. They can change the world.—Ned Svenborg

Told mainly through flashbacks, a 108-year-old man and former citizen of Cicely, Ned Svenborg, tells the story of Cicely's lesbian founders, Cicely and Roslyn. It is a tale of love, of hope, of conflict, and sadly of tragedy that forces Joel to really think about his relationship with Cicely and his place in its history.

SEASON 4 (1992–1993)

4.1 "Northwest Passages"

Directed by Dean Parisot
Written by Robin Green
Broadcast: 28 September 1992

> You get crow's feet and chicken chin. Your nips start heading south
> and your bum turns to yogurt!—Maggie (on turning thirty)

On the day of Maggie's thirtieth birthday, a fever during a solo camping
trip puts her into a delirious state in which she finds herself confronted
with the spirits of her dead ex-boyfriends: Rick, Glenn, David, Bruce, and
Steve. Meanwhile, Chris and Ruth-Anne teach Marilyn to drive, and
Maurice, stricken with repetitive strain injury from writing his memoirs,
wanders through Cicely dictating his life into a voice recorder (much to
the annoyance of his fellow Ciceleans).

4.2 "Midnight Sun"

Directed by Michael Katleman
Written by Geoffrey Neigher
Broadcast: 5 October 1992

> I didn't know you Jewish people were tall enough to care about basket-
> ball.—Maurice

Several days without darkness and the resulting sleep deprivation send
Joel into hyperdrive, channeling his newfound energy and knowledge of
basketball into coaching the Quarks, Cicely's basketball team, and lusting
after Maggie.

4.3 "Nothing's Perfect"*

Directed by Nick Marck
Written by Diane Frolov and Andrew Schneider
Broadcast: 12 October 1992

I just have this feeling that if I take pi well past all this static, take pi to ten million, twenty million digits, that I'll find something really incredible. Not just a pattern, not just an order, but a sign. A mathematical sign.—Amy (talking about pi)

An allergy to cats prevents the coupling between Chris and mathematician and doctoral student Amy, whom he is brought into contact with after accidentally running over her dog. Meanwhile, Maurice's patience is tested when an antique clock that he has ordered from Germany, which is assembled by the highly energetic specialist Rolf, fails to tell the time accurately.

Recap

A drive through the mountainous landscape sets into motion the key theme of "Nothing's Perfect." As wheels turn going, and Chris's pickup crosses paths with Red's coming, the theme of the circle, the cycle of time, is established. Red is delivering to Maurice a four-hundred-year-old clock imported from Germany (along with its eccentric clock restorer and fitter, Rolf). Meanwhile, unbeknownst to him, Chris is about to be pulled into his own karmic cycle defined by the taking of a life—that of a dog named Rusty—and giving, in the form of finding love with Amy (an academic and mathematician who is obsessed with the equation for pi) to whom Rusty belonged. Confronted by a slight malfunction, the clock confronts Maurice's growing obsession with time, in relation to which, over the course of the episode, he comes to terms with the fact that he has no control over it. Meanwhile for Chris, a string of pet deaths—first Rusty and then Paul, a parakeet—forces him to sacrifice something of his own, his motorbike, which he pushes off a cliff in the name of love. Life and death, gain and loss, love and love loss.

4.4 "Heroes"

Directed by Charles "Chuck" Braverman
Written by Jeffrey Vlaming
Broadcast: 19 October 1992

Tooley's going to experience things we can only imagine. He's going to soar like an albatross, plunge like a grayling into the crystal waters, and start on a fling of his own to places that we can only ponder in the daylight and experience in our dreams.—Chris

The funeral of Tooley, an old friend who had a profound relationship and influence on Chris, weighs heavily on the resident DJ, all while Cicely is visited by English rock star Brad Bonner (played by Adam Ant), whom Ed films and Shelly crushes on, much to Holling's jealousy.

4.5 "Blowing Bubbles"

Directed by Rob Thompson
Written by Mark B. Perry
Broadcast: 2 November 1992

> I'm not the one who's talking about hot-waxing the elephant man here.—Joel
> Drop dead, Fleischman.—Maggie

Cicely's newest resident, Mike Monroe, a hyper-allergic ex-lawyer who lives in a geodesic dome, attracts the attention of Maggie and the judgmental frustration of Joel. Meanwhile, the recently unemployed investment banker Matthew, son of Ruth-Anne, rekindles his relationship with his mother when he suddenly turns up in her store, having left his career behind and looking to start afresh in Cicely crafting fishing hooks.

4.6 "On Your Own"

Directed by Joan Tewkesbury
Written by Sy Rosen and Christian Williams
Broadcast: 9 November 1992

> Ed, are you hallucinating?—Joel
> Oh, yeah, but not right now.—Ed

A besotted Maggie—wearing dresses, cooking for and catering to Mike's needs—facilitates a meeting between Maurice and ex-lawyer Mike concerning Maurice's will, because he wishes to add Duk Won as a benefactor. Meanwhile, Marilyn is visited by her romantic interest, the "flying man," Enrico Ballati, who has since left the circus to start his own touring show and happens to be passing through Cicely with hopes of rekindling their unique romance.

4.7 "The Bad Seed"

Directed by Randall Miller
Written by Mitchell Burgess
Broadcast: 16 November 1992

> Cranes carry this heavy mystical baggage. They're icons of fidelity and happiness. The Vietnamese believe cranes cart our souls up to heaven on their wings.—Chris

Just as Marilyn moves out of her family home and Maggie helps her find her ideal place, Jackie—a con artist who claims to be a daughter that Holling knew nothing about—moves into town, disrupting Holling's every day and having a negative influence on Shelly.

4.8 "Thanksgiving"

Directed by Michael Fresco
Written by David Assael
Broadcast: 23 November 1992

> I'm to believe that this tomato was simply Ed's way of saying season's greetings?—Joel (after being pelted by a tomato by Ed)

Thanksgiving means two things in Cicely: the Thanksgiving feast and the Native Alaskan population throwing tomatoes at white people. Tomatoes on a crisp, clean shirt are not the only surprise in store for Joel, who discovers he owes the state of Alaska another year of service on his "sentence" due to inflation on the dollar. And just as Joel feels suspended in Cicely, Maggie's relationship with Mike moves on to the next level.

4.9 "Do the Right Thing"

Directed by Nick Marck
Written by Diane Frolov and Andrew Schneider

Broadcast: 30 November 1992

> People are simply incapable of prolonged, sustained goodness.—Joel

Both Maurice's memoirs, Holling's bar, and Maggie's piloting are brought to a standstill in this episode. Former KGB member Viktor visits Maurice with the offer to purchase a dossier containing embarrassing information; the Brick is inspected by the thorough health inspector, Jason; and news of the death of a colleague in a plane accident has a profound impact on her outlook.

4.10 "Crime and Punishment"

Directed by Rob Thompson
Written by Jeff Melvoin
Broadcast: 14 December 1992

> We've been over what I'm supposed to say, and I've got to tell you, it's pretty persuasive stuff, but is it the whole truth? It's a *slice* of truth, a morsel, a fraction. It's a piece of the pie, certainly not the whole enchilada, and now that I've been thinking about it, I don't think I could tell the whole truth about anything. That's a pretty heavy burden because we all just view the world through this little piece of Coke bottle. Is there such a thing as objective truth? I wonder.—Chris

Maurice enlists ex-lawyer Mike to defend Chris in this episode, in which, as the title suggests, the criminal past of Cicely's resident DJ catches up with him and he is brought before a judge to answer for them. While his past looms above him, working against his favor, his present contributions to the community help to even the odds.

4.11 "Survival of the Species"

Directed by Dean Parisot
Written by Denise Dobbs
Broadcast: 4 January 1993

> My own sex, I hope, will excuse me if I treat them like rational creatures instead of viewing them as if they were in a state of perpetual

childhood, dismissing these pretty feminine phrases which men condescendingly use to soften our slavish dependence, and despising that sweet docility of manners supposed to be the sexual characteristics of the weaker vessel. I wish to show that the first object of laudable ambition is to obtain a character as a human being, regardless of the distinction of sex.—Mary Wollstonecraft (quoted by Maggie)

Tensions over the management of an archaeological site on Maggie's property, in which ancient relics are unearthed, forces the women of Cicely to reclaim Maggie's yard and the excavation for themselves. Meanwhile, Ed spends time with Mike after a series of nightmares prompts him to consider his carbon footprint, and Holling gives a troubled young boy named Brad a job at the Brick.

4.12 "Revelations"

Directed by Daniel Attias
Written by Diane Frolov and Andrew Schneider
Broadcast: 11 January 1993

> Oh woman! Lovely woman! Nature made thee
> To temper man: we had been brutes without you!
> Angels are painted fair, to look like you:
> There's in you all that we believe of heaven;
> Amazing brightness, purity, and truth,
> Eternal joy, and everlasting love.—Chris (quoting Thomas Otway's *Venice Preserv'd*)

While Ruth-Anne upsets Maurice by settling the debt on her general store, thus owning it outright, Joel finds his waiting room empty of patients, which tests his patience, and Chris's world is empty of sound as he retreats to a monastery for spiritual guidance, inviting Bernard to fill his shoes at KBHR.

4.13 "Duets"

Directed by Win Phelps
Written by Geoffrey Neigher
Broadcast: 18 January 1993

Five guys? Yes, I admit that's strange. But there is no cause and effect
here.—Mike
Yes, there is. I'm the cause, death is the effect.—Maggie (on her
"boyfriend curse")

One-Who-Waits returns to Ed in this episode with news of the identity
and location of his father, Pete. Mike and Maggie's romance gets physical; however her "boyfriend curse" lingers in the air between them, pre-
venting them from getting closer. And finally, Holling becomes frustrated
with a rude, blind piano tuner who slaves away on the piano at the Brick.

4.14 "Grosse Pointe, 48230"

Directed by Michael Katleman
Written by Robin Green and Mitchell Burgess
Broadcast: 1 February 1993

> Poor Jane, always getting the fuzzy end of the lollipop.—Maggie's
> grandmother

On the promise of courtside-seat tickets to a basketball game, Joel is
persuaded to accompany Maggie, as her boyfriend, on a family visit to
Grosse Pointe, Michigan. While Joel gets along with Maggie's family,
tensions mount when Joel is introduced to Maggie's jealous ex-boyfriend,
Jed, who still holds feelings for Maggie.

4.15 "Learning Curve"

Directed by Michael Vittes
Written by Jeffrey Vlaming
Broadcast: 8 February 1993

> I'll be in my office should a patient choose to darken our door.—Joel

As Holling studies for the high school diploma that he never gained and
Maggie butts heads with a new schoolteacher whose views on a woman's
role in contemporary society differ from her own, Joel frets over Marilyn's safety after she takes a vacation in Seattle but fails to check into her
hotel.

4.16 "Ill Wind"

Directed by Rob Thompson
Written by Jeff Melvoin
Broadcast: 15 February 1993

> They say it's an ill wind that bloweth no man to good. I think our own
> Dr. Joel Fleischman will attest to that. For those of you who missed it,
> Maggie scored a one-round decision over Dr. Fleischman last night.
> Right jab to the old honker. Pow! TKO What better sign that the coho
> winds are once again upon us. . . . My advice this year, don't fight
> them; embrace them. Know your enemy.—Chris

Tensions mount in "Ill Wind" as Joel and Maggie's passion grows to a
point of violence and carnal desire, and Maurice feels obligated to Chris
after Chris saves his life.

4.17 "Love's Labor Mislaid"

Directed by Joe Napolitano
Written by Jeff Melvoin
Broadcast: 21 February 1993

> Sometimes, Maggie, you just have to go for it. Grab for the gusto. Go
> for the plunge.—Mike

The carnal desire from the previous episode has a short-term memory in
this episode, it seems, as Maggie forgets having sex with Joel. Meanwhile, Ed is confronted with the predicament of an arranged marriage to
someone he is not attracted to, and Holling and Ruth-Anne venture to find
a rare bird that has been sighted in the area.

4.18 "Northern Lights"

Directed by Bill D'Elia
Written by Diane Frolov and Andrew Schneider
Broadcast: 1 March 1993

> Continuous unremitting darkness has been known to send some people
> into an emotional tailspin, so the management here at KBHR radio

suggests locking away the firearms. The desire to stick that .45 between the teeth can get pretty strong at times, so why invite temptation?—Bernard

While Chris is once again out of inspiration and unable to work, Joel
refuses to work when his vacation is denied by the state. After avoiding
acting on her impulses, Maggie confronts her "boyfriend curse" and acts
on her attraction to Mike. Meanwhile, Maurice confronts an ex-marine-
turned-panhandler about his life and career decisions.

4.19 "Family Feud"

Directed by Adam Arkin
Written by David Assael
Broadcast: 8 March 1993

> Anyway, I know a couple of us have been down the aisle with these
> people before. Maybe this time they'll make it to the altar. We'll keep
> our collective fingers crossed.—Chris (referencing Holling and Shel-
> ly's wedding)

The unveiling of a totem pole by Leonard stirs a rift between two of
Cicely's tribes due to its historical association. Meanwhile, Shelly's life
is disrupted by fantasies of dancers—fantasies that can only be stopped if
Holling takes her hand in marriage, which he accepts.

4.20 "Homesick"*

Directed by Nick Marck
Written by Jeffrey Vlaming
Broadcast: 15 March 1993

> Thanks for showing me the outside of your house, Maurice. I especial-
> ly enjoyed the imaginary flower garden.—Ed

With Mike's illness suddenly cured, he makes the decision to leave Cicely, rejecting Maggie in favor of his environmental cause. While Maggie
and Mike's relationship comes to an end, Holling and Shelly's marriage
is tested when Shelly redecorates Holling's room, much to his distaste.

Meanwhile, Maurice revisits a memory of a minor betrayal of his brother, Malcolm, when he has the contents of his Oklahoma home moved to Cicely.

Recap

Descending the stairs, a child, Malcolm, blurs the line between fantasy and reality (as *Northern Exposure* often does), occupying a dream space in which Maurice has the opportunity to sit down and apologize to his brother for something he did in the past (stealing a toy fish from his brother). An act of confession and of forgiveness for an event in the past remedies the feelings and guilt experienced (by Maurice) in the present.

4.21 "The Big Feast"

Directed by Rob Thompson
Written by Mitchell Burgess and Robin Green
Broadcast: 22 March 1993

> Maurice J. Minnifield, our generous host, friend, and employer, I'm sure I join everyone in saying thank you for these very fine eats and drinks. You are a real American. You're an ex-marine and astronaut. You are America. You're rich, you're rapacious, you're progress without a conscience, paving everything in its path. You're 5 percent of the earth's population, yet consuming 25 percent of the earth's natural resources. You pay a lot of taxes; you do a lot of charity work—most of it is tax deductible, but your heart is in the right place. One thing's for certain: you have impeccable taste in the booze.—Chris (toasting Maurice)

Joel is left out of Minnifield Communications's twenty-fifth anniversary celebration due to the betrayal of Maurice's trust when he reported him to the IRS. But while Joel is left out, Adam takes over as head chef, and Eve helps Shelly re-create a bottle of 1929 Château Latour that Shelly accidentally breaks, without Maurice or Adam suspecting a thing.

4.22 "Kaddish, for Uncle Manny"*

Directed by Michael Lange

Written by Jeff Melvoin
Broadcast: 3 May 1993

> You need nine guys on a field to play baseball and ten Jews in a room
> to say Kaddish.—Joel

As one of a very limited number of Jews in Alaska, Joel's sense of
isolation grows stronger and is particularly felt when he is hit with the
news of the death of his uncle Manny and is unable to carry out a Kaddish
for his deceased relative due to being the only member of the Jewish faith
residing in Cicely. Chris on the other hand continues a long feud with the
Miller brothers, and Shelly is upset when Holling is chosen as Marilyn's
dance partner.

Recap

A series often defined by the theme of resisting to change—particular
Joel's inability to adapt and to accept Cicely and its denizens—"Kaddish,
for Uncle Manny" provides us with a glimpse of the opposite, as Joel
embraces the collective, the community, his fellow man, to enable him to
grieve the loss of his uncle via a performed Kaddish.

4.23 "Mud and Blood"

Directed by Jim Charleston
Written by Diane Frolov and Andrew Schneider
Broadcast: 10 May 1993

> Ed! Look at this plant.—Maggie
> OK. [Pauses.] Doesn't appear to be doing anything unusual, Mag-
> gie.—Ed

It is spring once again in Cicely. With the change of season, Maurice
feels lucky and purchases a truffle pig; Maggie is overcome with a sense
of optimism; and Holling, misinterpreting Chris's advice, becomes obsessed with the need to undertake hard labor in order to achieve a sense of
value and meaning.

4.24 "Sleeping with the Enemy"

Directed by Frank Prinzi
Written by Mitchell Burgess and Robin Green
Broadcast: 17 May 1993

> My nips are as big as double-drop chocolate cookies.—Shelly

The ghosts of war—specifically the Korean War—get in the way of Maurice's approval of his son Duk Won's fiancée, given that she is the daughter of his enemy. While heritage is very much affecting the lives of Duk Won and his partner, tradition and identity are precarious things in the eyes of Ed, who sees dubbing *The Prisoner of Zenda* (John Cromwell 1937) into the native language of Tlingit as an act of cultural preservation.

4.25 "Old Tree"

Directed by Michael Fresco
Written by Diane Frolov and Robin Green
Broadcast: 24 May 1993

> Be good to yourself, Cicely. Go out and plant a wet one on a tree.— Chris

Taking a break from diagnosing the human (and on occasion animal) population of Cicely, Joel is tasked by Maurice with performing a checkup on "Old Vicky"—an ancient tree located on his land. As if this task is not strange enough for Joel, every time he comes in contact with Maggie, he has an accident. Meanwhile, Shelly finds that she is unable to speak, only sing.

SEASON 5 (1993–1994)

5.1 "Three Doctors"

Directed by Daniel Attias
Written by Diane Frolov and Andrew Schneider

Broadcast: 20 September 1993

> Sometimes the mind, for reasons we don't necessarily understand, just
> decides to go to the store for a quart of milk.—Joel

While Ed finds himself waking up in unusual places around Cicely—
according to Leonard, an apparent calling from the spiritual world for one
to become a shaman—Joel is bound to the bed, having succumbed to a
local illness.

5.2 "The Mystery of the Old Curio Shop"

Directed by Michael Fresco
Written by Rogers Turrentine
Broadcast: 27 September 1993

> Excuse me, would you ladies mind postponing your trenchant literary
> critique so we can continue with our little medical practice here?—Joel

Long homesick for New York City and for a sense of connection to his
faith and community, an excited Joel discovers signs of the Yiddish language in Tlingit. While Joel tracks his culture, a worried Maurice confronts his health and mortality once more after suffering a mild heart
attack, and Maggie, left off the guest list for her father's wedding, escapes
into the mysteries of Nancy Drew.

5.3 "Jaws of Life"

Directed by Jim Charleston
Written by Robin Green and Mitchell Burgess
Broadcast: 4 October 1993

> Something I've been wondering about lately—mirrors, you know. You
> hold two of them facing each other, And what's on 'em? I don't
> know.—Ed

While Chris reflects on his outlook on life after coming across medication
that will improve his chances of exceeding the typically short lifespan of
the Stevens men, Maurice comes face-to-face with his doppelgänger, at

least physically, in the form of a to-scale wax replica sent by Madame Tussauds.

5.4 "Altered Egos"

Directed by John Coles
Written by Jeff Melvoin
Broadcast: 11 October 1993

> Oh God. Oh my God. I'm sitting here eating seeds and having a serious conversation about winter clothing.—Joel

While on one hand in this episode Joel laments his apparently declining New York City street smarts and Marilyn breaches doctor-patient confidentiality to snoop through the health records of the men she is dating, Bernard's new girlfriend, an ex-lover of Chris's, comes between the half brothers.

5.5 "A River Doesn't Run through It"

Directed by Nick Marck
Written by Jeff Melvoin
Broadcast: 25 October 1993

> Now, it says right here—I'm not making this up—"Be there or be square." I don't know what that means, so I'm not taking any chances. I'm gonna be there.—Chris

This episode features a cameo from a young Jack Black as a high schooler who invites Maggie to be his high school's homecoming queen. Meanwhile, wealth status and a land sale cause a rift between the two richest men in Cicely: Maurice and the newly listed local millionaire, Lester Haines (Apesanahkwat).

5.6 "Birds of a Feather"

Directed by Mark Horowitz
Written by Robin Green and Mitchell Burgess

Broadcast: 1 November 1993

> The Eagle wasn't always the Eagle. The Eagle, before he became the Eagle, was Yucatangee, the Talker. Yucatangee talked and talked. It talked so much it heard only itself. Not the river, not the wind, not even the Wolf. The Raven came and said, "The Wolf is hungry. If you stop talking, you'll hear him. The wind, too. And when you hear the wind, you'll fly." So he stopped talking and became its nature, the Eagle. The Eagle soared, and its flight said all it needed to say.—Marilyn

Herb and Nadine Fleischman, Joel's parents, visit Cicely, and Nadine has a profound experience. After forging a spiritual bond with Marilyn, who informs her that she is spiritually connected to the Eagle—a truth that Joel has trouble believing—Nadine survives a fall from a cliff during a hike, claiming that she flew to safety.

5.7 "Rosebud"

Directed by Michael Fresco
Written by Barbara Hall
Broadcast: 8 November 1993

> The path to our destination is not always a straight one, Ed. We go down the wrong road, we get lost, we turn back. Maybe it doesn't matter which road we embark on. Maybe what matters is that we embark.—Leonard

While the town attempts to recruit Joel for Cicely's volunteer fire department, an offer he turns down, Maurice tasks Ed with organizing a film festival dedicated to the career of Orson Welles, which brings famous New Hollywood film director Peter Bogdanovich (*Targets* [1968], *The Last Picture Show* [1971], and *Paper Moon* [1973]) to town to lend a helping hand.

5.8 "Heal Thyself"

Directed by Michael Katleman
Written by Diane Frolov and Andrew Schneider

Broadcast: 15 November 1993

> Low self-esteem is the root cause of practically all the pain and misery
> in the world. It's what drives war, and torture, and genocide. It's what
> evil is. Do you think Hitler liked himself? Or Cortez? We hate others
> because we hate ourselves.—Leonard

A little green man symbolizing low self-esteem haunts Ed, forcing him to
confront his self-doubt. Meanwhile, Maggie grows estranged from her
social circle at the local laundromat after buying her own washer-dryer,
and Holling is thrown out of a class for expectant parents because of his
childish interruptions.

5.9 "A Cup of Joe"

Directed by Michael Lange
Written by Robin Green and Mitchell Burgess
Broadcast: 22 November 1993

> I think the saying is better to have tried and failed than not to have
> tried at all, and if they didn't say it, they should have.—Chris

While Chris swots for his pilot's license and Marilyn enters detective
mode, investigating the theft of the petty cash, a historical event drives a
stake between Holling and Ruth-Anne concerning a fatal blizzard and the
consumption of Ruth-Anne's grandfather by Holling's grandfather.

5.10 "First Snow"

Directed by Daniel Attias
Written by Diane Frolov and Andrew Schneider
Broadcast: 13 December 1993

> *Bon hiver*, Cicely.—Chris

Devastation lingers in the minds of both Joel and Maurice in this episode.
For Joel, he is devastated by the loss of a patient who predicts her pend-
ing death, despite having nothing wrong with her, and for Maurice, it is
Shelly's confession that she never loved him, despite saying that she did.

5.11 "Baby Blues"

Directed by Jim Charleston
Written by Barbara Hall
Broadcast: 3 January 1994

> Like Woody Allen says, "It's worse than dog eat dog. It's dog doesn't
> return dog's phone calls."—Ed

Literal and symbolic babies hang over the heads of the characters involved in this episode. The stories of others' experiences of childbirth put Shelly on edge; the realization of a shared dislike of babies brings Maggie and Joel into agreement; and Ed's baby—his screenplay for *The Shaman*—is threatened by an interested, but interfering, Hollywood agent.

5.12 "Mr. Sandman"

Directed by Michael Fresco
Written by Diane Frolov and Andrew Schneider
Broadcast: 10 January 1994

> Maybe candy is just candy.—Marilyn

Holling, Maggie, Joel, Maurice, and Ron experience each other's dreams and deepest, darkest desires under the active Aurora Borealis, leading to a deep understanding of family, a disdain for food, and an embarrassment over a woman's footwear fetish.

5.13 "Mite Makes Right"

Directed by Michael Vittes
Written by Diane Frolov and Andrew Schneider
Broadcast: 17 January 1994

> Life is everywhere. The earth is throbbing with it; it's like music. The
> plants, the creatures, the ones we see, the ones we don't see, it's like
> one, big pulsating symphony.—Maggie

An allergy to bedbugs sees Maggie obsess over dust mites, to the point of seeing them, personified, at the Brick. Meanwhile, Maurice's purchase of a collectable violin attracts the unwanted attention of an obsessive professional violinist named Cal (Simon Templeman).

5.14 "A Bolt from the Blue"

Directed by Michael Lange
Written by Jeff Melvoin
Broadcast: 24 January 1994

> I know Adam is a walking pathologist, but the guy's never hurt anybody, not that I know of. I mean, threats of imminent danger are just his way of saying "good morning."—Joel

Joel attempts to reason with a recently fired Forestry Service fire lookout who wants to end his life of isolation; Ed survives being struck by lightning and is left contemplating the event's larger significance; and Adam sabotages Maurice's Presidents' Day fireworks display due to his paranoia.

5.15 "Hello, I Love You"

Directed by Michael Fresco
Written by Robin Green and Mitchell Burgess
Broadcast: 31 January 1994

> My masculinity doesn't hinge on—on whether or not I knit.—Joel

As her due date comes around, Shelly encounters Miranda, a young girl, at the laundromat and is convinced that she is her future child. Meanwhile, trapper Walt reveals his love for Ruth-Anne when the two are left stranded in a car overnight due to a storm.

5.16 "Northern Hospitality"

Directed by Oz Scott
Written by Barbara Hall

Broadcast: 28 February 1994

> The first song I played on that Kmart turntable my first day of freedom.—Chris

> You haven't vacuumed, Fleischman? What's this, petrified corn chips?—Maggie

Shelly travels to Canada to register her daughter, and Holling follows, fearing that she will not come back. Meanwhile, a suicide note naming Chris rattles the resident DJ, who ponders his potential part in the deceased's tragic fate. Joel, with the help of Maggie, attempts to throw a party to make up for his lack of social events during his time in Cicely.

5.17 "Una Volta in L'Inverno"

Directed by Michael Vittes
Written by Jeff Melvoin
Broadcast: 7 March 1994

> Morning, Cicely. 8:00 a.m., muchachos. Time to finish those flapjacks, knock back that second cup of joe, and get ready to greet the day.—Chris

The seasonal darkness drives Walt to addiction—not to substances but to artificial light, which comes in the form of a customized illuminated visor. Under the tutorship of Shelly, Ruth-Anne learns Italian to enable her to read Dante's *The Divine Comedy* in its native tongue. Meanwhile, Maggie, Joel, and, unexpectedly, Ed are stranded together during a blizzard.

5.18. "Fish Story"

Directed by Bill D'Elia
Written by Jeff Melvoin
Broadcast: 14 March 1994

> Time is but the stream I go a-fishing in.—Chris (quoting Henry David Thoreau)

On a fishing trip, Joel catches a legendary fish, causing him to have a Jonah fantasy. Meanwhile, in the real world of Cicely, Holling takes up a hobby, paint by numbers, and Ruth-Anne, frustrated by the confines of her store and irritated by her customers, hits the open road on Chris's motorcycle, riding with a group of leather-clad motorcyclists.

5.19 "The Gift of the Maggie"

Directed by Patrick McKee
Written by Robin Green and Mitchell Burgess
Broadcast: 28 March 1994

> The orchid, the aristocrat of the flower family. The most sophisticated plant on earth. Clearly a cut above. But it's got petals like everybody else. The lowly daisy, the cheap carnation, half-baked azalea. Like these, the orchid needs warmth. It needs care and kindness to get by. These flowers need you people. No, I need you.—Maurice

Maurice is forced to temporarily live with Holling and Shelly after a fire breaks out at his house; pleased with a diagnosis he makes, Joel falls depressed having no one to share the diagnosis with; and, in a *Deer Hunter*–like scene, Chris is unable to shoot a buck during a hunting trip.

5.20 "A Wing and a Prayer"

Directed by Lorraine Senna Ferrara
Written by Robin Green and Mitchell Burgess
Broadcast: 11 April 1994

> Bathe my window, make it flow, melt it as the ice will go.—Chris
> (quoting Robert Frost, "To the Thawing Wing")

Father McKerry visits Cicely to baptize Holling and Shelly's daughter. In the meantime, against his better judgment, Ed betrays Ruth-Anne's trust by discussing her romance with Walt with the whole town.

5.21 "I Feel the Earth Move"

Directed by Michael Fresco

Written by Jed Seidel
Broadcast: 2 May 1994

> Marriage. Why do we do it? Everybody knows the stats. One in two marriages end up in broken dishes and a trip to Tijuana. Is it loneliness? Partly. Is it teamwork? Definitely. Things just kind of go easier when there's two of you. One of you can wait in line at the movie theater while the other guy parks the car. Get better seats that way. Better room rate when it's a double. Are you ready to file jointly? . . . Above you is the sun and sky. Below you, the ground. Like the sun, your love should be constant, like the ground, solid. Are you both OK with that? In that case, I now pronounce you married.—Chris

The wedding of Ron and Eric is the event of the season. While romance is in the air for some, for others, such as Holling, it brings out their ruthless inner businessman, as Holling promises to cater the whole event at a bargain price, despite his better judgment, in order to take business away from another caterer.

5.22 "Grand Prix"

Directed by Michael Lange
Written by Barbara Hall
Broadcast: 9 May 1994

> Ed, you're dealing with the demon of external validation. You can't beat external validation. You want to know why? Because it feels so good.—Ed's little green man

The return of Ed's little green man sees him confront yet another aspect of his character. Ed's journey is backdropped by Cicely's first wheelchair race, for which Maurice has his eye on the prize, and Marilyn's contractor boyfriend Ted (Tim Sampson) has professional grievances with the wealthy Lester Haines.

5.23 "Blood Ties"

Directed by Thomas R. Moore
Written by Robin Green and Mitchell Burgess

Broadcast: 16 May 1994

As Cicely competes with another town over who can donate the most blood, the discovery of a woman who shares Ed's rare blood type leads to him investigating if she is his long-lost mother. Meanwhile, Jed, Maggie's ex-boyfriend from Grosse Pointe, Michigan, visits Cicely with the hope of getting back together.

5.24 "Lovers and Madmen"

Directed by James Hayman
Written by Jeff Melvoin
Broadcast: 23 May 1994

> First I thought it was numbness, shock, the inability to believe that a just God could allow someone to destroy a gold mine of prehistoric knowledge for a year's worth of Salisbury steak. . . . Life is a mystery. One man's life-altering experience is another man's tenderloin. I'm one of you now. I'm a Cicelean.—Joel

Maurice resorts to bribery to see that the obsessive violinist, Cal, is released from the mental asylum to play at Officer Barbara Semanski's birthday event. Meanwhile, Joel discovers a preserved woolly mammoth in the melting ice, promising to be the historical scientific discovery of the year.

SEASON 6 (1994–1995)

6.1 "Dinner at Seven-Thirty"

Directed by Michael Fresco
Written by Diane Frolov and Andrew Schneider
Broadcast: 19 September 1994

> We're blind and we're ignorant.—Chris

After consuming a healing remedy that Ed has concocted, Joel's reality is flipped on its head. He is a medical professional, back in Manhattan. Not only is his career alternative to his reality, but so is his relationship status.

He is married to Shelly. Meanwhile, the rest of Cicely assume a variety of alternative roles in his imagination: Maurice is his doorman; Maggie, an au pair for their—Joel and Shelly's—children; Holling, a celebrity entertainer; Ed, a Wall Street investor; Chris, Bernard's assistant; and Ruth-Anne, Joel's boss. While in some ways the ideal, quickly it becomes a nightmarish alternative reality that forces Joel to reevaluate his position on his daily life in Cicely.

6.2 "Eye of the Beholder"

Directed by Jim Charleston
Written by Robin Green and Mitchell Burgess
Broadcast: 26 September 1994

> A te e a nostra figlia e a tutte les generazione (To you and our daughter and to all generations).—Chris

An auction connects a number of narrative threads in this episode: Maurice donates a case of wine that has aged badly, which is bought by a proud Holling, much to Maurice's guilt, and Maggie is filled with regret for having donated an antique bank that was gifted to her by her grandmother. Meanwhile, away from the auction, Ed, assuming once again the mantle of Cicely's private eye, investigates a suspected insurance scam committed by Hayden Keyes.

6.3 "Shofar, So Good"

Directed by James Hayman
Written by Jeff Melvoin
Broadcast: 3 October 1994

> Stay out of this, Your Highness. We had a revolution to get rid of people like you, you know.—Ruth-Anne

A visiting English aristocrat is catered to by a committed Maurice, keen to impress her by organizing a fox hunt. Meanwhile, Holling is hard on himself for having not been there for his daughter, Jackie, who is up to her old tricks, and Joel's Yom Kippur goes a little different than expected.

6.4 "The Letter"

Directed by Jim Charleston
Written by Meredith Stiehm
Broadcast: 10 October 1994

> Oh, I'm sorry. You probably want to be alone with your manifesta-
> tion.—Ed

Time catches up with itself in this episode when Maggie opens and reads a letter that she wrote to herself when she was fifteen. The letter causes Maggie's thirty-year-old self to enter into a defensive dialogue with her younger self over her life and career choices. Meanwhile, Joel has a cancer scare, Chris is rejected by his barber over his countercultural politics, and Shelly measures the impact of a chain letter on her life.

6.5 "The Robe"

Directed by Lorraine Senna
Written by Sam Egan
Broadcast: 17 October 1994

> Chris in the morning solo once again, bidding a fond adieu to my good friend, Esau. Hope the next wayward soul who finds him learns as much as I did from my brief, intense apprenticeship. It's funny: all the qualities that flow so naturally from Esau like water from a spring melt are qualities that are in me, and embracing them means embracing Esau's black-and-white world, turning my back on the rainbow, letting one piercing note drown out the orchestra or one persuasive voice silence a clambering chorus. I don't know, Esau; maybe your straight-from-the-hip answers ring truer than my own fuzzy search for enlight-enment. Sometimes we just need the uncertainty, and if I ever figure out exactly why, maybe then we'll have an act worth taking on the road.—Chris

In partnership with the Johns Hopkins School of Medicine, Joel carries out a medical study that Ed accidentally jeopardizes. While tampered data speaks for Joel's research findings, a ventriloquist dummy speaks for Chris, offering the denizens of Cicely advice. And lastly, Shelly's dreams

see her tempted by an offer from the devil himself, disguised as a sales-
man.

6.6 "Zarya"

Directed by Jim Charleston
Written by Diane Frolov and Andrew Schneider
Broadcast: 31 October 1994

> As a scientist, I am not sure anymore that life can be reduced to a class
> struggle, to dialectical materialism, or any set of formulas. Life is
> spontaneous and it is unpredictable. It is magical. I think that we have
> struggled so hard with the tangible that we have forgotten the intan-
> gible.—Joel (in the character of Mikhail)

As this sixth and final season nears an end and the series's future feels
ambiguous, this episode, like "Cicely" (3.23), ventures into the past, exploring a romantic entanglement between none other than Princess Anastasia and Vladimir Lenin, Lenin's personal physician (played by Rob
Morrow), Anastasia's lady-in-waiting (played by Janine Turner), and
Marilyn's grandfather (played by Darren Burrows).

6.7 "Full Upright Position"

Directed by Oz Scott
Written by Robin Green and Mitchell Burgess
Broadcast: 7 November 1994

> Ladies and gentlemen, today we're here to honor electricity, the charge
> that charges everything from those electrons snapping in our brain to
> our father the sun. What's the sun? It's kind of like a brain. Electro-
> magnetic field, solar flares sparking back and forth from those nerve
> cells. We're all one, folks, giant blobs of electricity, all of us. Positive
> and negative, electromagnetic fields just circling each other. Positive,
> negative, north, south, male, and female. Looking for that electric
> moment. Magnet to magnet, opposites attract.—Chris

A flight bound for Moscow, with Joel and Maggie on board, is stranded
on the runway. The wait heightens the tensions between the twosome

over the nature of their "will they/won't they?" relationship, resulting in a proposal from Joel to Maggie, which Maggie accepts. Meanwhile, always the tortured artist, Chris struggles to find inspiration from his latest subject, electricity, and Maurice attempts to reshape the image of a young relative from the wrong side of the tracks.

6.8 "Up River"

Directed by Michael Fresco
Written by Diane Frolov and Andrew Schneider
Broadcast: 14 November 1994

> She gave me more than just a sweater vest that night. She gave me all this. Nothing. She gave me nothing. That's what I need. No phone book, no Game Boy, no pasta maker, TV Guide. Nowhere to go, nothing to do. Is that what you need?—Joel

After Joel and Maggie's attempt at living and being together romantically fails, Joel leaves Cicely altogether, abandoning his professional post and his friendships with the people of Cicely. Maurice sends Ed to Manonash, a settlement where Joel is reportedly residing and practicing medicine, living with a small tribe. When Ed arrives, Joel tells him of the events that led to him finally cracking and leaving Cicely altogether. Meanwhile, Chris's trailer undergoes a problematic upgrade, the fault of a bad contractor, and Ruth-Anne falls madly for Walt.

6.9 "Sons of the Tundra"

Directed by Michael Vittes
Written by Jeff Melvoin
Broadcast: 28 November 1994

> My God. A week ago, I was at Starbuck's having a decaf latte with friends, and now I'm on the trail of a larcenous rodent.—Michelle

History repeats itself as Cicely's newest residents, Phil and Michelle Capra, a doctor and a journalist from Los Angeles, who, much like Joel before them, struggle to adapt to life in rural Alaska. Meanwhile, tensions rise between Holling and Shelly over Holling's desire to join a gentlemen's club (from which the episode takes its name) that only admits men, and Ed travels to the future after consuming a trout.

6.10 "Realpolitik"

Directed by Victor Lobl
Written by Sam Egan
Broadcast: 12 December 1994

> This is unbelievable! If somebody had told me a month ago I'd be playing golf by moonlight in the Alaska wilderness.—Phil

While Maggie, in her new post as mayor, does battle with the town concerning her first proposed order of business, Chris, unlike the rest of Cicely's denizens, finds himself attracted to her new position. Meanwhile, Joel plays a round of golf with Phil, and Marilyn gains a new companion in the form of a retired sled dog.

6.11 "The Great Mushroom"

Directed by James Hayman
Written by Diane Frolov and Andrew Schneider
Broadcast: 4 January 1995

> We'll cut everything in half and serve buffet.—Michelle

Maggie and Joel reconcile in Manonash after Maggie visits him on his birthday, feeling responsible for his rash exit from Cicely and fearful for his life, given nightmares linked to her "boyfriend curse." Meanwhile, Cicely's newest residents, Phil and Michelle, host a dinner party for the town in an attempt to integrate.

6.12 "Mi Casa, Su Casa"

Directed by Daniel Attias
Written by Robin Green and Mitchell Burgess
Broadcast: 11 January 1995

Dr. Joel Fleischman in nature. Not exactly the man you knew. He couldn't see past the Hudson River if he tried. He likes his fish smoked or preferably hand sliced from Zabars on a sliced bagel served with onions. Nature, to him, was an irritant. Birds didn't sing; they woke him up. A body of water wasn't life; it was a golf hazard.—Joel

In this episode Joel is visited by another Cicelean, this time his former secretary, Marilyn, causing him to question himself and his decisions. Meanwhile in Cicely, Maurice misplaces responsibility on Ed to look after his house while he is out of town, and Shelly and Holling look for their own home, making Holling apprehensive.

6.13 "Horns"

Directed by Michael Fresco
Written by Jeff Melvoin
Broadcast: 18 January 1995

How come when men get horny it's OK, but when women get horny it's a disease?—Shelly

Joel is formally released from his contract with the state of Alaska and is free to leave; Maurice's latest business venture, bottling Cicely's freshwater, has unusual side effects for each gender; and escaped asylum patient, violinist, and born performer Cal Ingraham finds that the lack of an audience is causing him great pain and self-doubt.

6.14 "The Mommy's Curse"

Directed by Michael Lange
Written by Robin Green and Mitchell Burgess
Broadcast: 1 February 1995

I think it's them, Mary-Margaret. Men. They have no fortitude. They're always dying or skedaddling off at the first sign of trouble. So tell me this, who is left to pick up the pieces, ship the body, clean out the closets? Us! And they have the audacity to call us the weaker sex.—Jane (Maggie's mother)

Walt and Ruth-Anne's relationship is tested when Walt is employed at Ruth-Anne's general store. Meanwhile, Maurice is struck with jealousy over the nature of Holling's friendship with new physician Phil, and Maggie extends the remit of her supposed "boyfriend curse" to include the families of her partners as well as the men themselves.

6.15 "The Quest"*

Directed by Michael Vittes
Written by Diane Frolov and Andrew Schneider
Broadcast: 8 February 1995

> I used to think of all the billions of people in the world, and of all those people, how was I going to meet the right ones? The right ones to be my friends, the right one to be my husband. Now I just believe you meet the people you're supposed to meet.—Maggie

Maggie is enlisted by Joel on a spiritual quest to find the Jeweled City of the North. Meanwhile in Cicely, Phil and Michelle are the victims of unwanted drama and attention from their fellow Ciceleans: Joel's absence catches up with his dear friend Chris, who takes a harsh stance on Phil, suing him for medical malpractice, and Holling and Shelly find out that Michelle has been asked to review the Brick's cuisine.

Recap

Journeys end within the narrative, and beyond, in this episode titled "The Quest," which is as much about closing the book on Joel and releasing him from Cicely as it is about Morrow being released from his contract with the studio. The episode serves to facilitate the journey and to console the audience at home who have bonded with Joel. "The Quest" balances this beautifully through Chris, who, like critics of the series and critics of Phil, first experiences anger then acceptance; Maggie, who is ready to let go; and Joel, who has been, for fifteen episodes, hanging on. "The Quest," though sad, is a release—a release from the purgatorial state that Joel's hero's journey and indeed the series has been held in for quite some time.

6.16 "Lucky People"

Directed by Janet Greek
Written by Diane Frolov and Andrew Schneider
Broadcast: 15 February 1995

> I've been thinking about Roslyn and Cicely. They didn't need men
> because they had each other, a significant other. It doesn't matter if the
> cat's in pants or pedal pushers. I don't think we're supposed to fly
> solo.—Chris

Whereas it only took Joel a morning in Cicely to realize his distaste for all
it stood for, the same realization catches up to Phil and Michelle in this
episode. Meanwhile, both Chris and Maggie relish their love for the town
and its history by faithfully restoring the Model T Ford that Cicely and
Roslyn arrived in the town in, just in time for the Founders' Day parade.

6.17 "The Graduate"

Directed by James Hayman
Written by Sam Egan
Broadcast: 8 March 1995

> I bet you if Tom Hanks had played Nosferatu, eighty domestic,
> easy.—Ed

The acquisition of Cicely's local theater for her portfolio teaches Maggie
a thing or two about the perils of running a business, especially when
enlisting the likes of Ed and Heather Haines. For Chris, his master's
degree is jeopardized by two conflicted professors. Meanwhile, for Holling, his generosity toward Patrick Dulac, a young man he has been
sending money to for a quarter of a century, causes Patrick to believe that
Holling is his father.

6.18 "Little Italy"

Directed by Stephen Cragg
Written by Jeff Melvoin
Broadcast: 15 March 1995

I want to tell you about the time my friend Chris Stevens flung a piano with a medieval siege weapon known as a trebuchet. Chris is our local DJ, a self-taught, ex-con, mail-order minister with a passion for the transcendent. The piano in question was a 1943 Baldwin upright— good, solid mahogany which had been hauled all the way to Alaska. . . . Ed knew that Maggie ended up with this piano and had no use for it. Chris got it free of charge, and the fling was on. Chris told us all to meet him out at Ivory Springer's farm where . . . flew into space, leaving a vapor trail of broken keys in its wake, and when at last it fell to earth and broke into a million pieces, our spirits were elsewhere, somewhere still aloft in the clouds.—Ruth-Anne

The prevailing theme in this episode is battle: Ruth-Anne grapples with success after being interviewed on National Public Radio (NPR); Maggie grapples with the mayoral responsibilities that she was otherwise unaware of when she signed up for the job, namely marriage counseling; and Phil battles with two warring families in Cicely's Little Italy neighborhood.

6.19 "Balls"

Directed by Scott Paulin
Written by Jeff Melvoin
Broadcast: 6 April 1995

You know what they say—life throws you a gutter ball, you got to slap on the old rosin bag and step up to the line.—Chris

Romantic relationships are under the microscope in this episode in which Holling and Shelly's spare room is occupied by Michelle after she leaves Phil; Ed is put between a rock and a hard place when Heather's father, Lester, offers to fund his film only if he ends his relationship with his daughter; and Chris pursues his romantic attraction to Maggie, all narratives set against the backdrop of a bowling championship.

6.20 "Buss Stop"

Directed by Daniel Attias
Written by Robin Green and Mitchell Burgess
Broadcast: 24 April 1995

The theater is like a virus. It changes people—alters them. In a place like Cicely where you've got so many independent spirits, it's even more virulent. Petty jealousies. Creative differences. All kinds of little spats. Then, finally, there's a suspicious fire in the barn of the leading man. People come up here to reinvent themselves, rewrite the book so to speak. They're not the kind of people who easily take direction.— Maurice

Journalist Michelle finds it hard to turn her talents toward stage direction when she attempts to put on a rendition of William Inge's 1955 play *Bus Stop*, only to be met with blackmail and anger from the people of Cicely in response to her casting choices.

6.21 "Ursa Minor"

Directed by Patrick McKee
Written by Sam Egan
Broadcast: 12 July 1995

> Do we have anything you can spray on furniture to keep bears off, like Bear Away?—Ed

An orphaned bear cub sees Ed transfer his efforts from guiding people to helping animals when he temporarily becomes a surrogate parent for the cub. Meanwhile, Cicely's decreasing population troubles Maurice; Chris uses his dreams to locate the source of the issues affecting his relationship with Maggie; and Michelle gives her relationship with Phil another go.

6.22 "Let's Dance"

Directed by Michael Vittes
Written by Sam Egan
Broadcast: 19 July 1995

> Manners are the happy way of doing things. Each, once a stroke of genius or love, now repeated and hardened into usage. They form at last a rich varnish, with which the routine of life is washed and its details adorned. If they are superficial, so are dewdrops which give

such depth to the morning meadows.—Chris (quoting Ralph Waldo Emerson, *The Conduct of Life & Nature & Other Essays*)

A road trip for Officer Barbara Semanski and Maurice as they escort escaped mental patient Cal back to the state hospital causes Officer Semanski to realize her deep affection for Maurice. Meanwhile, Marilyn leads a class in traditional social conduct and manners according to eighteenth-century traditions, which is attended by Chris and Phil.

6.23 "Tranquility Base (Our Town)"

Directed by Michael Fresco
Written by Robin Green, Mitchell Burgess, and Jeff Melvoin
Broadcast: 26 July 1995

There's an old Yiddish proverb: when you don't know where you're going, every road will take you there.—Rabbi Schulman

Chris regrets ending his relationship with Maggie; Michelle's personality grates on Phil; and Barbara's behavior causes Maurice to rethink proposing to her—all events that occur under the roof of Maurice's new lodge, named "Tranquility Base" (from which the episode takes its name), where Maurice invites them to spend a few days.

APPENDIX B

Fan Survey

Halfway through this project I shared a link to the various *Northern Exposure* fan groups online. The link was for an online questionnaire addressing several questions that had been racing through my head as I was writing this book. Over two hundred fans (229 to be specific) generously took the time to complete this questionnaire, for which I am very grateful. Here is a summary of the responses to that questionnaire (all unedited).

Did you watch *Northern Exposure* when it was first broadcast on TV between 1990 and 1995?
In response to this question, 189 replied that they did see the series when it was first broadcast on television. Meanwhile 40 did not.

Are you a member of any *Northern Exposure* fan groups online?
Little to my surprise, this question attracted a staggering 191 yes. Meanwhile, the 28 who answered no need our help to connect to one another; 10 did not respond.

If you answered yes above, which fan groups are you a member of?
The answers to this question include the following:

- /r/northernexposure on Reddit

- Return to Cicely
- NOEX
- Return to Cicely—Small Group
- KBHR South
- Chef Adam
- KBHR 57am
- Club NX
- Northern Exposure Lovers
- Tranquility Base
- Moosechick
- Fans of Moosefest

Unsurprisingly, a lot of family and beloved *Northern Exposure* online groups were listed in the responses to this question. For anyone looking to start their online journey, take the list above as a menu of social media accounts you are welcome to join!

Have you ever attended a *Northern Exposure* fan event (such as Moosefest, for example)?
Thirty-one answered yes to this question, which is understandable, given that we are a global group of *Northern Exposure* fans. It was good to read that those who had attended an event were taking advantage of not only annual Moosefests in Roslyn but KBHR broadcasts online. Meanwhile, there were a few "I hope to visit Roslyn one day and buy a beer at the Brick." To them I say, let's hope there are two empty stools at the bar. It's my round.

What do you think is the value of fan communities? (Optional)
This was a very interesting question that attracted some fascinating replies. Some of which I have included below.

- "Huge. It helps to maintain alive the feeling, which often is a common feeling. It helps us recreate that magic spirit of Cicely; in the community we don't talk about things that divide us but about what we have in common, though with different points of view and different meanings. In Italy there aren't so many people who have followed and loved the series, so for me it is important the connec-

tion with other fans. Moreover, I love to get in touch with people from all over the world."
- "A place to share our collective love for a mystical utopian Cicely where we would all like to live."
- "Fan communities are foundational to any show's endurance and longevity; without dedicated, responsive fans, shows exist without meaning. Often, so-called 'cult' fandoms provide the most intense, though rewarding, appreciation of TV shows/films, and *Northern Exposure* (given its limited viewership) falls into such a category. The internet accommodates many such groups through online forums and portals and engenders a sociability entirely unique to mainstream social media platforms."
- "I have become great friends with so many members of the groups I am in. We all get along well, despite how completely different we all are. We seem to have varied political views, for example, and yet respect each other. This is not something that I see often in other groups. The fans of NX are as special as the show is. We believe we have a special connection!"
- "Nostalgia is enjoyed best when shared." [I love this one.]
- "The concentrated internet 'camaraderie' of shared information, opinions, preferences, emotions, memories and inside jokes with 'kindred spirits.' (And I appreciate the 'safe space' limitations on political, sexually explicit and other negative expressions which make it all more fun.)"
- "I love being in a place where people understand the lasting value of this show, its uniqueness, and its unmatched writing."
- "Camaraderie. Good conversation can also help someone deepen their appreciation—in a sense, being able to articulate something you knew but didn't know that you knew."
- "Cultural memory." [Very important.]
- "Keeping the series relevant."
- "Well, for one thing, it let's one know they are not alone in their fandom. Like-minded individuals can meet as strangers and form friendships that last a lifetime."
- "Feeling connected to the Big Mushroom."
- "To learn about events where I can possibly connect with the stars or creators of the show."

- "The exchange of opinions and perspectives that keep the show fresh after thirty years."

What does *Northern Exposure* mean to you?
I really hope the responses to this question make it back to those involved in making the series, just so they can see the positive impact the series has on peoples' lives. Here are some of those responses:

- "A special and positive way of understanding life."
- "A great deal! As a researcher into small-town American narratives, *Northern Exposure* represents a significant confluence of my interests in American studies. The accents of Americana evoked in the neon flash of the Brick's bar sign, the familiar storefronts and proximal houses along 'Main Street' that we enter via the opening credits, the tinny sound of Chris Steven's voice on KHBR as heard through a truck stereo; these are the indices of small-town America's appeal that *Northern Exposure* renders so perfectly. It is a show about our innate ability to make a place home, even somewhere as remote and frigid as Cicely. Relationships seem amplified in the cozy, quiet streets of the titular Alaskan burg. Buildings seem cozier, their stoves warmer. A show that melds regionalism with magic realism, Americana with drama, *Northern Exposure* is a show that wears its heart on its lumberjack-plaid sleeve, and to watch it is to inhabit, however briefly, a town that seems too perfect, too innocent, a community for this huge, complicated world."
- "It was a show that my mother and I watched together."
- "NX is a community where we all have a place. It is a quieter, safer place to be. When I am viewing the show, it is as if all is well in the world. Every character feels like a friend. Some of the 'friends' are closer than others, but they are all special."
- "It was offbeat and imaginative, where most TV series are extremely formulaic. The stories and characters had an intelligent, thoughtful, literary feel to them. An excellent example was the episode where Chris read *Paddle-to-the-Sea*. And of course, the Alaskan setting was also part of its charm."
- "It soothes the soul."
- "Community."
- "Cicely, Alaska, was a refuge for me as a teenager in the '90s."

- "The lesson I got from Northern Exposure was that kindness is the more important thing we can give to each other; that it's never wrong to welcome a stranger, even one who doesn't want to be there; and human creativity is boundless."
- "It's the reason I moved to the Pacific Northwest."
- "Hard to put into words . . . it's a show that captured your attention and took you away like a good book. But while making you laugh, making you think, and even teaching a thing or two at times."
- "My absolute favorite TV show of all times. We watched it every week in my girlfriend's (now wife of twenty-five years) dorm room." [This one appeals to the nostalgic romantic in me.]
- "Where David Chase came from. And a moose. Or was it an elk?"
- "Spiritual, grounding, mystical, funny, romantic, dramatic."

Are there any aspects about *Northern Exposure* that you find problematic today (i.e., representations of gender, race, sexuality, identity, culture, and heritage)?

- "Although speaking from a position of privilege, I can't help but feel the show's inclusion of native Americans, African Americans (Bernard is, admittedly, too infrequent) and the lesbian love story at the center of its most acclaimed episode ('Cicely') is remarkably progressive, especially given the era's sitcoms (*Seinfeld, Frasier*, etc.), which were comprised exclusively of white lead characters. *Northern Exposure* may be set in a small town, but it rebuffs the conservatism one might associate with such a setting and embraces a host of various perspectives and narratives that feel, even now, authentic and genuine."
- "How bluntly homophobic Maurice was, how insulting Joel was throughout the series. Even Maggie was a bit sexist."
- "Man . . . I mean . . . obviously Maurice says *many* problematic things, but it's in order to teach us a lesson about why that's wrong. There are things here and there, but overall, the show was extremely 'woke' and was probably the first place I heard about climate change."
- "Lots of product plugs! Some of the representations of native peoples seemed problematic at times. However, Ed's journey could be read as a journey of him finding his relationship to his indigeneity."

- "Maggie's feminism, such as it is: she wants a man, changes herself for Mike, gets on a high horse about the artifacts in her yard, and she was violent to Joel (throwing things, punching him)."
- "Maggie being enraged by Joel not having sex with her while she was asleep in Juneau was creepy as hell. There was also a bit of cultural appropriation that I am more uncomfortable with now than I was when it originally aired."
- "Native Americans played by non–Native Americans. Some of Maurice's overt homophobia. This was indicative of the times, but it does grate on me."
- "It's sexist, unfortunately, and it isn't so much a question of aging well or badly. The show doesn't even attempt to tackle the feminist issues of the time (bearing in mind this was the political atmosphere of the time). Instead, any insecurities that a female character (i.e., Maggie) might face are addressed with a mocking eye roll. Women are presented as hot tempered, irrational, and emotive. The show continuously pushes the idea that male and female differences are a biological fact. Somehow, Chris, a fairly adolescent and surfaced character, has the final word on any feminist issues. Many episodes are aimed around the premise of tricking female characters into sex. See season 3, episodes 4, 5, 20, and 21 (where Joel enjoys fooling Maggie into thinking they had sex while she was sleeping). The relationship between Holling and Shelley is frighteningly inappropriate. The question of their age would be less glaring if it weren't for Holling's constant infantilizing of Shelley (e.g., season 4, episodes 1 and 7)."
- "Some of Maurice's reactions and responses to Ron and Eric would not make it on television today. But being gay myself, I don't take offense to how those episodes were written for that time. On a positive note, I think Maurice grew to accept them but always seemed on guard to not show that he did have respect and an actual affection for them and their contribution to "his" growing town. Maurice's character and understanding did grow with the series. Certainly more than the writers allowed Joel's character to grow until the sixth season."
- "Holling & Shelly; he's so obsessed with her body and her youth."
- "Maggie being upset that Joel did not rape her did *not* age well at all—that plotline always made me cringe, but it's worse now than

ever. The show's basic attitude of tolerance and acceptance helps make up for a lot (Ron and Eric were clearly ahead of their time in representing a gay couple as just regular people, for instance, and as a professional disability advocate, I've always appreciated the blind piano tuner in "Duets"), but moments like that still stand out. Also, Joel's Judaism does sometimes hew a bit too close to stereotypes. He isn't an unrealistic character (at least by the show's standards), but some of the implicit assumptions about "New York Jews"—that we're all invariably supportive of Israel, that we all assume that someone must have Germanic names to be Jewish, etc.—are, again, not unprecedented in real life, but I think come off more as norms than personality quirks of Joel himself, and that makes me a little uncomfortable. Oh, and I wish they could excise the references to Trump, but that's another story."

- "Maurice's homophobia and machismo is a bit uncomfortable to watch."
- "Overemphasis on women getting married."

Do you have a favorite episode?

OK, so many responses to this one, so I have picked the top five (in terms of times listed). The most popular episode that appeared was "Seoul Mates," followed by "Aurora Borealis: A Fairy Tale for Big People." These were closely followed by "Three Amigos," "Cicely," and "Kaddish, for Uncle Manny." Some of the runners-up for the top five include "Burning Down the House," "The Big Kiss," "Spring Break," "Wake Up Call," "Three Doctors," and "Lost and Found."

For me these answers confirmed the consensus on certain episodes. I was particularly pleased to see several mentions of "Three Amigos" in there, but where is the love for "Soapy Sanderson"?

APPENDIX C

Books about *Northern Exposure*

If *Northern Exposure* has taught me anything, it is that nothing exists in a vacuum. All is connected. This book is not the first, nor do I think it will be the last, book about *Northern Exposure*. In the kaleidoscope of work on *Northern Exposure*, this book is only a fragment. *The Northern Exposure Book* (1993), written by Louis Chunovic, has long been considered a sacred text for *Northern Exposure* fans—an early entry in the library of *Northern Exposure* books that provides a complete inside-out look at the series while it was originally on air (1990–1995). While Chunovic's book is a great companion to the series, other books have gone in a different direction, each offering a unique take on the series. For example, Patricia Kelly's *The Tao of Northern Exposure* (2020), David Boersema's *Northern Exposure and Philosophy* (2018), and Chunovic's other publication, *Chris in the Morning: Love, Life and the Whole Karmic Enchilada* (1993), all use the series as a way of introducing, and in some instances exploring, complex concepts and philosophy. Meanwhile, both *Northern Exposed* (2013) by Darren Burrows and *Exposing Northern Exposure* (1992) by Scott Nance offer behind-the-scenes explorations of the series's production. *Northern Exposures: Photographs* (1994) by Rob Morrow is a revealing visual, personal glimpse behind the curtain from the actor's personal photo collection. *Northern Exposure: Letters from Cicely* (1992) by Ellis Weiner imagines the personal worlds of the denizens of Cicely through letter form. And finally, one of my favorites, *The North-*

ern Exposure Cookbook (1994), by Ellis Weiner, is a companion to the television series like no other—inviting viewers and fans to re-create dishes inspired by the series.

OTHER THINGS *NORTHERN EXPOSURE*

In addition to the excellent books committed to the series detailed above, there are a growing number of other resources for *Northern Exposure* fans to get their fix. Both Moosechick Notes and the *Northern Exposure* wiki are excellent websites and resources for detailed, quick reference information, as well as links to an expansive archive, containing new "clippings" and photographs. Likewise, one cannot help but recommend (and thank) the wonderful people behind the two *Northern Exposure* podcasts—*The Alaskan Riviera* and *Northern Overexposure*—along with the team behind "KBHR South" for their hours of commitment to the series and the endless entertainment that they provide.

NOTES

PROLOGUE

1. Anon. "What Is a 'Cwtch'?," University of South Wales, accessed 26 February 2018, https://www.southwales.ac.uk/story/926.
2. Ibid.
3. Ibid.
4. Ibid.

I. ROSLYN

1. Di Salvatore, "City Slickers," 41.
2. Kershner, "Roslyn—Thumbnail History."
3. Ricks, "To Tour Alaska, Head East on 1-90."
4. Di Salvatore, "City Slickers," 41.
5. Phillips, *Concept Marketing for Communities*, 32.
6. Interview with Will Carroll.
7. Di Salvatore, "City Slickers," 41.
8. Anon. "Venture into the Wild 'American Alps.'"
9. Skelton, "What's It Like in Cicely, Alaska?"
10. I make specific reference to Roslyn making its small-screen debut here, as Roslyn has previously featured as the filming location in several films. These include the 1977 film *Joyride* (Joseph Ruben)—an R-rated film about a group of teenagers who leave Los Angeles and drive north to Alaska, committing robbery and taking hostages along the way—and *The Runner Stumbles* (Stanley Kramer

1979), starring Dick Van Dyke and Kathleen Quinlan, in which Roslyn was a stand-in for Isadore, Michigan.

11. Doan, "Magical Realism."

12. "Pilot," season 1, episode 1. Originally broadcast 12 July 1990.

13. John Aylward, who plays Joel's unnamed passenger on the flight from New York City to Anchorage, also plays the character Red, who appears later in the series, a bush pilot who provides air taxi between Cicely and Anchorage. It is unestablished in "Pilot" if the unnamed passenger and Red are the same character.

14. Schwartz's awards for the score of *Northern Exposure* were the first of many. Both of his scores for the main titles of *Wolf Lake* and *Deadwood* would go on to receive Emmy Award nominations for Outstanding Main Title Theme Music in 2002 and 2004, respectively, and he would receive two consecutive BMI TV Music Awards for *Rules of Engagement* in 2006 and 2007.

15. We know that in real life the moose's name was Morty thanks to several articles run in the likes of *Entertainment Weekly* (see Garey 1992) that named the beloved animal. Sadly, however, as the *Los Angeles Times* reported, Morty— who was an orphaned moose brought to Washington from Alaska—died in 1994 of a mineral deficiency (see Associated Press, 1994).

16. *American Progress* (1872) is a commercial painting commissioned by George A. Crofutt for western travel guide *Crofutt's Western World*. The partnership between John Gast and George A. Crofutt resulted in the image of what the Autry describes as a "beautiful and charming female . . . floating westward through the air, bearing on her forehead the 'Star of Empire.' . . . In her right hand she carries a book . . . the emblem of education and . . . national enlightenment, while with the left hand she unfolds and stretches the slender wires of the telegraph, that are to flash intelligence throughout the land" (Anon, the Autry museum's collections webpage).

17. Countless cultural products after Gast's *American Progress* replicated the codified images in their visual, written, or aural constructions of the American frontier: the dime novels (or "penny dreadfuls") of the latter half of the nineteenth century (*Malaeska, the Indian Wife of the White Hunter* by Ann S. Stephens), comics of the 1930s (*The Virginian* by Owen Wister and *Riders of the Purple Sage* by Zane Grey) and literature spanning the twentieth century (from *The Big Sky* by A. B. Guthrie Jr. to *Blood Meridian* by Cormac McCarthy); Western films, such as *The Great Train Robbery* (Edwin S. Porter 1903), *Stagecoach* (John Ford 1939), *Shane* (George Stevens 1953), and *3:10 to Yuma* (Delmer Davies 1957); televised Westerns, from *Gunsmoke* (1955–1975), *Bonanza* (1959–1973), and *Little House on the Prairie* (1974–1983) to *Deadwood* (2004–2006; 2019) and *Hell on Wheels* (2011–2016); and digital games, most

notably Rockstar Games's Red Dead franchise, which includes *Red Dead Revolver*, *Red Dead Redemption*, and *Red Dead Redemption II* (2004–).

18. Phillips, *Concept Marketing for Communities*, 32.

19. Anon. "A Town Goes Alaskan for 'Northern Exposure.'"

20. Anon. "Roslyn Historical Museum: Northern Exposure."

21. Ibid.

22. Di Salvatore, "City Slickers," 41.

23. Phillips, *Concept Marketing for Communities*, 32–33.

24. Ibid.

25. Nailon, "Roslyn Still Rides 'Northern Exposure' Fame."

26. Skelton, "What's It Like in Cicely, Alaska?"

27. Ibid.

28. Phillips, *Concept Marketing for Communities*, 32.

29. Anon. "A Town Goes Alaskan for 'Northern Exposure.'"

30. Di Salvatore, "City Slickers," 41.

31. Ibid. 41–42.

32. Anon. "A Town Goes Alaskan for 'Northern Exposure.'"

33. The famous Roslyn Cafe mural was painted in 1980. The apostrophe "s" was added for the series and later removed. As of 2019, the mural still exists, though the café itself has changed hands.

34. *Northern Exposure*'s primary fan site, Moosechick Notes, provides a comprehensive illustrated map and key of the numerous sites to see in Roslyn for the *Northern Exposure* fan-tourist. This can be found at https://www.moosechick.com/RoslynSite.html.

35. Phillips, *Concept Marketing for Communities*, 32.

36. Ibid.

37. Skelton, "What's It Like in Cicely, Alaska?"

38. Ibid.

39. Ibid.

40. Phillips, *Concept Marketing for Communities*, 32.

41. Ibid.

42. Nailon, "Roslyn Still Rides 'Northern Exposure' Fame."

43. Grindeland, "Moosefest's Last Reunion to Honor 'Exposure.'"

44. Seattle Times Staff, "Moosefest's Last Reunion."

45. Phillips, *Concept Marketing for Communities*, 33–34.

46. Grindeland, "Moosefest's Last Reunion to Honor 'Exposure.'"

47. Ibid.

48. Anon. "Moosefest: The Northern Exposure Fan Festival."

49. Nailon, "Roslyn Still Rides 'Northern Exposure' Fame."

50. Ibid.

51. Interview with Will Carroll.

52. Quoted by Joel in "Pilot," season 1, episode 1. Originally broadcast 12 July 1990.

53. "The Final Frontier," season 3, episode 20. Originally broadcast 27 April 1992.

54. "Aurora Borealis: A Fairy Tale for Big People," season 1, episode 8. Originally broadcast 30 August 1990.

55. This book was completed between 2017 and 2021. The series turned thirty years old on 12 July 2020.

56. Harrison, "The Essential TV Shows You Can't Find on Netflix, Amazon or Now TV."

57. Thompson, *Television's Second Golden Age.*

2. PAGING "DR. SNOW"

1. Lazic, "Missing Twin Peaks? There's Never Been a Better Time to Watch Northern Exposure."

2. Acevedo, "The Writers Panel #343."

3. The season 7 ATX Festival panel, which ran between 7 and 10 June 2017, included cocreator Joshua Brand along with writer-producers Robin Green and Mitchell Burgess; producer Cheryl Bloch; and actors Rob Morrow, Janine Turner, Cynthia Geary, and Adam Arkin. The full panel discussion can be found on the ATX Festival's YouTube channel under the title "ATX Festival Q&A: Northern Exposure (2017)," 25 August 2017.

4. Acevedo, "The Writers Panel #343."

5. Matz, "Joshua Brand: Writer/Show Creator."

6. Ibid.

7. Ibid.

8. Ibid.

9. Ibid.

10. Botte, "Cult-Classic 'The White Shadow' Still Resonates 40 Years Later."

11. Matz, "Joshua Brand: Writer/Show Creator."

12. Genzlinger, "John Falsey, Creator of Acclaimed TV Series, Is Dead at 67."

13. Matz, "Joshua Brand: Writer/Show Creator."

14. Ibid.

15. Lance Luria, MD, is credited as "medical advisor" on the first two episodes of *St. Elsewhere.*

16. Matz, "Joshua Brand: Writer/Show Creator."

17. Taken from anecdote from Brand in Matz.

18. Sepinwall, "St. Elsewhere."

19. Matz, "Joshua Brand: Writer/Show Creator."

20. VanDerWerff, "St. Elsewhere."

21. O'Connor, "TV: NBC's Stylish 'St. Elsewhere.'"

22. Wittmer, "The Best and Worst TV Series Finales of All Time."

23. Ibid.

24. Anon. "Peabody: St. Elsewhere."

25. For explorations of so-called quality TV, see Feuer, Kerr, and Vahimagi, *MTM: "Quality Television"*; Thompson, *Television's Second Golden Age.*

26. VanDerWerff, "St. Elsewhere."

27. Feuer, Kerr, and Vahimagi, *MTM: "Quality Television,"* 25.

28. For a more comprehensive exploration, see Feuer, Kerr, and Vahimagi, 56.

29. Thompson, "Rx for Success."

30. Sepinwall, "St. Elsewhere."

31. O'Connor, "TV Reviews: Kiley and Saint Co-star in 'A Year in the Life.'"

32. Ibid.

33. Matz, "Joshua Brand: Writer/Show Creator."

34. Thompson, *Television's Second Golden Age.*

35. Matz, "Joshua Brand: Writer/Show Creator."

36. Stecker, "WGAW's Laurel Award for Television to Honor Joshua Brand and John Falsey."

37. Ibid.

38. Wittmer, "The Best and Worst TV Series Finales of All Time."

39. Bill Forsyth described *Local Hero* as a "moderate success" in an interview on the DVD bonus feature. While the film failed to capture the immediate attention of the US audience, performing poorly at the box office, it gained something of a cult reputation with audiences ten to fifteen years after its release, according to Forsyth. Regardless of the box office, *Local Hero* garnered universal praise from critics in the United States and UK alike and was awarded a British Academy Film Award for Best Direction (where it was also nominated for a total of seven awards in 1983); a National Board of Review Award in 1983 for Top Ten Films; and two Best Screenplay awards for Bill Forsyth at the National Society of Film Critics and New York Film Critics Circle, respectively, in 1984.

40. Taken from the *Criterion Collection* copy for *Local Hero.*

41. Ibid.

42. Kehr, "Never Cry Wolf."

43. Matz, "Joshua Brand: Writer/Show Creator."

44. Ibid.

45. Ibid.

46. Acevedo, "The Writers Panel #343."

47. "Cicely," season 3, episode 23. Originally broadcast 18 May 1992.

48. "Pilot," season 1, episode 1. Originally broadcast 12 July 1990.

49. "Aurora Borealis: A Fairy Tale for Big People," season 1, episode 8. Originally broadcast 30 August 1990.

50. Lazic, "Missing Twin Peaks? There's Never Been a Better Time to Watch Northern Exposure."

51. Acevedo, "The Writers Panel #343."

3. "THE PARIS OF THE NORTH"

1. Lavery, *The Essential Cult TV Reader*.

2. Ibid., 3.

3. Gwenllian-Jones and Pearson, *Cult Television*, xii, quoted in Lavery, *The Essential Cult TV Reader*, 3, emphasis Lavery's.

4. Hills, *Cult Television*, 137.

5. Lavery, *The Essential Cult TV Reader*, 3.

6. Quoted by Ned Svenborg in "Cicely," season 3, episode 23. Originally broadcast 18 May 1992.

7. Quoted by Pete Gilliam in "Pilot," season 1, episode 1. Originally broadcast 12 July 1990.

8. "Pilot," season 1, episode 1. Originally broadcast 12 July 1990.

9. Campbell, *The Hero with a Thousand Faces*, 23.

10. Bakhtin, *The Dialogic Imagination*.

11. Mikhail Bakhtin conceptualized the "chronotope"—meaning time space—in his examination of literary narrative traditions in *The Dialogic Imagination*; see the chapter "Forms of Time and of the Chronotope in the Novel: Notes toward a Historical Poetics."

12. My overview here is a simplification of Campbell's. In *The Hero with a Thousand Faces*, 23, Campbell writes, "A hero ventures forth from the world of common day into a region of supernatural wonder (x): fabulous forces are there encountered and a decisive victory is won (y): the hero comes back from this mysterious adventure with the power to bestow boons on his fellow man (z)."

13. Campbell, *The Hero with a Thousand Faces*, 23–24.

14. Darowski and Darowski, *Frasier: A Cultural History*, xi.

15. "Goodnight Seattle," season 11, episodes 23 and 24. Originally broadcast 13 May 2004.

16. "Pilot," season 1, episode 1. Originally broadcast 12 July 1990.

17. "Birds of a Feather," season 5, episode 6. Originally broadcast 1 November 1993.

18. We get a sense of Joel's conservative politics in the series, especially in the episode "Democracy in America," season 3, episode 15. Originally broadcast 24 February 1992.

19. "Cicely," season 3, episode 23. Originally broadcast 18 May 1992.

20. Quoted from Ned Svenborg in "Cicely," season 3, episode 23. Originally broadcast 18 May 1992.

21. Lavery and Cain, "Quirky Quality Television: Revisiting Northern Exposure."

22. Doan, "Magical Realism."

23. Description taken from Barry Corbin's official website.

24. Ibid.

25. "A Kodiak Moment," season 1, episode 7. Originally broadcast 23 August 1990.

26. "Brains, Know-How, & Native Intelligence," season 1, episode 2. Originally broadcast 19 July 1990.

27. "Seoul Mates," season 3, episode 10. Originally broadcast 16 December 1991.

28. Taken from the character description for Shelly Tambo on the website "ShareTV."

29. "Sex, Lies and Ed's Tape," season 1, episode 6. Originally broadcast 16 August 1990.

30. "Only You," season 3, episode 2. Originally broadcast 30 September 1991.

31. Quoted by Shelly in "A Kodiak Moment," season 1, episode 7. Originally broadcast 23 August 1990.

32. Quoted by Shelly in "Dreams, Schemes and Putting Greens," season 1, episode 4. Originally broadcast 2 August 1990.

33. Here, I am referring to Ed's super-8 documentary "Cicely," which he makes in "Soapy Sanderson," season 1, episode 3. Originally broadcast 26 July 1990.

34. Doan, "Magical Realism."

35. Billy Drago—the stage name for American actor William Eugene Burrows Jr.—had a rich career in film and television, playing mainly antagonists in the likes of *Pale Rider* (Clint Eastwood 1985) and *The Untouchables* (Brian De Palma 1987), and in television, *The Adventures of Brisco County, Jr.* (1993–1994), *The X-Files*, and *Charmed* (1998–2006).

4. FROM CRITICALLY ACCLAIMED TO CANCELED

1. Stevens, "30 Years On."

2. "Pilot," season 1, episode 1. Originally broadcast 12 July 1990.

3. Doan, "Magical Realism."

4. "Aurora Borealis: A Fairy Tale for Big People," season 1, episode 8. Originally broadcast 30 August 1990.

5. "War and Peace," season 2, episode 6. Originally broadcast 13 May 1991.

6. "Aurora Borealis: A Fairy Tale for Big People," season 1, episode 8. Originally broadcast 30 August 1990.

7. For a further exploration of *Northern Exposure*'s magical realist tendencies, see Doan, "Magical Realism."

8. "Goodbye to All That," season 2, episode 1. Originally broadcast 8 April 1991.

9. "Seoul Mates," season 3, episode 10. Originally broadcast 16 December 1991.

10. "Three Amigos," season 3, episode 16. Originally broadcast 2 March 1992.

11. "Oy Wilderness," season 3, episode 3. Originally broadcast 7 October 1991.

12. "Democracy in America," season 3, episode 15. Originally broadcast 24 February 1992.

13. "The Bumpy Road to Love," season 3, episode 1. Originally broadcast 23 September 1991.

14. "Cicely," season 3, episode 23. Originally broadcast 18 May 1992.

15. "War and Peace," season 2, episode 6. Originally broadcast 13 May 1991.

16. Matz, "Joshua Brand: Writer/Show Creator."

17. Ibid.

18. Ibid.

19. Ibid.

20. "Seoul Mates," season 3, episode 10. Originally broadcast 16 December 1991.

21. "Lost and Found," season 3, episode 17. Originally broadcast 9 March 1992.

22. "Cicely," season 3, episode 23. Originally broadcast 18 May 1992.

23. "Sleeping with the Enemy," season 4, episode 24. Originally broadcast 17 May 1993.

24. "The Big Feast," season 4, episode 21. Originally broadcast 22 May 1993.

25. "Get Real," season 3, episode 9. Originally broadcast 9 December 1991.

26. "On Your Own," season 4, episode 6. Originally broadcast 9 November 1992.

27. "The Bad Seed," season 4, episode 7. Originally broadcast 16 November 1992.

28. "Crime and Punishment," season 4, episode 10. Originally broadcast 14 December 1992.

29. "Revelations," season 4, episode 12. Originally broadcast 11 January 1993.

30. "Mud and Blood," season 4, episode 23. Originally broadcast 10 May 1993.

31. "Love's Labor Mislaid," season 4, episode 17. Originally broadcast 21 February 1993.

32. "Kaddish for Uncle Manny," season 4, episode 22. Originally broadcast 3 May 1993.

33. "Hello, I Love You," season 5, episode 15. Originally broadcast 31 January 1994.

34. "Heal Thyself," season 5, episode 8. Originally broadcast 15 November 1993.

35. Cerone, "'Northern Exposure,' Star in Icy Dispute."

36. Engstrom, "Morrow Leaving with Mixed Emotions."

37. Ibid.

38. "Full Upright Position," season 6, episode 7. Originally broadcast 7 November 1994.

39. "Up River," season 6, episode 8. Originally broadcast 14 November 1994.

40. "Sons of the Tundra," season 6, episode 9. Originally broadcast 28 November 1994.

41. "Realpolitik," season 6, episode 10. Originally broadcast 12 December 1994.

42. "Balls," season 6, episode 19. Originally broadcast 6 April 1995.

43. "The Quest," season 6, episode 15. Originally broadcast 8 February 1995.

44. Crowe, "The Lights Slowly Dim on 'Northern Exposure.'"

45. Ibid.

46. Ibid.

47. Ibid.

48. Ibid.

49. Ibid.

50. Ibid.

51. Ibid.

52. "The Quest," season 6, episode 15. Originally broadcast 8 February 1995.

53. "Tranquility Base (Our Town)," season 6, episode 23. Originally broadcast 26 July 1995.

54. Quotes by Chris to Joel in "Soapy Sanderson," season 1, episode 3. Originally broadcast 26 July 1990.

5. NORTHERN EXPOSURE

1. Thompson, *Television's Second Golden Age.*
2. Matz, "Joshua Brand: Writer/Show Creator."
3. Thompson, *Television's Second Golden Age*, 31.
4. Ibid.
5. Rothman, "The Scathing Speech That Made Television History."
6. Newcomb, *TV: The Most Popular Art*, 256.
7. Thompson, *Television's Second Golden Age*, 32.
8. "Thanksgiving," season 4, episode 8. Originally broadcast 23 November 1992.
9. Murray, "Northern Exposure, 'Thanksgiving.'"
10. Anon. "Why Northern Exposure Still Stands as One of the Greatest Shows Ever Made."
11. Ibid.
12. Harrison, "The Essential TV Shows You Can't Find on Netflix, Amazon or Now TV."
13. Doan, "Magical Realism."
14. "Russian Flu," season 1, episode 5. Originally broadcast 9 August 1990.
15. Ibid.
16. Harrison, "The Essential TV Shows You Can't Find on Netflix, Amazon or Now TV."
17. Thompson, *Television's Second Golden Age*, 149–78.
18. Ibid., 150.
19. Feuer, "Town Meetings of the Imagination."
20. Doan, "Magical Realism."
21. Ibid.
22. Jacobs, "With 'Molly of Denali,' PBS Raises Its Bar for Inclusion."
23. Ibid.
24. Shafer, "Alaskan Timeosaurs and Interplanetary Human Spaghetti," 389.
25. Wilson, Gutiérrez, and Chao, *Racism, Sexism and the Media*, 99.
26. Gatzke, "'Northern Exposure': A Site for Hegemonic Struggle?"
27. Corey Davorin's time-lapse can be found under the title "Dismantling KBHR (Timelapse)," on his YouTube channel, "Tooley Lives," published 18 January 2016, accessed 23 December 2020, https://www.youtube.com/watch?v=0lrBYD6yHHA&feature=share.
28. D'Ambrosio, "Northern Exposed: Darren Burrows' Return to Cicely."
29. Ibid.
30. Frederik, "Get to Know Veep and Arrested Development Composer David Schwartz."
31. Harris and Pryor, "On the Set of 'Northern Exposure.'"

32. Harrison, "The Essential TV Shows You Can't Find on Netflix, Amazon or Now TV."

33. Ibid.

34. Ibid.

35. Lazic, "Missing Twin Peaks? There's Never Been a Better Time to Watch Northern Exposure."

36. Anon. "Why Northern Exposure Still Stands as One of the Greatest Shows Ever Made."

37. McKairnes, "'Northern Exposure' at 30."

38. McConnell, "Northern Exposure," 20.

39. Lavery and Cain, "Quirky Quality Television: Revisiting Northern Exposure."

40. "The Quest," season 6, episode 15. Originally broadcast 8 February 1995.

EPILOGUE

1. Stevens, "30 Years On."

APPENDIX A

1. In 2019, I circulated a questionnaire to fans associated with the various *Northern Exposure* social media fan accounts. One of the questions included was, "What is your favorite episode?" The results of this questionnaire are published in appendix B.

BIBLIOGRAPHY AND FILMOGRAPHY

Acevedo, Aristotle. 2017. "The Writers Panel #343: Northern Exposure." *Nerdist*, 18 July 2017. https://nerdist.com/the-writers-panel-343-northern-exposure.

Addley, Esther. 2010. "Your Next Box Set: Northern Exposure." *Guardian*, 22 October 2010. https://www.theguardian.com/tv-and-radio/2010/oct/22/northern-exposure-next-box-set.

Anon. N.d. "Venture into the Wild 'American Alps.'" *National Geographic*. https://www.nationalgeographic.com/travel/national-parks/article/north-cascades-national-park.

———. 1984. "Peabody: St. Elsewhere." 1984. http://www.peabodyawards.com/award-profile/st.-elsewhere.

———. 1991. "A Town Goes Alaskan for 'Northern Exposure.'" *New York Times*, 17 June 1991.

———. 2015. "Why Northern Exposure Still Stands as One of the Greatest Shows Ever Made." *Outcryer*, 10 July 2015. http://www.outcryer.com/northern-exposure-anniversary.

———. 2018. "What Is a 'Cwtch'?" *University of South Wales* (blog), 26 February 2018. https://www.southwales.ac.uk/story/926.

———. 2020. "Bill Forsyth Local Hero." *Criterion Collection* (blog), 2020. https://www.criterion.com/films/28709-local-hero.

———. 2020a. "Moosefest: The Northern Exposure Fan Festival." *Moosefest: The Northern Exposure Fan Festival* (blog), accessed 1 November 2020. http://www.moosefest.org.

———. 2020b. "Roslyn Historical Museum: Northern Exposure." Accessed 1 September 2020. http://www.roslynmuseum.com/northern-exposure.html.

Bakhtin, Mikhail. 1990. *The Dialogic Imagination: Four Essays*. Translated by Michael Holquist. Austin: University of Texas Press.

Botte, Peter. 2018. "Cult-Classic 'The White Shadow' Still Resonates 40 Years Later." *New York Post*, 2018. https://nypost.com/2018/11/27/cult-classic-the-white-shadow-still-resonates-40-years-later.

Brannon, Jody. 1992. "Thanks to 'Exposure,' Tiny Roslyn Is a Star." *Variety*, 18 May 1992.

Burrows, Darren. 2013. *Northern Exposed*. Film Farms.

Campbell, Joseph. 2008. *The Hero with a Thousand Faces*. 3rd ed. Bollingen Series 17. Novato, CA: New World Library.

Carroll, Will. 2020. Interview with Will Carroll, University of Birmingham. Subject: "Small Town American Fictions."

Cerone, Daniel. 1992. "'Northern Exposure,' Star in Icy Dispute: Television: Holdout Rob Morrow Is Sued by Universal. He Reportedly Wants His $30,000-per-Episode Salary Doubled." *Los Angeles Times*, 2 July 1992. https://www.latimes.com/archives/la-xpm-1992-07-02-ca-1993-story.html.

Chunovic, Louis. 1993. *The Northern Exposure Book*. Boxtree.

Cooks, Leda M., and Roger C. Aden. 1995. "Northern Exposure's Sense of Place: Constructing and Marginalizing the Matriarchal Community." *Women's Studies in Communication* 18 (1): 1–17.

Crawford, Iain. 1994. "Reading TV: Intertextuality in Northern Exposure." *Mid-Atlantic Almanack: The Journal of the Mid-Atlantic Popular/American Culture Association*, no. 3:14–22.

Crowe, Jerry. 1995. "The Lights Slowly Dim on 'Northern Exposure': Television: The Loss of a Main Character and Its Time Slot Were the Beginning of the End for One of CBS' Most Popular Prime-Time Programs." *Los Angeles Times*, July 12. https://www.latimes.com/archives/la-xpm-1995-07-12-ca-22915-story.html.

D'Ambrosio, Brian. 2017. "Northern Exposed: Darren Burrows' Return to Cicely." *HuffPost*, 8 May 2015. https://www.huffpost.com/entry/northern-exposed-darren-b_b_7241774.

Darowski, Joseph, and Kate Darowski. 2017. Frasier: *A Cultural History*. Lanham, MD: Rowman & Littlefield.

Di Salvatore, Bryan. 1993. "City Slickers: Our Far-Flung Correspondents." *New Yorker*, 22 March 1993.

Doan, Brian. 2015. "Magical Realism." 20 July 2015. https://www.rogerebert.com/demanders/magical-realism-nothern-exposure-25-years-later.

Engstrom, John. 1994. "Morrow Leaving with Mixed Emotions." *Deseret News*, 5 December 1994. https://www.deseret.com/1994/12/5/19146377/morrow-leaving-with-mixed-emotions.

Fahy, Thomas, ed. 2008. *Considering David Chase: Essays on the Rockford Files, Northern Exposure and The Sopranos*. Jefferson, NC: McFarland.

Feuer, Jane. 2010. "Town Meetings of the Imagination: Gilmore Girls and Northern Exposure." In *Screwball Television: Critical Perspectives on* Gilmore Girls, edited by David Scott Diffrient and David Lavery, 148–65. New York: Syracuse University Press.

Feuer, Jane, Paul Kerr, and Tise Vahimagi. 1984. *MTM: "Quality Television."* London: BFI.

Frederik, Brittany. 2019. "Get to Know Veep and Arrested Development Composer David Schwartz." *Hidden Remote*, 15 June 2019. https://hiddenremote.com/2019/06/15/veep-composer-david-schwartz.

Gatzke, Jennifer. 2003. "'Northern Exposure': A Site for Hegemonic Struggle?" Department of Anthropology, University of Idaho, April 2003. https://www.webpages.uidaho.edu/sense-place/northernexposure.htm.

Genzlinger, Neil. 2019. "John Falsey, Creator of Acclaimed TV Series, Is Dead at 67." *New York Times*, 11 January 2019. https://www.nytimes.com/2019/01/11/obituaries/john-falsey-dead.html?auth=login-email&login=email.

Grindeland, Sherry. 2005. "Moosefest's Last Reunion to Honor 'Exposure.'" *Seattle Times*, 28 June 2005. https://archive.seattletimes.com/archive/?date=20050628&slug=grin28e.

Gwenllian-Jones, Sara, and Roberta E. Pearson, eds. 2004. *Cult Television*. Minneapolis: University of Minnesota Press.

Harris, Mark, and Kelli Pryor. 1991. "On the Set of 'Northern Exposure.'" *Entertainment Weekly*, 26 July 1991. https://ew.com/article/1991/07/26/set-northern-exposure-2.

Harrison, Phil. 2018. "The Essential TV Shows You Can't Find on Netflix, Amazon or Now TV." *Guardian*, 12 July 2018. https://www.theguardian.com/tv-and-radio/2018/jul/12/the-essential-tv-shows-you-cant-find-on-netflix-amazon-or-now-tv?CMP=Share_iOSApp_Other.

Hecht, Michael. 2002. "Jewish American Identity: A Communication Theory of Identity Analysis of the Television Series Northern Exposure." *Journal of Communication* 52 (4): 852–69.

Hills, Matt. 2002. *Cult Television*. New York: Routledge.

Jacobs, Julia. 2019. "With 'Molly of Denali,' PBS Raises Its Bar for Inclusion." *New York Times*, 15 July 2019. https://www.nytimes.com/2019/07/15/arts/television/molly-of-denali-alaska-native-pbs.html.

Johnson, Allan. 1995. "Long Goodbye." *Chicago Tribune*, 4 July 1995. https://www.chicagotribune.com/news/ct-xpm-1995-07-04-9507040005-story.html.

Johnson, Jessica, and Josef Raab. 1994. "The Utopian Community of Northern Exposure." *Popular Culture Review* 5 (2): 73–85.

Kasindorf, Jeanie. 1991. "New Frontier: How 'Northern Exposure' Became the Spring's Hottest TV Show." *New York Magazine*, 27 May 1991.

Kehr, Dave. 1983. "Never Cry Wolf." *Chicago Reader*, 1983. https://www.chicagoreader.com/chicago/never-cry-wolf/Film?oid=1051020.

Kershner, Jim. 2009. "Roslyn—Thumbnail History." *History Link*. https://www.historylink.org/File/9239.

Lavery, David. 2010. *The Essential Cult TV Reader*. Lexington: University Press of Kentucky.

Lavery, David, and Jimmie Cain. 2006. "Quirky Quality Television: Revisiting Northern Exposure." Special issue, *Critical Studies in Television: Scholarly Studies for Small Screen Fictions* 1 (2): 2–5.

Lavery, David, and Robert J. Thompson. 2002. "David Chase, The Sopranos, and Television Creativity." In *This Thing of Ours: Investigating The Sopranos*, 18–25. New York: Columbia University Press.

Lazic, Elena. 2017. "Missing Twin Peaks? There's Never Been a Better Time to Watch Northern Exposure." Little White Lies, 2017. https://lwlies.com/articles/twin-peaks-northern-exposure-90s-cult-tv-show.

Matz, Jenni. 2017. "Joshua Brand: Writer/Show Creator." Television Academy Foundation: The Interviews. https://interviews.televisionacademy.com/interviews/joshua-brand.

McCabe, Janet, and Kim Akass. 2007. *Quality TV: Contemporary American Television and Beyond*. London: I. B. Tauris.

McConnell, Frank. 1993. "Northern Exposure." *Commonweal* 120 (19): 19.

McKairnes, Jim. 2020. "'Northern Exposure' at 30: How the Quirky Summer CBS Drama Changed TV." *USA Today*, 10 July 2020. https://eu.usatoday.com/story/entertainment/tv/2020/07/10/northern-exposure-turns-30-looking-back-quirky-cbs-drama/3224245001.

Murray, Noel. 2010. "*Northern Exposure*, 'Thanksgiving.'" *A.V. Club* (blog), 18 November 2010. https://tv.avclub.com/northern-exposure-thanksgiving-1798223281.

Nailon, Jordan. 2016. "Roslyn Still Rides 'Northern Exposure' Fame." *Kitsap Sun*, 27 February 2016. https://eu.kitsapsun.com/story/travel/2016/02/27/roslyn-still-rides-northern-exposure-fame/94258712.

Newcomb, Horace. 1974. *TV: The Most Popular Art*. Garden City, NY: Anchor.

O'Connor, John J. 1982. "TV: NBC's Stylish 'St. Elsewhere.'" *New York Times*, 16 November 1982.

———. 1986. "TV Reviews: Kiley and Saint Co-star in 'A Year in the Life.'" *New York Times*, 15 December 1986.

Phillips, Rhonda. 2002. *Concept Marketing for Communities: Capitalizing on Underutilized Resources to Generate Growth and Development*. Westport, CT: Praeger.

Porter, Michael J. 1996. "The Function of Scenes in Television Narratives." *Creative Screenwriting* 1 (2): 94–116.

Porter, Rick. 2018. "'Northern Exposure' Revival with Rob Morrow in the Works at CBS." *Hollywood Reporter*, 20 November 2018. https://www.hollywoodreporter.com/live-feed/northern-exposure-revival-rob-morrow-works-at-cbs-1163110.

Pringle, Mary Beth, and Cynthia L. Shearer. 1994. "The Female Spirit of Northern Exposure's Cicely, Alaska." *Mid-Atlantic Almanack: The Journal of the Mid-Atlantic Popular/American Culture Association* 3:34–39.

Ricks, Ingrid. 1993. "To Tour Alaska, Head East on 1-90." *Seattle Times*, 27 May 1993.

Romeyn, Esther, and Jack Kugelmass. 1996. "Writing Alaska, Writing the Nation: Northern Exposure and the Quest for a New America." In *"Writing" Nation and "Writing" Region in America*, edited by Theo D'haen and Hans Bertens, 252–67. Amsterdam: VU University Press.

Rothman, Lily. 2016. "The Scathing Speech That Made Television History." *Time*, 9 May 2016. https://time.com/4315217/newton-minow-vast-wasteland-1961-speech.

Rucker, Allen. 2000. *The Sopranos: A Family History*. New York: New American Library.

Seattle Times Staff. 2005. "Moosefest's Last Reunion to Honor 'Exposure.'" *Seattle Times*, 28 June 2005. https://www.seattletimes.com/seattle-news/eastside/moosefests-last-reunion-to-honor-exposure.

Seitz, Matt Z. 2015. Mad Men *Carousel: The Complete Critical Companion.* New York: Abrams.

Sepinwall, Alan. 2018. "'St. Elsewhere': Why You Should Revisit TV's Groundbreaking Medical Drama." *Rolling Stone*, 31 October 2018. https://www.rollingstone.com/tv/tv-features/stream-this-show-st-elsewhere-hulu-groundbreaking-medical-drama-747833.

Shafer, Nathan. 2020. "Alaskan Timeosaurs and Interplanetary Human Spaghetti: A Regional Look at Augmented Reality in Special Classrooms." In *Augmented Reality in Education*, edited by Vladimir Geroimenko, 387–411. London: Springer Nature.

Skelton, Renee. 1992. "What's It Like in Cicely, Alaska?" *Washington Post*, 22 March 1992. https://www.washingtonpost.com/archive/lifestyle/tv/1992/03/22/whats-it-like-in-cicely-alaska/144678cb-6b30-4dd8-8332-d9d25875f293.

Stecker, Joshua. 2012. "WGAW's Laurel Award for Television to Honor Joshua Brand and John Falsey." *Hollywood Reporter*, 19 December 2012. https://www.hollywoodreporter.com/news/wgaws-laurel-award-television-honor-405114.

Stevens, Ashlie D. 2020. "30 Years On, the Magical Realism of 'Northern Exposure' Is a Gentle Balm for Our Cabin Fever." *Salon*, 10 September 2020. https://www.salon.com/2020/09/10/northern-exposure-30th-anniversary-tribute-cabin-fever.

Taylor, Annette M. 1994. "Landscape of the West in Northern Exposure." *Mid-Atlantic Almanack: The Journal of the Mid-Atlantic Popular/American Culture Association* 3:23–33.

———. 1996a. "Cultural Heritage in Northern Exposure." In *Dressing in Feathers: The Construction of the American Popular Culture*, edited by S. Elizabeth Bird, 229–44. Boulder, CO: Westview Press.

———. 1996b. "Northern Exposure and Mythology of the Global Community." *Journal of Popular Culture* 30 (2): 75–85.

Thompson, Robert J. 1996. *Television's Second Golden Age: From Hill Street Blues to ER.* Syracuse, NY: Syracuse University Press.

———. 2006. "Rx for Success How 'St. Elsewhere' Influenced Today's Top Medical Dramas." *Washington Post*, 17 December 2006. https://www.washingtonpost.com/archive/lifestyle/tv/2006/12/17/rx-for-success-span-classbankheadhow-st-elsewhere-influenced-todays-top-medical-dramasspan/8c07f8eb-ce67-45f3-90b4-b11cdddbd59a.

———. 2007. "Preface." In *Quality TV: Contemporary American Television and Beyond*, edited by Janet McCabe and Kim Akass, xvii–xx. New York: I. B. Tauris.

Underwood, Willard A., and Janice M. Underwood. 1999. "The Image of America through a Contemporary Alaskan Model: Northern Exposure's Celebration of Diversity." In *The Image of America in Literature, Media, and Society*, edited by Will Wright and Steven Kaplan, 358–60. Pueblo: University of Colorado.

VanDerWerff, Emily Todd. 2012. "St. Elsewhere." *A.V. Club* (blog), 12 March 2012. https://tv.avclub.com/st-elsewhere-1798230318.

Wilcox, Rhonda V. 1993. "'In Your Dreams, Fleischman': Dr. Flesh and the Dream of the Spirit in Northern Exposure." *Studies in Popular Culture* 15 (2): 1–13.

Williams, Betsy. 1993. "North to the Future: Northern Exposure and Quality Television." *Spectator* 13 (3): 28–39.

———. 1994. "North to the Future: Northern Exposure and Quality Television." In *Television: The Critical View*, edited by Horace Newcomb, 141–54. Oxford: Oxford University Press.

Wilson, Clint C., II, Félix Gutiérrez, and Lena M. Chao. 2013. *Racism, Sexism and the Media: Multicultural Issues into the New Communications Age.* 4th ed. Los Angeles: Sage Publications.

Wittmer, Carrie. 2018. "The Best and Worst TV Series Finales of All Time, from 'The Americans' to 'Seinfeld.'" *Business Insider*, 16 June 2018. https://www.businessinsider.com/best-and-worst-tv-finales-of-all-time-the-americans-30-rock-breaking-bad-2018-6?r=US&IR=T.

Zoglin, Richard. 1991. "A Little Too Flaky in Alaska." *Time*, 20 May 1991. http://content.time.com/time/subscriber/article/0,33009,972958,00.html.

Zurawik, David. 2003. *The Jews of Prime Time.* Hanover, NH: Brandeis University Press.

TELEVISION SERIES

Adventures of Brisco County, Jr. (1993–1994), Fox
All in the Family (1971–1979), CBS
Amazing Stories (1985–1987), NBC
Americans, The (2013–2018), FX
Anger Management (2012–2014), FX
Arrested Development (2003–2006), FX; (2018–2019), Netflix
A-Team, The (1983–1987), NBC
Ben Casey (1961–1966), ABC
Better Call Saul (2015–), AMC
Beverly Hills, 90210 (1990–2000), Fox
Billions (2016–), Showtime
Blood & Oil (2015), ABC
Bob Newhart Show, The (1972–1978), CBS
BoJack Horseman (2014–2020), Netflix
Bonanza (1959–1973), NBC
Boone (1983–1984), NBC
Buffy the Vampire Slayer (1997–2003), WB
Charmed (1998–2006), WB
Cheer (2020), Netflix
Cheers (1982–1993), NBC
Chicago Hope (1994–2000), CBS
China Beach (1988–1991), ABC
City Hospital (1951–1953), CBS
Columbo (1968–1971), NBC; (1989–2003), ABC
Connors, The (2019–), ABC
Criminal Minds (2005–2020), CBS
CSI: Crime Scene Investigation (2000–2015), CBS
Dallas (1978–1991), CBS
Dawson's Creek (1998–2003), WB
Deadwood (2004–2006), HBO
Delvecchio (1976–1977), CBS
Designated Survivor (2015–2017), ABC; (2019), Netflix
Dick Van Dyke Show, The (1961–1966), CBS
Doc Martin (2004–), ITV
Doctor Who (1963–), BBC One
Doogie Houser, M.D. (1982–1993), ABC
Dr. Kildare (1961–1966), NBC
Ed Sullivan Show, The (1948–1971), CBS
Ellen (1994–1998), ABC
Empty Nest (1988–1995), NBC
ER (1994–2009), NBC
Frasier (1993–2004), NBC
Freaks and Geeks (1999–2000), NBC
Friday Night Lights (2006–2011), NBC
Friends (1994–2004), NBC
Full House (1987–1995), ABC
Fuller House (2016–2019), Netflix
Game of Thrones (2011–2019), HBO
General Hospital (1963–), ABC
Gilmore Girls (2000–2007), WB and CW; (2019), Netflix
Glee (2009–2015), Fox
Godless (2017), Netflix
Good Doctor, The (2017–), ABC
Good Place, The (2016–2020), NBC

Good Wife, The (2009–2016), CBS
Grey's Anatomy (2005–), ABC
Gunsmoke (1955–1975), CBS
Happy Days (1974–1984), ABC
Hart of Dixie (2011–2015), CW
Hell on Wheels (2011–2016), AMC
Hill Street Blues (1981–1987), NBC
I'll Fly Away (1991–1993), NBC
I'll Fly Away: Then and Now (1993), NBC
Island Son (1989–1990), CBS
Kay O'Brien (1986–1987), CBS
Kids' Court (1988), CBS
King of the Hill (1997–2010), Fox
Knight Rider (1982–1986), NBC
Kolchak: The Night Stalker (1974–1975), ABC
Little House on the Prairie (1974–1983), NBC
Lou Grant (1977–1982), CBS
Mad Men (2007–2015), AMC
Madam Secretary (2014–2019), CBS
Marcus Welby, M.D. (1969–1976), ABC
Mary Tyler Moore Show, The (1970–1977), CBS
M*A*S*H (1972–1983), CBS
Matlock (1986–1992), CBS; (1992–1995), ABC
Medic (1954–1956), NBC
Medical Centre/Calling Dr. Gannon (1969–1976), CBS
Medium (2005–2009), NBC; (2009–2011), CBS
Middle, The (2009–2018), ABC
Modern Family (2009–2020), ABC
Molly of Denali (2019), PBS Kids
Monarch of the Glen (2000–2005), BBC One
Murphy Brown (1988–1998; 2018), CBS
My So-Called Life (1994–1995), ABC
New Amsterdam (2018–), NBC
Nightingales (1989), NBC
90210 (2008–2013), CW
Northern Exposure (1990–1995), CBS
Numb3rs (2005–2010), CBS
NYPD Blue (1993–2005), ABC
O.C., The (2003–2007), Fox
One Tree Hill (2003–2006), WB; (2006–2012), CW
Operation Petticoat/Petticoat Affair (1977–1979), ABC
Parenthood (2010–2015), NBC
Parks and Recreation (2009–2015), NBC
People v. O. J. Simpson: American Crime Story, The (2016), FX
Phantom of the Opera, The (1990), NBC
Picket Fences (1992–1996), CBS
Quantum Leap (1989–1993), NBC
Quincy, M.E. (1976–1983), NBC
Ranch, The (2016–2020), Netflix
Rhoda (1974–1978), CBS
Riverdale (2017–), CW
Rosanne (1988–1996; 2018), ABC
Roswell (1999–2002), WB/UPN
Roswell: New Mexico (2019–), CW
Rules of Engagement (2007–2013), CBS
Sabrina the Teenage Witch (1996–2003), ABC

Schitt's Creek (2015–2020), CBC Television
Seinfeld (1989–1998), NBC
Sex and the City (1998–2004), HBO
Simpsons, The (1989–), Fox
Sopranos, The (1999–2007), HBO
Spin City (1996–2002), ABC
St. Elsewhere (1982–1988), NBC
Street Time (2002–2003), Showtime
Strong Medicine (2000–2006), Lifetime
Switch (1975–1978), CBS
Thick of It, The (2005–2012), BBC Four and Two
Thirtysomething (1987–1991), ABC
Thorn Birds, The (1983), ABC
Trapper John, M.D. (1979–1986), CBS
Twin Peaks (1990–1991), ABC
Twin Peaks: The Return (2017), Showtime
United States of Tara, The (2009–2011), Showtime
Virgin River (2019–), Netflix
Waltons, The (1972–1981), CBS
West Wing, The (1999–2006), NBC
White Shadow, The (1978–1981), CBS
Whole Truth, The (2010), ABC
Will & Grace (1998–2005; 2017–2018), NBC
Wolf Lake (2001), CBS
Wonder Years, The (1988–1993), ABC
X-Files, The (1993–2002; 2016–2019)
Year in the Life, A (1986), NBC
7th Heaven (1996–2007), WB (1996–2006)/CW (2006–2007)

FILMS

Amistad. Directed by Steven Spielberg. Rhode Island: Dreamworks Pictures, 1997.
Big Business. Directed by Jim Abrahams. California: Touchstone Pictures, 1988.
Blue Velvet. Directed by David Lynch. North Carolina: De Laurentiis Entertainment Group, 1986.
Casualties of War. Directed by Brian De Palma. California: Columbia Pictures, 1989.
Clash of the Titans. Directed by Desmond Davis. Buckinghamshire: Charles H. Schneer Productions, 1981.
Cleopatra. Directed by Joseph L. Mankiewicz. Andalucía: Twentieth Century Fox, 1963.
Cliffhanger. Directed by Renny Harlin. Colorado: Canal+, 1993.
Comfort and Joy. Directed by Bill Forsyth. Glasgow: Lake (Comfort and Joy), 1984.
Cry-Baby. Directed by John Waters. Baltimore: Universal Pictures, 1990.
Doc Hollywood. Directed by Michael Caton-Jones. US: Warner Bros. 1991.
Dune. Directed by David Lynch. Arizona: Dino De Laurentiis Company, 1984.
Elephant Man, The. Directed by David Lynch. England: Brooksfilms, 1980.
Eraserhead. Directed by David Lynch. Los Angeles: American Film Institute (AFI), 1977.
First Blood. Directed by Ted Kotcheff. US: Anabasis Investments, 1982.
Good Morning, Vietnam. Directed by Barry Levingson. Bangkok: Touchstone Pictures, 1987.
Grease. Directed by Randall Kleiser. Los Angeles: Paramount Pictures, 1978.
Great Train Robbery, The. Directed by Edwin S. Porter. New Jersey: Edison Manufacturing Company, 1903.
Gregory's Girl. Directed by Bill Forsyth. North Lanarkshire: Lake Films, 1980.
Hamlet. Directed by Bill Colleran and John Gielgud. New York: Theatrofilm, 1964.

Hercules. Directed by Ron Clements and John Musker. US: Walt Disney Pictures, 1997.

The Hobbit trilogy. Directed by Peter Jackson. Otago: Metro-Goldwyn-Mayer (MGM), 2012–2014.

Intolerance. Directed by D. W. Griffiths. Los Angeles: Triangle Film Corporation, 1916.

It's a Wonderful Life. Directed by Frank Capra. California: Liberty Films, 1946.

Jason and the Argonauts. Directed by Don Chaffey. Italy: Charles H. Schneer Productions, 1963.

Joyride. Directed by Joseph Ruben. Washington: Joyride Productions, 1977.

Kill Your Darlings. Directed by John Krokidas. New York: Killer Films, 2013.

Last Picture Show, The. Directed by Peter Bogdanovich. US: BBS Pictures, 1971.

Local Hero. Directed by Bill Forsyth. Aberdeenshire: Enigma Productions, 1983.

Lord of the Rings trilogy. Directed by Peter Jackson. Wellington: New Line Cinema, 2001–2003.

Love Is Strange. Directed by Ira Sachs. New York: Parts and Labor, 2014.

M.A.S.H. Directed by Robert Altman. Los Angeles: Aspen Productions, 1970.

Meet the Parents. Directed by Jay Roach. Port Washington: Universal Pictures, 2000.

My Big Fat Greek Wedding. Directed by Joel Zwick. Toronto: Home Box Office (HBO), 2002.

My Big Fat Greek Wedding 2. Directed by Kirk Jones. Toronto: HBO Films, 2016.

Nashville. Directed by Robert Altman. Tennessee: ABC Entertainment, 1975.

Never Cry Wolf. Directed by Carroll Ballard. British Columbia: Walt Disney Pictures, 1983.

O Brother, Where Art Thou?. Directed by Joel Coen and Ethan Coen. Mississippi: Touchstone Pictures, 2000.

Pale Rider. Directed by Clint Eastwood. California: The Malpaso Company, 1985.

Paper Moon. Directed by Peter Bogdanovich. US: The Directors Company, 1973.

Percy Jackson and the Lightning Thief. Directed by Chris Columbus. Las Vegas: Fox 2000 Pictures, 2010.

Percy Jackson: Sea of Monsters. Directed by Thor Freudenthal. British Columbia: Fox 2000 Pictures, 2013.

Prisoner of Zenda, The. Directed by John Cromwell. California: Selznick International Pictures, 1937.

Quiet Man, The. Directed by John Ford. Ireland: Argosy Pictures, 1952.

Quiz Show. Directed by Robert Redford. California: Hollywood Pictures, 1994.

Raising Helen. Directed by Gary Marshall. New York: Touchstone Pictures, 2004.

Rebel without a Cause. Directed by Nicolas Ray. US: Warner Bros. 1955.

Runner Stumbles, The. Directed by Stanley Kramer. Washington: Twentieth Century Fox, 1979.

Serendipity. Directed by Peter Chelsom. Toronto: Miramax, 2001.

Serpico. Directed by Sidney Lumet. US: Artists Entertainment Complex, 1973.

Sex and the City. Directed by Michael Patrick King. New York: New Line Cinema, 2008.

Sex and the City 2. Directed by Michael Patrick King. Morocco: New Line Cinema, 2010.

Shane. Directed by George Stevens. Wyoming: Paramount Pictures, 1953.

Stagecoach. Directed by John Ford. California: Walter Wanger Productions, 1939.

Steel Magnolias. Directed by Herbert Ross. Louisiana: TriStar Pictures, 1989.

Sullivan's Travels. Directed by Preston Sturges. Los Angeles: Paramount Pictures, 1941.

Targets. Directed by Peter Bogdanovich. US: Saticoy Pictures, 1968.

That Sinking Feeling. Directed by Bill Forsyth. Glasgow: Lake Films, 1979.

3:10 to Yuma. Directed by Delmer Davies. Arizona: Columbia Pictures, 1957.

To All the Boys I've Loved Before. Directed by Susan Johnson. Vancouver: Awesomeness Films, 2018.

To All the Boys: P.S. I Still Love You. Directed by Michael Filmognari. Vancouver: Ace Entertainment, 2020.

Twin Peaks: Fire Walk with Me. Directed by David Lynch. France: CIBY 2000, 1992.

Untouchables, The. Directed by Brian De Palma. Chicago: Paramount Pictures, 1987.

Vanishing Point. Directed by Richard C. Sarafian. Arizona: Cupid Productions, 1971.

Volcano. Directed by Mick Jackson. Los Angeles: Twentieth Century Fox, 1997.

WarGames. Directed by John Badham. Culver City: United Artists, 1983.

Warriors, The. Directed by Walter Hill. New York: Paramount Pictures, 1979.

DIGITAL GAMES

Never Alone (2014), Upper One Games.
Red Dead Revolver (2004), Rockstar San Diego.
Red Dead Redemption (2010), Rockstar San Diego.
Red Dead Redemption II (2018), Rockstar Studios.

LIST OF FIGURES

(In order of appearance in the book)

Sketch inspired by the Roslyn Cafe mural in the opening sequence of *Northern Exposure*. Illustrated by Michael Samuel.

Sketch inspired by the location of Dr. Joel Fleischman's practice in *Northern Exposure*. Illustrated by Michael Samuel.

Sketch inspired by Dr. Joel Fleischman's postcard sent to Maggie O'Connell in "The Quest" (6.15) in *Northern Exposure*. Illustrated by Michael Samuel.

Sketch inspired by Maurice's NASA hat, which he is seen wearing throughout *Northern Exposure*. Illustrated by Michael Samuel.

Sketch inspired by the sign outside the Brick tavern in Roslyn, Washington. Illustrated by Michael Samuel.

Sketch inspired by the DJ microphone in the KBHR radio studio in *Northern Exposure*. Illustrated by Michael Samuel.

Sketch inspired by Ed's film camera. Illustrated by Michael Samuel.

Sketch inspired by Maggie O'Connell's plane in *Northern Exposure*. Illustrated by Michael Samuel.

Sketch inspired by Dr. Joel Fleischman's return to New York City in "The Quest" (6.15) in *Northern Exposure*. Illustrated by Michael Samuel.

INDEX

ABC, 17, 31
ACE Eddie Award, 75
Alaskan Natives, 88
Allen, Woody, 61
All in the Family, 85
Altman, Robert, 17, 59
AMC, 31
Amazon Prime Instant Video, 31
American Progress, 5
The Americans, 20
Arrested Development, 4
The A-Team, 63
A Thousand Acres, 23
ATX Television Festival, 15, 18, 39, 96
August: Osage County, 58
A Year in the Life, 33–34, 35
"Bachelors", 23

BAFTA, 47
Bakhtin, Mikhail, 44
the Beatles, 20
Ben Casey, 16
Bergen, Candice, 15
Bergman, Ingmar, 61
Better Call Saul, 53
Beverly Hills, 90210, 4
Billions, 47
Blood & Oil, 53
Blue Velvet , 85
Blu-ray, 9
BMI Music Award, 4

The Bob Newhart Show, 27
Bochco, Steven, 21, 84
Boone, Richard, 16
Breaking Bad, 53
Brolin, James, 16
Buffy the Vampire Slayer, xi, 85, 87

Calling Dr. Gannon, 17
Camelot, 58
Campbell, Joseph, 44
Capaldi, Peter, 36
Carroll, Will, 2, 11
Carter, Thomas, 23
Cascade Mountains National Park, 3
Casualties of War, 62
CBS, vii, xi, 12, 15, 17–18, 21, 24, 25, 31,
    35, 67, 73, 78, 79, 87, 96, 103
CBS TriStar Pictures, 22
Chamberlain, Richard, 16–17
Channel 4, xi
Cheer, 23
Cheers, xi, 46
Chicago Hope, 77–78
China Beach, 17
Cine-Nevada, 5
City Hospital, 16
Clash of the Titans, 45
Cliffhanger, 63
Columbia University, 3, 20, 47, 48, 104
Columbo, 53
Comfort and Joy, 36

The Connors, 96
COVID-19, 101
Criminal Minds, 77
Cry-Baby, 62
CSI: Crime Scene Investigation, 62
Cult Television, vii, xi, 12, 41, 43, 65
Cultural Memory, 12

Dallas, 53, 63
David Schwartz, xii, 4, 75, 96–97
Dawson's Creek, 23
Deadwood, 4
Delvecchio, 21
De Palma, Brian, 62
Designated Survivor, 47
The Dick Van Dyke Show, 27
Directors Guild of America, 72
Di Salvatore, Bryan, 3, 7
Doogie Howser, M.D., 17
Dramedy, 17, 39, 86
Draper, Don, 23
Dune, 85
DVD, xii, 9, 11, 79, 97

The Ed Sullivan Show, 20
The Elephant Man, 85
Ellen, 53
Emmys, 24, 34, 35, 53, 57, 60, 72, 75, 117
Environmentalism, 88–89
ER, xi, 32
Eraserhead, 85

Fandom, 92–95
Fellini, Federico, 61
Feminism, 89–92
Feuer, Jane, 31
First Blood, 21
fish-out-of-water, 3, 36, 37
Florrick, Alicia, 23
The Forever War, 23
Frasier, xi, 46–47, 77, 161
Freaks and Geeks, 79
Friday Night Lights, 23, 63
Friends, xi
Frost, Mark, 67, 83
Fuller House, 96
Full House, 96
FX, 20, 31

Game of Thrones, 29
Gandolfini, James, 23
Gast, John, 5
General Hospital, 16
Gilmore Girls, 86, 87
Glee, 23
Godless , 53
Golden Globe Awards, 34, 60, 72
The Good Doctor, 32
Good Morning, Vietnam, 59
The Good Place, 4
The Good Wife, 23
Goodwin, Richard, 47
Grammer, Kelsey, 46
Grease, 62
Gregory's Girl, 36
Grey's Anatomy, 32

Haldeman, Joe, 23
Hamlet, 58
Happy Days, 85
Harris, Neil Patrick, 17
HBO (Home Box Office), 19, 31, 86
Hercules, 45
hero's journey, 44–51
Hill Street Blues, 21, 27, 29, 32, 53, 82, 84, 86
Hirsch, Judd, 21
The Hobbit, 45
Homer's *Odyssey*, 45
Hooker, Robert, 17
Howard, Ken, 23
Hulu, 31

I'll Fly Away, 72, 73
Iowa Writers' Workshop, 23, 25
Island Son, 17

Jason and the Argonauts, 45

Kafka, Franz, 50
Kalember, Patricia, 17
Kay O'Brien, 17
Dr. Kildare, 16, 30
Kiley, Steven, 16
Kill Your Darlings, 58
King of the Hill, 53
Klugman, Jack, 17
Kolchak: The Night Stalker, 21

Korean War, 17, 117, 135
Kozoll, Michael, 21

Lancaster, Burt, 36
Lazic, Elena, 15, 39
Local Hero, 36–38
The Lord of the Rings, 45
Los Angeles, 16, 20–22, 26, 76, 77, 149,
    167n10
Lou Grant, 27
Love Is Strange, 58, 62
Lynch, David, 67, 83–85

Madam Secretary, 58
Mad Men, 58
Marcus Welby, M.D., 16
Margulies, Julianna, 23, 30, 82
M*A*S*H, 17
M*A*S*H: A Novel about Three Army
    Doctors, 17
Massey, Raymond, 16
Matlock, 53
Matz, Jenni, 25, 71
Medic, 16
Medical Center, 16
medical drama, 15–17
Medium, 77
Meet the Parents, 77
Metamorphosis, 50
The Middle, 58
Modern Family, 53
Molly of Denali, 88
Moonlighting, 85
Moore, Mary Tyler, 27
MTM Enterprises, 27
Murphy Brown, 15, 18, 53, 96
My Big Fat Greek Wedding, 59
My So-Called Life, 23

Nailon, Jordan, 11
NASA, 54
Nashville, 59
National Register of Historic Places, 5
Native American representation, 88, 89–92
NBC, 17, 22, 27, 30, 31, 33, 34, 73, 96
Netflix, 23, 31, 47, 96
Never Alone, 88
Never Cry Wolf, 37–38
New Amsterdam, 32

New York, 2, 3, 15–16, 19, 20, 22–23, 26,
    30, 37, 38–39, 47, 48, 51, 68, 69, 70,
    71, 73, 77, 78, 79, 98
New Yorker, 23, 33
New York Times, 26, 30, 33, 86
Nightingales, 17
Northern Exposure: Brand, Joshua, ix, 3, 5,
    13, 15, 18–23, 25–35, 36–37, 38–39,
    48, 50, 52, 60, 61, 71–74, 83, 84, 85,
    87, 96, 104, 107, 170n3, 170n5,
    170n11, 170n13, 170n16, 170n17,
    171n19, 171n33, 171n35, 171n36,
    171n43, 174n16, 176n2, 181, 182; the
    Brick, 7, 9, 11, 12, 51, 52, 57, 62,
    69–70, 93, 104, 107, 109, 112, 118,
    128, 129, 130, 141, 152, 158, 160, 187;
    cancellation, 9, 13, 67, 78, 79; Chase,
    David, 75, 78, 86, 161, 180, 181;
    Cicely, Alaska, xi, xii, 3, 4, 12, 19, 39,
    50, 65, 68, 73–74, 79, 95, 97, 104, 111,
    119, 122, 127, 151, 160; diversity, xiii;
    Falsey, John, 3, 13, 15, 18–19, 22–23,
    25–29, 31, 32, 33–35, 38, 39, 41, 48,
    60, 71–76, 83, 84, 85, 87, 96, 104, 107;
    KBHR, 7, 9, 12, 54, 59, 92–93, 95, 104,
    129, 131, 158; Moosechick Notes, 58,
    94–95, 158, 166; Moosefest, 9–11;
    Northern Exposed, 62, 95, 165; opening
    credit sequence, xi, xiii, 5, 7, 12, 97;
    Roslyn, Washington, xi, 1–3
Numb3rs, 47, 77
NYPD Blue, 62, 84

O Brother, Where Art Thou?, 45
The O.C., 23
O'Connor, John J., 30, 33–34
One Tree Hill, 53
Operation Petticoat, 25
Outcryer, 83

Paltrow, Bruce, 23
Paltrow, Gwyneth, 23
Paltrow, Jake, 23
Parenthood, 53
Parks and Recreation, 87
PBS, 88
Peabody Award, 30–31, 73–74, 83
Peabody, George Foster, 30

The People v. O. J. Simpson: American Crime Story, 47
Percy Jackson, 45
Petticoat Affair, 25
Phillips, Rhonda, 6, 8–9
Picket Fences, 79, 86
Pleshette, Suzanne, 17
Presley, Elvis, 20
Private Lives, 58
Pulitzer Prize, 23
"quality TV", 31, 86

Quantum Leap, 63
Queens, 19, 47
The Quiet Man, 54
Quincy, M.E., 17, 21
"quirky television", 86–87
Quiz Show, 47

Rebel without a Cause, 33
Redford, Robert, 47
Remembering America: A Voice from the Sixties, 47
Rhoda, 27
Rhys, Matthew, 20
Riverdale, 23
Roberts, Pernell, 17
Rosanne, 96
Roswell, 96
Roswell: New Mexico, 96
Rules of Engagement, 4, 168n14
Russell, Keri, 20
Ryan, Maureen, 18, 96

Scorsese, Martin, 61
Seattle Times, 9
Seattle, WA, xi, 1, 3, 5, 6, 9, 33, 38, 46–47, 130
Seinfeld, 83, 85, 161
Sepinwall, Alan, 29, 32
Serpico, 27
Sex and the City, 59
The Simpsons, xi, 83
sitcom, 15, 46–47, 85, 96, 161
small-town America, 1–3, 11–12
Smiley, Jane, 23
The Sopranos, 23, 75, 86
Soprano, Tony, 23
Spielberg, Steven, 61–62

Spin City, 53
sports drama, 23
St. Elsewhere, 20, 29–32, 33, 35, 38, 48, 71, 73, 82, 86
Stewart, Byron, 23
Street Time, 47
Switch, 21

television's "first golden age", 81
television's "second golden age", 13, 35, 81–82, 86
That Sinking Feeling, 36
The Thick of It, 36
Thompson, Robert J., 31, 72, 74, 81, 83, 86, 87
Tinker, Grant, 27–28, 29
To All the Boys, 59
Tony Award, 58
Twin Peaks, 67, 79, 83–86, 96
Twin Peaks: Fire Walk with Me, 84
Twin Peaks: The Return, 84

United States of Tara, 59
USA Today, 98

Vanishing Point, 59
Volcano , 59

Waitress, 58
Walt Disney, 37, 45
The Waltons , 53
WarGames, 53
The Warriors, 59
Washington Post, 6, 31
Washington State Film and Video Office, 5
Waters, John, 62
Wayne, John, 54–55
The West Wing, xi, 17
The White Shadow, 23, 23–28
Whitman, Walt, 54, 55, 87, 90, 104
The Whole Truth, 47
Will and Grace, 96
The Wonder Years, 59
Writer's Guild of America, 25, 35, 36, 38

The X-Files, 62, 96, 173n35

Young, Robert, 16

ABOUT THE AUTHOR

This book was written and illustrated by Dr. Michael Samuel. Michael is a lecturer in film and television studies at the University of Bristol. He previously taught at the University of Warwick, the Royal Holloway University of London, the University of Birmingham, and the City University of New York (CUNY). He has published widely in the areas of film, television, technology, and digital games in several books and peer-reviewed journals. He is the coeditor of a special dossier on BBC Four for *100 Years of the BBC* (Critical Studies in Television 2022) and of two edited collections, including *Streaming and Screen Culture in the Asia-Pacific* (2022) and *True Detective: Critical Essays on the HBO Series* (2017). He is currently writing a book about British television and heritage. Most significantly, he is a huge *Northern Exposure* fan.